"Dr Korner's work represents a profound language-centred movement in psychotherapy. It is an examination of language at the core of our most vulnerable human characteristic: the cohesion of self, or the co-ordination of competing 'selves'. Building on the tradition from Hughlings Jackson, Janet and James, through to today – in the Conversational Model of Meares and Hobson – Korner investigates the development of the self as extensions of a personal, historical and evolutionary continuum. Language here encompasses the web of latent patterns in communication by which the metaphors and more general choices we make reconnect patients with the quickened core of life's positive narratives. In the uncovering of such personal value, meaning potential opens out, even in painful cases of Personality Disorder."

– **David G. Butt**, Associate Professor, Linguistics Department, Faculty of Medicine, Health and Human Sciences, Macquarie University, Sydney, Australia

"This book is a must read if you are interested in human relationships, what it means to be human and how psychotherapy can help people in distress. The fundamental basis of the book is that humans develop through interactions with others, symbolized by the very earliest form of communication, the human cry.

Modern psychological treatments have tended to regard humans as isolates, separate, contained organisms, who regulate emotions via internal thought processes, without much reference to the outside world. Korner is an advocate of the Conversational Model of Therapy, which views self as arising from a matrix of mutual relations with key others, starting at birth and continuing throughout life. The therapy, as it name implies, pays close attention to language and how meaningful contact and communication is shared between people.

The main chapters of the book focus on 'living language', 'the feeling body' and 'making meaning'. Korner seamlessly weaves discussions on language, philosophy and human development to explain the human condition, and the central importance of feeling. In the final chapter, 'The Long Conversation' he addresses the impact of trauma on the developing person and draws upon examples from human civilization to argue how this can be addressed both in therapy and in day to day life. He uses the example of 'The Dreaming' – the Australian Indigenous Peoples' understanding of the world, its creation and how life should be lived – to offer a model of healing and unity for individuals and society.

This is a deeply thought-provoking book, which mixes theory and clinical material in a stimulating and, at times, entrancing way. It is a wonderful addition to our current understanding of how therapies work and can be read by therapists, clients and anyone who is interested in the human psyche."

– **Professor Elspeth Guthrie**, Professor of Psychological Medicine, University of Leeds, UK

"Anthony Korner is a doctor who appreciates the life story of each patient who seeks his care. He attends to their unique experiences of illness with pain, with acceptance for the sense of shame that goes with admission to others of being unwell. He knows that speaking about these personal experiences gives them meaning to be shared and a chance of help with mutual understanding. His book is a story of stories, a telling of how life has been negotiated and what it needs from sympathetic listening of family and other kind friends, including those educated in the science of bodily well-being and emotional health."

– **Colwyn Trevarthen**, Professor (Emeritus) of Child Psychology and Psychobiology, School of Philosophy, Psychology and Language Sciences, The University of Edinburgh, Scotland, UK

"This beautifully written book develops the newly emergent idea that the central experience of living we call self comes into being in the context of a particular kind of therapeutic conversation. The author highlights the integration of language and feeling as the basis of this creation. The book shows the reader how communicative exchanges can be transformative. These exchanges are embodied. The author's argument is supported by research data concerning the timings of language and breathing. This book is an important contribution to a further understanding of therapeutic action."

– **Emeritus Professor Russell Meares**, University of Sydney, Australia

"In this intellectually rich and clinically relevant volume, Dr Korner provides a new understanding of how psychotherapy provides an opportunity for the client to reframe and integrate feelings into a powerful personal narrative of optimism. We learn that language, as a mental structure, frames meaning and helps form the boundary of mental activities that we experience as the self. But most importantly, we are reminded that our biology limits our capacity to experience the positive attributes of being a human and that the expression of these positive features through psychotherapy is predicated on our ability to feel safe, which is dependent on opportunities to regulate our physiological state via reciprocal social interactions."

– **Stephen W. Porges**, PhD, Professor of Psychiatry, University of North Carolina, USA; Distinguished University Scientist, Kinsey Institute, Indiana University, USA

Communicative Exchange, Psychotherapy and the Resonant Self

In *Communicative Exchange, Psychotherapy and the Resonant Self*, Anthony Korner demonstrates how important communication and resonance are to the development of a sense of self. This process of realization is embedded in social relatedness and is intrinsically tied to language.

Uniquely presenting a collaborative approach to research, this book illuminates the potential for change that lies in therapy that engages both heart and mind between patient and therapist, as well as demonstrating how language and relating are fundamental to psychotherapy. Korner explains how language engenders growth through communicative processes that shape lives and personality. Korner helps the reader see how communicative exchanges can be transformative. Brimmed with emotive clinical material, literary illustrations and reports of first-hand life experience, Korner demonstrates how the combination of knowledge and evocation of feeling in human connection is central to psychotherapeutic process.

An intersubjective approach to research is put forward as exemplar of how the minds of both patient and therapist might be employed in furthering understanding of psychotherapeutic process. This book will be an essential resource for mental health clinicians involved in psychodynamic psychotherapy, as well as more generally to people interested in understanding human connections.

Anthony Korner, PhD, is a clinical senior lecturer in psychiatry at Westmead Clinical School, University of Sydney. He lives with his wife in Sydney and has worked as a psychiatrist and psychotherapist for over 30 years. He has also completed a PhD in linguistics. He has interests in theatre, music, philosophy and time with family.

Communicative Exchange, Psychotherapy and the Resonant Self

Roads to Realization

Anthony Korner

LONDON AND NEW YORK

First published 2021
by Routledge
2 Park Square, Milton Park, Abingdon, Oxon OX14 4RN

and by Routledge
52 Vanderbilt Avenue, New York, NY 10017

Routledge is an imprint of the Taylor & Francis Group, an informa business

© 2021 Anthony Korner

The right of Anthony Korner to be identified as author of this work has been asserted by him in accordance with sections 77 and 78 of the Copyright, Designs and Patents Act 1988.

All rights reserved. No part of this book may be reprinted or reproduced or utilised in any form or by any electronic, mechanical, or other means, now known or hereafter invented, including photocopying and recording, or in any information storage or retrieval system, without permission in writing from the publishers.

Trademark notice: Product or corporate names may be trademarks or registered trademarks, and are used only for identification and explanation without intent to infringe.

British Library Cataloguing-in-Publication Data
A catalogue record for this book is available from the British Library

Library of Congress Cataloging-in-Publication Data
A catalog record for this book has been requested

ISBN: 978-0-367-19652-3 (hbk)
ISBN: 978-0-367-19653-0 (pbk)
ISBN: 978-0-429-20372-5 (ebk)

Typeset in Times New Roman
by Apex CoVantage, LLC

Contents

	Preface	viii
1	Cry and response	1
2	Living language and the resonant self	31
3	Heart and soul: the feeling body	62
4	Making meaning together: the realization of value	85
5	Two minds greater than one: an intersubjective approach to research	116
6	Becoming who we are: personal realization	139
7	The long conversation	163
	References	190
	Index	206

Preface

It's hard to say where things begin. The profession of psychotherapy is still young. In my estimation, it is emerging as a discipline that seeks to integrate a scientific outlook with the artistic and creative currents of human life. In a few words, this is the agenda of *Communicative Exchange, Psychotherapy and the Resonant Self: Roads to Realization*.

As a youth I remember being torn between pursuit of a medical or scientific career, and surrendering to my artistic longings for expression. A path was taken via medicine, acting and psychiatry towards further study and clinical practice as a psychotherapist. Some years later, a higher degree in linguistics and involvement in teaching also contributed to the genesis of this book. Through all of this, I have always found that study needs to find expression in practice and in actions that can be felt and shared. Without feeling, things just don't seem real.

There are many conversations that have contributed to my development. Somehow, I find them all ongoing, even the ones with people now deceased. Before touching on a few of these relationships, I'll share a couple of experiences that seem like preludes to this book.

In the early 1980s I spent time in an acting course in Sydney, Australia. Naturally, acting was involved! Over my time in this course, my idea of acting and theatre changed substantially. At first, I imagined working hard on giving some kind of peerless performance that would "impress" the audience. Of course, this is a recipe for awkward declamatory efforts that leave the audience cold. It became clear that one had to work in relationship with others. While I make no claims of any great ability, I did find that from time to time things would just click. This usually followed a lot of rehearsal, sometimes well into the run of a particular performance. One had the sense that "it's really happening now". My observation of these moments included awareness in myself of a momentary shiver of recognition. More importantly, I could also see a simultaneous subtle shaking in my fellow actors on stage. There was something very exciting about this kind of experience, that remains vivid for me now.

For me, this anecdote captures what excites me about relationships and the potential for creating something of value between people. There have been similar experiences in other contexts, including psychotherapy. As I have discovered the Polyvagal Theory of Stephen Porges over the last two decades, I began to see this kind of positive experience as being supported by the autonomic nervous system (ANS), specifically the social engagement system which is central to Porges' thinking. For these developments to happen between people there needs to be a genuine communicative exchange. That's what makes it possible.

On the other hand, trauma gets in the way of creative conversations and the development of self. A second experience speaks to this.

> *In the 2000s my mother was having a difficult time. Like many people, she couldn't express her distress by crying. We were close. She tried to tell me what was going on for her. At one stage she said, "I wish I could cry. My body feels all dried up, like a desert". Sadly, it remained hard for my mother to find this avenue of relief.*

This moment crystallized what has been evident to me in a great number of situations in both my professional and personal life. The expression of emotion and being in touch with one's own vulnerability is a key to mental well-being. One of the main themes of this book is that of *cry and response*. It speaks to the need for our conversations to have the component of emotional expression as well as intellectual understanding.

The value of conversation and the particular kinds of conversation that nurture individuals have been the basis for the development of the Conversational Model of Psychotherapy, originally the work of Robert Hobson and Russell Meares.

There are many people who I would like to thank for their roles in supporting the birth of this book. My parents, both deceased in the last decade, speak to me still. My wife, Val, has provided the kind of devotion that permits my life to happen at all. Russell Meares introduced me to many of the concepts that I develop in these pages. I am also indebted to Dmitri Melkonyan who helped make sense of the autonomic and physiological data reported in Chapter 5. David Butt's enthusiasm and generosity provided an induction into the science of linguistics that has greatly enriched the work. The idea that *language lives* is another central theme of the book.

My children and grandchildren challenge me to find ways of reaching across generations and inspire me to join with them in creating our future. As with most of us, there is much joy and some pain in their unfinished stories and potentials. From the beginning, *significance* in life is about reciprocal relatedness. They never fail to remind me of this.

Since 1997, I have been involved in the public sector psychotherapy program established by Russell Meares in the 1980s in Sydney, Australia. Such programs are rare. My dedicated colleagues' devotion keeps the service going. They have all contributed to countless conversations on psychotherapy practice and theory. It has been, and is, a long conversation worth having. So, thanks to Loy Mclean, Phil Graham, Joan Haliburn, George Lianos, Tessa Philips, Kamal Touma, Janine Stevenson, Michael Williamson, Lea Crisante, Leo Van Biene, Jay Bains and Stephen Malloch. When morale has flagged, our educational support staff, Lynne Gallaty, and Michelle Phillips before her, have acted as "therapists to the therapists" and helped keep the boat afloat. Our many students continue to provide the necessary stimulus to help us think creatively. Watching them grow is one of the heart-warming rewards of my job.

Finally, I want to express thanks to the many people I have seen as patients over my professional life. It has been a privilege and, I hope, a partnership that has usually been mutually valued. I find that the partnership between therapist and patient to be the main source of learning in a clinical sense. Of course, I've had my own share of experiences as a patient, mostly positive. Human survival has always depended upon our capacity to work together and heal together. There is no life in isolation.

Chapter 1

Cry and response

Overview

Being is not something any of us do in isolation. Humans grow as *communicants* from the infant's first cry, or look and gesture of focused interest, and the different responses they bring from an attentive parent. In the cry we see human vulnerability, and in focused eye-to-eye contact and play a wish to share experience, the beginnings of participation in *communicative exchange*. *Significance* is found in our closest relationships as we engage in a spiral of play and communication. Language entwined with feeling allows growth in the sense of significance over time. Our nervous system is to be understood as providing a facilitating interface with the environment. Such facilitation involves the guiding of body movement and reception of feedback from the outset. Complex neural networks underpin a system of exchange that always has feeling as its representative in consciousness, a touchstone for well-being of *self*. The expansion of consciousness and the growth of self necessarily involve a gift for engaging in language. The singularity of self may be understood as an embodied *text*. We develop as *living symbols* in stories of relation to one another. We have evolved through care, play and conversation. Role transformations have evolved as age-related transformations to support these functions. In healthy relationships there is an element of giving in the exchange between two compassionate selves. We grow in conversations of feeling.

Communicative exchange

Imagine a time before money was a medium of exchange, before writing became a means of communication or before painting became a form of human representation. Stretching a little further, imagine an era when language in its human form was just beginning. What would we have in common with these early humans? We can be pretty certain that humans had a capacity to feel in interaction with the environment. Interpersonal interactions within the tribe or early social grouping would have been associated with a felt sense of significance as it is with other species who display complex and purposeful social behaviour. It's not difficult to imagine feeling-based communication as the primary vehicle of exchange for humans. We still see it with every newborn child, from the first cry and the response it evokes.

Feeling gives a sense of the situation we are in. It is also accompanied by a need for expression. Human communication took another step as language became symbolic, coming to represent more than just the immediate situation. As it developed, language must have done so in concert with feeling. Humans have an evolutionary investment in language and communication involving emotional investment renewed in each life where our sense of who we are and who we become is so intimately tied up with how we communicate both to ourselves and others. Born immature, we are shaped by the communicative environment. It provides pathways for the growth of relationships and skill acquisition. Human flourishing occurs through the relationships and communication that give our lives meaning. On the other hand, traumatic experience disrupts our ongoing sense of existence and bodily functioning. Trauma requires healing. For psychotherapy, a compassionate exchange of feeling through conversation is the vehicle for personal growth, healing and recovery.

Resonant selves and resonant worlds

This form of exchange that shapes human lives also keeps resounding within the body of the individual. Humans have a gift for "languaging", a creative process occurring within and between people. This relates to the musicality of language as it is performed. "Languaging" has been used to denote a "manner of living" dating back into pre-history:

> Indeed, our human **identity** is a systemic phenomenon, and in our opinion it arose in the primate evolutionary history to which we belong some three million years ago when languaging as a manner of living began to be systemically conserved generation after generation.
> (Maturana & Verdan-Zoeller, 2009, emphasis in original)

The property of musical resonance is that the resonating chamber helps sustain and transmit the notes within its body and towards the environment. For humans, our bodies are resonating chambers that not only sustain and transmit notes but also meaning that is held in enduring forms that go beyond the experience of the moment. Hence, we recall, in the flow of our associations, a line from a poem or a song, a famous speech, words from a loved one, images that speak to us or fictional characters who have captured our imagination. These all represent meaning potentials that are experienced in a felt way that is trans-modal and transtemporal rather than being determined by a specific sensory system or a single moment in time. This is a complex organization realized in "forms of feeling" that involve a total organization of experience rooted simultaneously in body and mind (Hobson, 1985).

A personal example may serve as illustration. As a pre-school child I remember my mother singing to me. There were many such songs. One that keeps resonating in my mind is the traditional song, "Early One Morning".

Early one morning, Just as the sun was rising, I heard a maiden crying in the valley below, O don't deceive me, O never leave me, How could you treat a poor maiden so?

As a child, I felt the song to be beautiful, especially because it was my mother singing it for me. Although my mother died a few years ago, I still hear her voice singing. It is an old song, so these days I also have a sense of many generations singing this same song. Beyond that, it speaks of meaning that arises in relationships of love and the suffering of the forsaken. My heart goes out to the maiden, this imaginary character who I never met. It seems the song could resonate through eternity. It's a personal legacy from my mother as well as a link to bygone days. A small thread in the intimate weave of culture and being that shapes my personal world.

Being human

How shall I live? Surely this question confronts us all over the course of a life. Answers prove hard to find, particularly in modern pluralistic societies lacking uniform beliefs and values. *How shall **we** live?* Phrased in the plural we are reminded of our essentially social nature. This question makes being human seem possible. It also has claim to an *a priori* significance in that individuality is preceded by the sense of *being-in-relatedness*. The earliest experience of significance occurs in the asymmetric relatedness of the carer-infant dyad. It lies at the core of human feeling throughout life.

The kind of existence we hope for is one where the individual has the opportunity to grow, respected within a community of people, each of whom has a uniquely realized life. *Person* and *self* are terms that are neither completely subjective nor objective. They are not things but rather refer to lives shaped in communicative interaction with the environment. From this perspective the evolution of self involves the investment of feeling in interaction with significant others in an environment of symbolically enriched exchange: a place of myth, narrative and possibilities. A person has a voice that is heard, to which there is a human response. This process of exchange takes centre stage in the process of psychological growth. This is in contrast to situations where human beings are treated as "non-persons" or "sub-humans", a situation all too often occurring today as it has throughout history. Here the individual is subject to a symbolically impoverished environment where communication tends to be reduced to command and punishment with little space for thought, action or imagination and hence limited opportunity for the development of mind.

Throughout life, the cry, the smile, laughter and the protest, amongst other natural signs, retain power to evoke and enliven human interactions. They herald participation in a relational world. The expression of human vulnerability is nowhere more clearly expressed than in the capacity to cry. It is symbolized in the image of the crying child or, to put it more dynamically, in the moving images of the crying child and the responding mother. It is essential to mental well-being not only for the infant but throughout life. Natural signs and affective expression enliven speech and the symbolic medium of language. They also convey something beyond words:

> *I remember the expression on my seven-year-old step-daughter's face. I had taken her to task for some minor matter, now forgotten, that had annoyed me. What I remember is the steely determination of her refusal to concede an inch. I knew I faced a choice: to enforce my authority or to let it go. The strength of feelings she conveyed was such that it was as if I'd "seen"* **her***, as her own person, for the first time. I let it go. I doubt she remembers it.*

Human stories unfold around countless episodes of this kind, mostly unremembered. There is always an element that is more than the events themselves, requiring symbolization and placement not only in the literal context of what happened but in the symbolic context of the myths and legends of each culture.

Our myths can be considered the truly symbolic dimensions of existence in that they pertain to that which does not correspond precisely to what is actually found in objective existence. They relate particularly to the area of *significance* linked to the system of cry and response or *self and other*. They deal with the experience of desire and care, intuitively recognized by self. In contrast, the world of science, involving facts and logical relations, can be seen in terms of propositions and concepts that exist, to a considerable extent, independently of self.

No one person can claim ownership of language. It is common property. Yet the individual development of complexity arising through the experience of communicative interaction in relationships of significance underpins the growing person. Her private flux of experience is the basis for the emergence of *self*, beginning in reciprocal interplay with significant others. Natural affective-expressive signs contribute in increasingly differentiated ways to human relatedness. Feeling retains a crucial importance in motivating people to communicate and realize their potential. Living in a world of reciprocal engagement requires constant adjustment and accommodation with experiences of integration, disintegration and mobility. Such is the non-linear path of personal realization.

Interpersonal experience precedes personal growth in knowledge and understanding. There is a change from semantic, or general, understanding of an issue towards a personal, emotionally invested understanding coupled with its social expression. Paradoxically for *self*, this involves movement from the abstract to the concrete, from something known "in theory" to something *felt* to be real.

Humans depend for a long time on the asymmetrical relationship between infant and carer, requiring extra parental care relative to other species. The impetus for this development seems to have been "provided by the evolution of a game the mother could play with her baby, which gave her pleasure, so rewarding her behaviour" (Meares, 2016, p. 10). People may seek and find significance in this game and its cultural elaborations at any age. It is the human *calling*.

Cry and response

The *cry*, an evocative synonym for *call*, is paradigmatic as an emotional gesture oriented, initially unconsciously, towards the need for connection and relatedness. It is an important beginning to the life of participation in a social network, a life of felt significance.

All states of mind have an element of feeling. The need for relatedness generates both powerful and nuanced feelings as part of self-experience in the interpersonal domain. In medical literature there is a tendency towards a mechanistic conception of emotion understood as a component of mental life. Recognition that feeling arises in a network of relatedness provides a different emphasis:

> The most significant historical change in the conceptualization of emotions by Western commentators has been the replacement of the implications of an agent's feeling for the integrity of, and their relation to, others in the community as the criterion for classifying emotions with each individual's sensory pleasure and biological fitness.
>
> (Kagan, 2007, p. 19)

In an historical sense there has been a shift away from fluctuations of feeling as a gauge of integrity in human relationships, towards attention on the individual as isolate, rendering emotion a "thing" to be associated with pleasure, pain, or biological advantage over others (ibid.). Such reification of emotion becomes empty, because it has no external referent or point of shared understanding. Given that affects arise in lived contexts, the *aliveness* of felt experience is lost.

Human feeling develops in relatedness where we "can't help but mean" (Halliday, 1975), despite the fact that clarity of meaning eludes us much of the time. Interactions are felt to be significant, even when that significance lies in what is lacking. From the outset there is a drive to seek what is needed from the environment. For humans the seeking of response and relationship is crucial to well-being.

Self emerges from a matrix of mutual relatedness where integrity grows through a dialectical process involving mutual responsibility (Samuels, 2015). This occurs through establishment of a sign-process with an affective-expressive and gestural basis, well before the subsequent emergence of symbolic language with its basis in conventional signs. This process is known as *semiosis*, a linguistic term introduced by C. S. Peirce to denote "any form of activity, conduct, or process that involves signs, including the production of meaning" (Bains, 2006). It adds significance to the spoken word and continues to operate throughout life.

The birth scene is surely one of the central moments of human life, transformative both literally and psychologically. Despite huge cultural variations in birthing practices, the basic facts of the scene are held in common. The emotional stakes are high and there is an awareness of the risk to the life of mother and baby. Where the birth proceeds well, there will have been a first step taken in the establishment of a bond critical to the infant and his or her subsequent development. Where there are complications, parents and the supporting community become involved in remedial action. Where this fails, it is catastrophic for personal development. The effort, across cultures, is towards the inclusion and induction of the infant into the family and community.

The sequence that occurs at birth can be taken as representative of cycles of communication that occur between infant and carers, subsequently iterated with enormous variation leading to the development of particular personalities and relationships. The infant is born and with the first breath *cries*. This is paradigmatic as a *mood sign* in terms of its interpersonal significance. Although the infant is not aware of doing anything in an intentional sense, unconsciously this is a communication, shared with other mammals, referred to as the *separation* or *isolation call* (MacLean, 1985; Newman, 2007). From the carer's perspective this cry is usually at the forefront of the consciousness of parents and other attendants. It is an "image given and received" (Buber, 1947), even though the "giving" of the infant occurs unconsciously. A healthy first cry will typically elicit a response that includes relief and joy at this announcement of new life.

The power of the human cry motivates those in the vicinity to *act* by taking measures to comfort and settle the infant, involving being held, warmed or assisted in any manner necessary at the time. Such measures are characteristic of the way, under reasonable conditions, that carers respond to distress in the infant: care must be provided. These can be contrasted with the responses that characterize states where the infant is expressing well-being, or interest in the environment, when the carer tends to match, amplify or otherwise encourage the infant, allowing the development of a field of play (Meares, 1990; Meares & Lichtenberg, 1995; Meares & Jones, 2009). The critical impact of the absence of adequate responsiveness has been dramatically illustrated by the infant's distress in response to the "still-face" situation, where the mother is instructed to cease responding, and maintain an immobile face to the alert infant who is seeking interaction (Tronick et al., 1978).

Emotive exchanges from birth are "language-like": "Infant crying and parental response is the first language of the new dyadic relationship" (LaGasse et al., 2005). The language referred to here is not, of course, a language in the sense of system of conventional signs. Nevertheless, it is the start of the semiotic process that characterizes human interaction. It provides the grounds for carer response crucial to the infant's early self-regulation. The cry of the infant, while initially reflex-like, nevertheless requires effort and in that sense is an active communication.

The pattern of call and response develops over the ensuing weeks and months and becomes increasingly differentiated with a range of calls and signs becoming known within the mutuality of the infant-carer dyad. While it remains an *indexical* language (linked to the present), there is a shift from *sign requiring action* to the knowledge that calls may be *just signals*, allowing increasing space for variable response and the emergence of play while the infant remains in a pre-verbal, pre-conceptual state (Bateson, 1954). Play in turn allows the dyad to establish a new space where the initiatives and agenda of the infant are encouraged. The child is no longer simply a recipient of care but becomes more clearly a participant in a creative process. The delicate expressions and gestures of the child allow the infant to *take the lead* in the dialogue with carer (Trevarthen, 1979, 2019).

The human cry has characteristics clearly shared with other members of the species, yet is also unique like a fingerprint, distinguishing the infant (for the mother) from other infants (Pinyerd, 1994). The communications that develop through the pattern of call and response become more particular to the dyad, as the process continues, including a progressive differentiation and individuation of the cry, as has been demonstrated in other primates (MacLean, 1985).

An infant gives the whole of his or her being to crying for its duration. While the call is a *powerful* signal to others, paradoxically it is usually understood as an indication of helplessness or vulnerability. At a whole person level, the situation of infant cry and maternal response presents the mother (parent) with an experience of a radical "otherness". The new parent is finally faced with a relationship where the other *cannot be understood as just another person like me* who I can "take or leave". Rather the new parent is faced with the singularity of this infant, here and now, "demanding my response" or, in an alternative construal, "*giving me responsibility*". The infant's need does not go away. In many cases the parent will be able to mobilize a sufficient response, often the beginning of a profound shift in consciousness from the position of *living for myself* to the position of *living for the other* (or for "self *and* other"). This is resonant with the philosophy of Emmanuel Levinas, where significance comes through orientation to the other and where guilt for the suffering of the other brings an experience of suffering that is meaningful for the individual in a way that the experience of one's own pain cannot be (for discussion, see Orange, 2010, pp. 93–97). The deepest level of bonding emerges from the ownership of responsibility for human vulnerability.

When human vulnerability can be clearly seen we often find others are stimulated to go beyond habitual ways of relating to extend themselves for the other. For example, a report from the sports pages of a daily newspaper, by no means unusual, describes the response of a football team to a vulnerable child (Lewis, 2010, p. 28). It tells of a child who at five years of age has a serious illness and very limited life expectancy. The child, a fan of the team, was brought on the field before and after the game and given a guard of honour at the end by the team who clapped him off. The team captain was reported to say, "*He hasn't got long left, the poor little kid, and we just wanted to make a dream come true. He gave us a lot of inspiration as well, going out there today*". The father was quoted as saying, "*He's always smiling, but today's a different smile. I'd say today is the best day of his life. You always hear bad stories about football clubs, but what they've done for my son and my family today, I could never repay them*". When confronted with true frailty people can respond in ways that give value to the most vulnerable amongst us. The team response ("*he gave us inspiration*") indicates that the child was motivating to the them, giving something back in a way that was not the result of any particular intention. Rather it is an example of the child as a *living symbol* analogous to the experience of the carer feeling *called* by an infant's expression of vulnerability.

While there has been an emphasis on the cry, other pre-conceptual communications appear predictably on the infant's developmental schedule. Some of the more obvious ones are the smile, laughter and the protest (tantrum). The smile and laughter, in particular, facilitate social engagement and shared enjoyment, factors of great importance to a developing sense of self as a centre of creative, social and personal exploration. Again, the infant's whole being is at times be given over to these communications. In each case there are powerful images given and received and the infant is becoming a differentiated *living symbol* in the minds of carers with whom he or she is intimately acquainted. So, even though the infant is not conscious of symbolism, he is participating, already an actor in the symbolic world. The infant is "a self-possessed . . . performer of many new rituals of social expression" (Trevarthen, 2008). While not constituting meaning in a conceptual sense, these communications are language-like "acts of meaning" (ibid.). The *performance* of communication reflects a strong association between speech and gestures in humans (Willems & Hagoort, 2007). The facial expression of the mother for the infant (and vice versa) can be considered the equivalent of a word or phrase in these exchanges (Meares, 2005).

The infant takes in reciprocal images given and received which become established as the rhythms of interaction and associated feeling states become familiar in the infant-carer relationship. The feeling of warmth and familiarity engenders security, necessary to a robust sense of self. The ongoing communications and quiet spaces that occur in this pre-reflective period are accompanied by a sense of valence and feeling associated with the interpersonal exchange characteristics of language that then continue throughout life as a barometer of the value of self-in-relationship. Since it is ever-present, feeling provides an internal measure, gauged by the self concomitantly with verbal exchanges. In a sense, feeling continues to operate outside conceptual space, lacking conceptual clarity for consciousness. Nor is it completely opaque, rather being reflected in the intuitive sense of situations. The self-in-relationship in this initial communicative system is the infant-self on the one hand and the parent-self on the other. Allowing the infant-self necessary "quiet" space is a feature of the interplay preventing over-stimulation and allowing exploration (Bowlby, 1988).

There is asymmetry in the early communicative space with the "wordless" infant and the more competent and powerful parent. All relationships are coloured by this asymmetry, as is the case in the situation of psychotherapy. The responsibility that the parent (or therapist) carries for holding a safe space where the child is recognized and given response, has been termed the *moral third*, highlighting the morality that forms the basis of nurturing relationships (Benjamin, 2004). This safe space then gives rise to the possibility of creative interplay, or a *creative third*, in the therapeutic context (Meares, 2005). As self-awareness enlarges to include awareness of the larger community, this sense of asymmetry remains insofar as each self finds itself dwarfed by the immensity of the world, to which it calls in the hope of reciprocal response. The triangulation involved in self-other relationships and self-world relatedness, also offers opportunities for growth, and for greater autonomy. The barometer that was established early in life still acts as a template for understanding the significance of feeling-based reciprocal exchange since "affects are the currency of the brain/mind economy that signal the survival value of objects and ways of acting in the world" (Panksepp & Burgdorf, 2003).

The cry as complex emotional expression

Therapy excerpt

Pt: I just .... I ..... it's like I wanted (my ex) there 'cause I'm used to it .....
.... (becomes emotional) I don't like to be reminded that he's gone. There you go ... there's feelings ....
.... I'm glad he's gone in a sense. I'm glad that the limbo is kind of over. I know where we stand. .... I'm glad of the separation but there's elements that I miss.

Th: Of course, 'cause you're telling me that he has a number of really positive features about him that he has been a good man in your life.

Pt: I miss him when I'm feeling bad he'll just give you a hug and sometimes you feel so much better you know it doesn't take away what I'm feeling or anything but I just don't feel alone with that feeling ....
.... I don't want him back but sometimes I miss the company ....
....

Th: ... it's a big change .... The idea of being alone ......

Pt: It sounds really childish huh? ...

This vignette, taken from a psychotherapy session, illustrates the recurring motif of the cry throughout life. In this case we are not talking about an infant although the display of emotion is taken as a sign, commented on by the patient. The patient finds it difficult to accept its value ("childish huh?"). The emotional expression, no less moving for occurring in adulthood, relates to issues of isolation and loneliness. In this session patient and therapist were recorded and a transcript made. A week later both independently rated the transcript in terms of *moments when my self-experience changed* (see also Chapter 5). This passage evoked a series of positively valenced ratings by the therapist, suggesting the expression of emotion was enlivening to the session.

It is thought that crying and laughing persist in adult life "because they are indispensable in expressing positive and negative feelings. . . . and convey a sense of commonality among all human beings" (Cardoso & Sabbatini, 2002). Crying can be therapeutic: "Weeping is perhaps the most human and most universal of all relief measures" (Menninger, 1963).

The cry is referred to in an evolutionary sense as the *separation call*. In psychotherapeutic practice, and in adult life, crying is to be understood as a complex emotional expression. Humans may be unique amongst mammals in crying *emotional* tears. We are "the animal that weeps" (Cardoso & Sabbatini, 2002). Over a lifetime, the significance of the cry becomes differentiated but not diminished. Far from being solely linked to distress, it is often associated with a sense of relief or healing (Menninger, 1963; Orloff, 2010).

Humans have characteristics of *paedomorphism*, the preservation of infant-like features, and *neoteny*, the preservation of infant-like functions, into adulthood (Cardoso & Sabbatini, 2002). The lack of facial hair, in humans, allows emotional expression to be more evident. In a species that stands upright, has binocular vision, and socially engages face-to-face, this enhances communicative capacity. Crying and other complex emotional expressions serve a social engagement function throughout life. While in adulthood many people prefer to cry in private (ibid.), it is possible to *cry like a baby* at any age, suggesting the original significance of the cry is retained throughout life. In psychotherapeutic practice it is not unusual to encounter patients who have difficulty with crying, finding this a distressing expressive deficiency.

While crying is expressive and may provide relief, prolonged crying can be exhausting and be associated with physiological strain (Pinyerd, 1994; Cardoso & Sabbatini, 2002). In infancy cries come to have a range of meanings and are recognized as signs of vigour as well as distress (Cross, 2009). Infants learn quickly that crying gets attention (Cardoso & Sabbatini, 2002). Cries can be aversive to carers, particularly those not well prepared for the parenting role. They may stimulate abusive behaviours (LaGasse et al., 2005). The cry is always occurring in a unique context, unconsciously symbolized in that space. It needs to be understood as a complex relational phenomenon, not as something occurring in isolation: "Man is not merely the symbol-using animal. He is constituted of symbols, and he symbolizes because that is his nature, not because he is driven" (Levenson, 2017).

Infant distress, expressed by crying, is not thought to be unduly painful compared to later affects such as shame or intense anxiety: "[infant] distress is not a toxic crippling affect which necessarily generates avoidance strategies, but rather promotes remedial strategies which can attack the sources of distress" (Tomkins, 1995, p. 119). Although crying in adults may be associated with relief or joy, it may be that sometimes relief relates to "stored up pain and sadness", so that while relief or happiness is experienced, the reaction may still be in relation to inner sadness (Cardoso & Sabbatini, 2002).

In the first months of life infants have some discriminative capacities that are more highly developed early but wane later. While infants become better over time at discriminating the voices of the birth culture and human faces, they become worse over the corresponding period, in discriminating voices of other cultures and faces of other species (Lewkowicz & Ghazanfar, 2006). This is evidenced by better matching of monkey faces and vocalizations by human infants at 4 and 6 months than is evident at 8 or 10 months (ibid.). The infant's capacity to incorporate into their own crying behaviours the prosodic features of native language speakers that they are exposed to in the neonatal period suggests a well-developed acoustic receptive system able to distinguish between prosodically different languages (Cross, 2009). Some studies indicate that infant crying is not purely reflexive but demonstrates quite early and sophisticated vocal learning (Mampe et al., 2009). This is thought to enhance the likelihood of caregiver-infant affiliation, and can be considered a demonstration that helplessness of infants is "more apparent than real" (Cross, 2009).

The human cry, in contrast to acquired language, is an innate form of expression. Not necessarily intended but none the less powerful or meaningful for that. It is one of the ways the neonate actively participates in interpersonal relatedness. At one level it is a signal but within the relational matrix it is also an indexical communication since it has a direct effect on the mother/carer that brings about a response. It is a real contingency in a non-iconic sense. This is to say it is actual rather than symbolic. At the same time the communication is iconic in that humans live in environments in which the image of an infant, and particularly a crying infant, are part of the cultural milieu just as are images of nurturing mothers and associated stories. Stories involve an animation of symbols. The fundamental role of animation in communicative systems is illustrated by the fact that infants, for a significant period, show little response to static inanimate objects (Ricks, 1979). The fact that the infant and mother are both alive and moving in relation to each other adds to the power of their "iconicity" for each other.

The "cry" needs to be recognized as a *sign* as well as a *signal*. In the conceptualization of the *sign* developed by C. S. Peirce, it fits with the definition of "qualisign: a quality which is a Sign. It cannot actually act as a sign until it is embodied" (Peirce, 1897). In keeping with his view of the significance of the *sign* in human life, the cry is a primary, powerfully embodied sign. For Peirce the living human body forms the basis for human symbols:

> There is no element whatever of man's consciousness that has not something corresponding to it in the word; and the reason is obvious. It is that the word or sign that man uses **is** the man himself. For, as the fact that every thought is a sign, taken in conjunction with the fact that life is a train of thought, proves that man is a sign; so, that every thought is an **external** sign, proves that man is an external sign. That is to say, the man and the external sign are identical, in the same sense in which the words homo and man are identical. Thus my language is the sum total of myself; for the man is the thought.
>
> (Peirce, 1897, p. 2)

This is an understanding of communication as a whole person phenomenon. "**All** symbolic behaviour is a projection of feeling" (Browning, 2017) where feeling itself represents the whole person integration of all sources of perception. Humans encompass and embody language, thought and feeling as *living symbols*. This holds true from the cradle to the grave. It is similar to the definition of *psyche* that identifies psyche simply with the living, breathing human being: "Socrates and Socrates' Psyche are identical. The psyche, in sum, is the living self" (Gregory, 1987).

The neuroscience of the cry and reciprocity

Neurological tissue derives *in embryo* from ectoderm, in an evolutionary sense the original boundary between simple organisms and the environment (Larsen, 2001). Although the human nervous system has great complexity and subserves many capacities, it can still be seen, at a basic level, as part of a *functional interface with the environment*, "linking this inner bodily world with the outer world" (Siegel, 2015). With the development of complex social organizations in mammals, it is not surprising that evolution may have been in the direction of complementary capacities consistent with social functions. On this view, the nervous system is seen more as a facilitator and mediator of behaviour, rather than "control centre". The widely prevalent view of the brain as a computer-like control centre is also challenged by recognition that language is necessary for higher-order consciousness (Edelman & Tononi, 2000, p. 104). This makes clear that higher consciousness cannot be considered the property of an "isolated brain". Indeed, in the same sense that "there is no such thing as an infant" (Winnicott, 1960), there is "*no such thing as an isolated brain*" (Korner et al., 2008; Siegel, 2015). Recognizing the brain-mind as facilitator rather than controller makes a big difference to how we see ourselves: it amounts to seeing the brain as part of a person rather than as a machine (McGilchrist, 2012).

In this section, a brief outline is given of some developments in understanding brain structure linked to vocal production. The contribution of Broca's area, in the left frontal lobe to verbal vocalization, and that of Wernicke's area, in the left temporal lobe, to receptive functions in verbal language are well recognized. These findings contributed to the view of the left cerebral hemisphere as dominant for language. More recently there has been recognition of the prominent role of the right cerebral hemisphere in relation to attention (McGilchrist, 2009, 2012) and early development (Schore, 1994, 2012), reflecting a current reappraisal of left hemispheric dominance.

It is argued that hemispheric lateralization is crucial to the way we engage with the world. Humans and other species simultaneously deploy two forms of attention, one that is focused and linked to grasping objects and one that is broader, keeping an eye, as it were, on conditions in the environment. This latter form of attention, mediated by the right hemisphere keeps us in tune with the "present moment" of reality and allows us to sense situations and their possibilities, in contrast to the left hemisphere which enables us to fix objects, analysing them in our own time (McGilchrist, 2012). During development and throughout life, forms of communication that engage the right hemisphere will be sensed as closer to the immediate concerns of self.

The *first language* of cry, response and feeling-based non-verbal vocalization is considered with reference to its role in later linguistic communication. *Vocal production and reception are the result of a coordination of networks, not the* simple product of one centre in the brain. The ensuing description highlights coordination not only within the individual but between individuals in the infant-carer dyad. The conceptual content, articulation and production of verbal language are significantly mediated through the left hemispheric centres mentioned earlier, although affective intonation and prosody, the more musical qualities of language, are primarily mediated through right hemispheric networks (Schore, 2012). Nonverbal vocalizations appear less related to neocortical structures.

The cry of the infant includes brainstem activity, as evidenced by the presence of cries, even in decorticate animals, or anencephalic infants (Newman, 2007; Solms, 2015). Structures in the midbrain, particularly the periaqueductal grey matter (PAG), are important, as evidenced by failure to cry in lesion studies (MacLean, 1985; Newman, 2007). In humans the development of the thalamo-cingulate circuitry appears necessary for the production of a *healthy* cry. Evidence from both stimulation and lesion studies supports a significant role for this part of the limbic system being involved, both in cry production and also in the receptive recognition of the cry (Newman, 2007). The anterior cingulate appears to have a role, not only in cry production, but in the "response" side of nurturing behaviour. The amygdala is another limbic structure shown to have a role in cry production in primates, with ablation associated with a "blunted" quality to the cry (Newman & Bachevalier, 1997). Evolution has provided neural networks where the response in the parent is closely and reciprocally organized relative to the infant. Oxytocin facilitates maternal responsiveness.

In terms of social-emotional, pre-semantic vocalization there is considerable evidence of conservative evolutionary process, where structures are retained that continue to serve functions in vocalization. Other mammals share the development of the thalamo-cingulate circuitry not evident in reptiles. In humans, this component of the limbic system is particularly highly developed (MacLean, 1985). The power of language relates closely to the sense of emotional conviction, which relates to functions of the central parts of the brain that form the limbic system (Panksepp, 2008). The motivation for speech remains strongly linked to "social motivational systems that we share with other mammals" (Panksepp, 2008). In primates, vocalization and brain circuits for emotional and intellectual function, are intertwined (Newman, 2003). It is likely that the "brain substrates underlying vocal communication fit into larger schemes" that are defining of **affective** neuroscience (Newman, 2003). While brainstem structures are essential for vocalization, the thalamo-fronto-cingulate circuits are implicated both in the experience of affect and the production of crying and laughter (Newman, 2003). In primates a range of limbic and closely related structures have been shown to be necessary to affect-based vocal production (Newman, 2003). It appears "the central core for vocal production seems to have changed little over millions of years" (Newman, 2003). Areas uniquely activated by exposure to infant cries in women include the medial thalamus; the medial prefrontal cortex; and right orbito-frontal cortex, with relative activation in the anterior and posterior cingulate cortex, compared to the control condition of "white noise" (MacLean, 1988).

Located in the central part of the brain, the "limbic lobe" (Broca, 1878) is considered an ancient mammalian formation. Observations in stimulation and seizure studies have provided evidence of strong feelings elicited by activity of this part of the brain. There appear to be three important functional divisions within the limbic system: the amygdala, concerned with "self-preservation", the septal division, involved in feeling and expressive states and the thalamo-cingulate division, that "looms large" in relation to distinctive mammalian characteristics (nurturance of young; audio-vocal communication; and play) (MacLean, 1985). These neural structures are crucial to the sense of a "core self" in communication (Panksepp & Burgdorfer, 2003).

When affective components are lost, communication lacks conviction, with loss of information and an effective dissociation of intellectual from emotional aspects of speech (Panksepp, 2008). When humans dissociate the left-brain mediated intellectual component of language from the affectively based right hemispheric and limbically mediated elements of language, circumstances arise where either intellect or emotion dominates for an individual (Newman, 2003). In the former case this is likely to manifest as a kind of empty rhetoric, while in the latter the person may be left "without a voice", in relation to states where emotional intensity interferes with speech.

The neural organization of feeling subserves an experienced component of communication continually active in semiotic and linguistic processes. Engagement at this level through responsive, reciprocal exchange is necessary to the process of change in psychotherapy. Superimposed upon this level of neural organization are the more specific language structures of the neocortex. The two systems are intertwined, both contributing to social intelligence and the power and conviction of speech.

Complex emotional expression in living language

The cry is the earliest form of vocal communication network in mammals. The progression in evolutionary terms is (1) mother responding to infant cry by retrieval, (2) mother calling back to crying infant, (3) emergence of other vocal signals, probably requiring more involvement of frontal cortex, that foster closer-ranged communication between mother and infant, and (4) the development of circuits for calling that promote integrity within larger social groupings (Newman, 2007).

The cry is communication in the sense of message and response. This is only one aspect of communication, which in the early period may be best thought of as being "in communication" in the sense of sharing mutual attention and responsiveness, and broadly "being in rhythm" (Bullowa, 1979). This sense of sharing involves being "in sync" and is different from the linear sequence of message-reception-response seen in linguistic analysis. To be *in communication* is more like a resonating system, a "rhythmic dovetailing" of one with the other (Browning, 2017). Whole person perception (*apperception*) integrated as feeling is crucial to this process (Browning, 2017) where "what is important . . . is not the negotiation of rules for establishing communication but the entering into a form of life that is communicative" (Reed, 1996, p. 126).

Mood signs, experienced as feeling, are intertwined with language, rather than having a one-to-one relationship. Affective experience often arises through linguistic expression, and, conversely, linguistic expression may arise out of affective states. Affect theorists highlight that affects occur in combinations and blends that can never be entirely captured by words (Tomkins, 1995; Kagan, 2007). These theorists differ in their approach to feeling. Tomkins follows Darwin in identifying fundamental affects, seen as universal, which are then considered separately and in combination (Tomkins, 1995; Darwin, 1872). Essentially, for Tomkins, affect is an entity, or "thing-like", and therefore potentially subject to mathematical description. This leads to a description of affective life as adding greatly to the range of human expression by providing additional degrees of freedom for any given expression.

In contrast, Kagan eschews mathematical description of affect: "there is no mathematics that comes close to describing the simplest emotion" (Kagan, 2007). For him, the crucial point is the recognition of a change in feeling that reflects the sense of integrity of the individual in their relational network (ibid.). He considers that cultural beliefs and scripts may significantly influence the appraisal of affect (ibid.). Emotion descriptor words, such as *happy* and *sad*, are inadequate in capturing the complexity of emotion, even though they are often used as proxies for emotional states. He gives the following example based on a cinematic depiction:

> *Leila is a young Muslim wife who, having discovered she cannot conceive, feels ashamed and guilty because she has failed to meet one of the imperatives of her community. Leila's mother-in-law asks her to permit her husband to take a second wife who might provide the desired son. Leila vacillates but agrees, and the night the new bride arrives in her home to consummate the marriage she flees, crying, to her parents' home.*

There is no word for such a state (Kagan, 2007, p. 9). By itself language cannot provide words that capture the complexity of the situation, or the blend of emotions implied. This complexity, however, is an essential component of language in its enriched, embodied, lived form.

Efforts to define language according to strict rules can be undone by variations of context, affective intonation and expression. The phrase "Colorless green ideas sleep furiously" was put forward as an example of language "not making sense" (Chomsky, 1975). However, even apparent nonsense can be reconstructed to make sense. Indeed, "No sooner do we read this ['colorless green ideas . . .'] than we think of possible readings. Uninspired ecological proposals, we understand after a couple of seconds thought, lie dormant in spite of the anger that gave rise to them" (Frayn, 2006, p. 313). The language of play, and personal life, can take on infinite permutations that are highly idiosyncratic. People live with a personal, private language not always seen in public displays. It is *language underground* whose purpose is not primarily for classifying the physical universe but rather a "means of creating a psychological universe" (Baum, 1977).

I had an experience of "language underground" following the death of my grandmother, involving crying. It illustrates, arguably, the complex and non-linear nature of feeling-based communication:

> *My grandmother suffered a major stroke. I was called and attended her, since my parents were away. Her doctor said her condition had deteriorated and that she required intravenous fluids and hospitalization. I understood that the prognosis was poor and questioned the value of resuscitation. Despite this, measures were taken to support life. The outcome was a little over 12 months in a nursing home where grandma was paralysed and unable to communicate. We all sensed her suffering and harboured regret that her life had been prolonged in such a painful way. She had been a strong, intelligent and independent woman. I had never seen her cry while alive. When she finally died there was a sense of relief. It was two or three years later that I had a dream involving a very clear image of grandma sobbing intensely, "crying like a baby". Somehow this seemed important to me: it was as if the suffering I had witnessed had finally been expressed. It became easier to imagine her at peace.*

The complexity of language can be captured by explicitly describing concurrent strata present in any linguistic expression. These are *phonology* (the system of sounds); *lexicogrammar* (the system of words and the way they are arranged); *semantics* (the system of meanings); and *context* (Halliday, 2004). Contextual contributions to meaning are complex and highly culturally determined, as in the case of *Leila* discussed earlier. The contribution of *self* to language is as *personal context* with *forms of feeling* playing a significant role, as in the story about my grandmother. The task in psychotherapy relates to capturing greater degrees of emotional complexity through linguistic expression rather than pronouncing on what cannot be defined in words. Kagan's vision is consistent with feeling as living process, a form of life intertwined with language.

Selves develop organically in relation to significant others and the environment. Recognition and personal realization emerge from the immediacy of these complex encounters since, "It is in the meeting with other selves that the self comes alive" (Charon, 2006). In conversation, self finds its home. Put another way, "I can only find myself in and between me and my fellows in a human conversation" (Hobson, 1985).

Crying and other expressions, gestures and vocalizations in the infant are seen to have a function as a "call for connection, or contact". They have positive value as initiators of the interactive "dance" of responsiveness between infant and carer, the *proto-conversation* (Trevarthen, 1974). While the *proto-conversation* is typically described as an interaction associated with well-being, the cry is also important in facilitating early relationship and connection. It is the forerunner of the development of language, part of a system of emotional interaction that has significance as the beginning of essential bonds which, when disrupted, cause significant distress at all ages. In communicative terms, the cry is a "cry *for* life" that modifies the life not just of the infant, but also of the parent. It is a *calling* in the true vocational sense, to the role of parent.

Self as emergent from the field of self and other

Communicative exchange between individuals provides the basis for growth of self and the emergence of an individual sense of self from within a field of self and other. The earliest phase of development is characterized by "the sense of an emergent self" (Stern, 1985) or alternatively as dominated by the "motivational system based on the psychic regulation of physiological requirements" (Lichtenberg, 1989). Both perspectives emphasize that these early forms of organization continue to be active throughout life. The phrase *emergent self* tends towards emphasis on the active role played by the infant in relation to the environment, while *psychic regulation of physiological requirements* highlights the infant as recipient not only of care but of images and communications reflecting the psychic qualities of carers and the environment. Both involve early integration of experience through forms of feeling that become characteristic for the individual.

Self is understood as process. If we understand humans as developing under the "rather simple evolutionary constraint of social dependency for survival" (Atzil et al., 2018), then we understand how the social environment is not only vitally salient in providing "the ultimate driving force for socially crafted brain development and learning" (ibid.) but also in providing the interpersonal basis of this process. There is self-organizing combined with mutuality, referred to as dual processes of *autopoiesis* and *consensuality* (Maturana, 1978).

At a personal level, the process is a living, growing *text* corresponding to the embodied experience of particular selves. Such a text increases in complexity over time, with a presumed corresponding increase in complexity in the associated brains and bodies. A *living text* implies something that cannot be reduced to words on a page: language and bodily feeling are involved. The involvement of other selves in the process means that development is understood as "a dialogical narrative process" (Rizzoli, 2016). Bodily states may be modified by provision of an evocative environment (e.g. a lullaby). While "Language is neither **of** the brain nor **in** the brain" (Schumann, 2007), it is likely that communication evokes responses in the developing mind that are formative for self.

The interplay between self and other involves processes of going out to the other and taking into self that are dynamic and continual, focused firstly on maintaining life and vital connections (homeostasis) and, secondly, on facilitating growth of self. The movement in this interplay has a circular quality, although one that *spirals* through time serving both homeostatic and developmental functions. The *growth* of self may be better thought of as an *allostatic process* in that stability requires continual matching and adjustment in a changing relational field.

Although scientific description tends towards objectification of these processes, they occur from an embodied spatial position that has an inherent duality (Merleau-Ponty, 1945). The field of view for self is not simply the "shifting figure and ground with an horizon" of objective description, but rather this field *and* a simultaneous field characterized by the actual body, sensed as enveloping self, from which there is an awareness in the visual field, of the tip of the nose, and the boundaries of the orbits, but not of the face. The face is open to the field of vision of the *other* (Merleau-Ponty, 1945). The position of self in relation to other (and to world) is "face-to-face". Taking this into account it can be seen how the processes of the proto-conversation depend upon both self and other. In a real sense I come to know myself, my own emotional responses and self-affectivity, through the facial and gestural display of others because my own spontaneous expressions and movements are not available to me in a manner that can be received, when my effort and attention is towards "giving out" to the other.

Where there is good enough care, there will be a sufficient illusion of safety for the infant to thrive. However, the situation is often traumatic although trauma may be neither overt, nor intentional, on the part of the parent. Consider the situation of an infant where the mother, at birth, experienced a perineal tear during delivery, leading her to comment that the infant "tore me apart" (Lichtenberg, 1989). Subsequently, the same mother had difficulty feeding the child, and was unable to make feeding an experience satisfying to the child. She also had trouble responding to the infant's cries, typically delaying her response. It wasn't that the mother was not making efforts to care. She was doing the best she could to respond and take advice. Still, the infant developed a failure to thrive (ibid.).

In a neurophysiological sense the earliest forms of implicit memory are in play for the infant. The importance of receptive processes, organized according to principles of apperception and affective valence, is evidenced by the extent to which autonomic *input* subserving social engagement dominates organization of the vagal nerve, with up to 80 per cent of the vagal nerve being devoted to *afferent* networks. Development of perceptual and affective organization is a prerequisite for more complex functioning. The movements of the infant also gradually cohere into felt knowledge of the body-in-action through procedural memory, an *action knowledge* of the body-in-the-world as opposed to conceptual knowledge. These forms of affectively-mediated, embodied organization remain critical to function throughout life although they become a focus for conscious attention mainly when there are failures in functioning. Normally attention is focused on its objects rather than on bodily functioning (Merleau-Ponty, 1945).

Higher level homeostatic process "reflects the coordination of behaviour, emotional tone and bodily state to successfully negotiate social interactions" (Porges, 2011). What is seen and felt at this level goes beyond objective data. They require a shared understanding not only of language but of relational, affective and symbolic processes. This implies a level of integration of the symbolic medium of language with the bodily experience of feeling. Developmentally this emergence begins at the stage Stern describes as the "sense of a subjective self" from about

7–9 months of age where "infants gradually come upon the momentous realization that inner subjective experiences, the 'subject matter' of the mind, are potentially shareable with someone else" (Stern, 1985). This also corresponds to the development of a relatively specific proto-language between infant and carer (Halliday, 1975).

The further transition to the "sense of a verbal self" is said by Stern to "drive a wedge between two simultaneous forms of interpersonal experience: as it is lived and as it is verbally represented. Experience in the domains of emergent, core and intersubjective relatedness, which continue irrespective of language, can be embraced only very partially in the domain of verbal relatedness" (Stern, 1985, p. 162). What is highlighted is the challenge of integrating experience in verbal form with affective life. This remains a central concern to self throughout life. This involves *narrative knowledge* that "enables one individual to understand particular events befalling another . . . not as an instance of something that is universally true but as a singular and meaningful situation" (Charon, 2006). The *"true voice of feeling"* (Hobson, 1985) reflects successful integration of the spoken word with affective experience through processes of symbolical expression that *fit analogically*, rather than mechanically or exactly, with the embodied, feeling self. Such a conception is imperfectly realized in actuality.

Getting it together: the neural ontology of complexity

The question remains as to what might be the objective and neural correlates of the development of *self*. Self is a notion that implies intrinsic activity within the mind with the duality of *I* and *me*, i.e. internal relatedness. Self can be multiple depending on context and role and yet also provides the individual with senses of unity, continuity and growth. In the characterization of self as "I, me and myself" (Meares, 2000), it is *myself* that denotes the zone of expansion or growth in contrast to the subject-object polarity of *I* and *me*. Growth depends on the development of a secure base and the sense of "warmth and familiarity" in the environment that pertains, as well as the experience of novelty and exploration.

The provision of a safe environment involves active input from others to maintain the infant's homeostasis. The notion of homeostasis implies regulation around an optimum range. It also implies a starting point around which regulation becomes organized. In terms of self this corresponds to what has been termed the *proto-self* which is defined in neural terms as, "a coherent collection of neural patterns which map, moment by moment, the state of the physical structure of the organism in its many dimensions" (Damasio, 2000). This is non-conscious and to be understood as a "reference point at each point in which it is", without language, powers of perception or knowledge (ibid., p. 153). Damasio sees this as the ground for the development of a *core self* which relates to the movements and patterns that are felt in the animations and interactions that constitute life associated initially with "primordial feelings" relating to the sense of existence (Damasio,

2012). Crucial to primordial feelings are centres in the brainstem. In particular Damasio highlights that the *nucleus tractus solitarius* and the parabrachial nuclei "receive a full complement of signals describing the state of the internal milieu in the entire body" (ibid.). He also cites the importance of the superior colliculi as a critical site for integration of sensory input and mapping in visual, auditory and somatic modalities (ibid.). Taken together these sites support the early experience of feeling as a whole person integration of both the internal and external environment.

While much neurophysiological investigation has taken place in relation to task performance, self implies growth in complexity of the individual when *not* involved in task performance. It is to be expected that non-task related activity would be found in the human brain and neural networks. Greater complexity in such activity could be consistent with emergence of a self that can take on relatively independent functioning as opposed to being dependent upon others for self-regulation. Hence one would expect shifts during development towards greater complexity in relation to neural structures that subserve communicative exchange involving both of the great human semiotic systems, that of affective expression and that of verbal language.

Investigations into brain function involving imaging techniques have involved subtraction techniques whereby images taken during a *rest* condition are subtracted from images taken during task performance with the expectation of highlighting those areas where there is increased activity during task performance, identifying areas of functionality in the brain. There have been consistent observations that in some areas task performance was associated with a paradoxical deactivation. In other words, these areas were more active during the *rest* condition. The areas which displayed this paradoxical activity were termed the *default mode of brain function* (Raichle et al., 2001). Recent literature refers also to the *default network* (Fair et al., 2008), *default mode network* (Otti et al., 2010) or *default system* (Raichle & Snyder, 2007). The network implicated is widespread, involving areas previously described as communication and affect regulation networks including the orbitofrontal cortex, the posterior cingulate area, the parahippocampal area and parts of the parietal and temporal cortex (Fair et al., 2008). It also seems "all areas of the brain have a high level of organized default functional activity" (Raichle & Snyder, 2007). The oscillations of the default network (DN) have been described "as spontaneous and continuous as heartbeat and breathing", suggesting an inherent rhythmicity in these functions (Otti et al., 2010).

It is perhaps not surprising that intrinsic networks of activity in the brain can be identified when one considers that the great majority of the brain's energy consumption supports communication between neurones (as much as 80%) (Raichle & Snyder, 2007). The additional burden on the brain related to momentary demands of the environment under normal conditions may be as little as 0.5–1 per cent of the brain's metabolic energy requirements (ibid.). While the functions of the default system remain a matter of speculation, investigators have related it to spontaneous, stimulus-independent thought, self-referential thought, the sculpting of communicative responses, introspection, interpreting, responding to and predicting the environment, serving an internal narrative function, empathy and future orientation (Raichle & Snyder, 2007; Otti et al., 2010; Fair et al., 2008; Hassabis et al., 2007).

Affective pattern recognition forms the basis of implicit *mental models* which have primary survival value in terms of anticipating experience in an environmental context (Siegel, 2015; Solms, 2015). The DN may reflect growth in the complexity of these models. Activity levels in the DN show an inverse relationship to sympathetic arousal and also show decreased activation during linearly directed mental activity (Fair et al., 2008). These networks show only sparse interconnections in children of 7–9 years of age compared to highly integrated connectivity by early adulthood consistent with a more autonomous forms of neural functioning (Fair et al., 2008). It might be anticipated that factors like trauma may impact upon the development of neural integration.

The DN is a promising candidate as objective correlate of *self*. It is hard to know what the experiential correlate of increased complexity might look like. Complexity develops outside awareness and we don't always realize our capacities consciously. Given that "the elemental form of consciousness (is) affect" (Solms, 2019), it is likely that integration of self is not a purely neo-cortical matter:

> *I had an experience in a therapy group where I found myself simultaneously (or at least rapidly alternating between) laughing and crying. This was experienced as a profound relief at the time. On reflection it seems to me to have involved something like an integrative expression of my contradictory and confusing personal world. It helped that the therapist at the time commented that he had "seen such states before".*

Significance: an evolutionary perspective

Significance, as feeling in relationship, provides a level of meaning constitutive of human lives yet distinct from semantic meaning that emerges in language in more specific forms. It is shared with other mammals.

The evolutionary developments that set mammals apart from other species are: "(1) nursing in conjunction with maternal care; (2) audiovocal communication for maintaining maternal-offspring contact; and (3) play" (MacLean, 1985). The *first language*, with its audiovocal, affective basis, is substantially present not only in humans but also across mammalian species, who have invested their energies towards the *family*: "When mammals opted for a family way of life, they set the stage for one of the most distressful forms of suffering. A condition that, for us, makes being a mammal so painful is having to endure separation or isolation from loved ones and, in the end, the utter isolation of death" (ibid., p. 415). Significance relates in a fundamental way to exchanges involving *care, maintenance of contact* and *co-created fields of interest, enjoyment and exploration*. The extent to which this is shared across species points to an elemental level of significance, very much in the fabric of human *being*, without which it would not be possible to have a sense of self or to develop as individuals in a world of self and other. The evolutionary history of these developments gives a context for the particular development, in humans, of language.

The forerunners of mammals are known as *therapsids*. These mammal-like reptiles had developed cranial characteristics similar to mammals. It has been suggested that cooling environmental conditions may have led to these creatures retaining their eggs and possibly to the development of placentation (MacLean, 1985). The earliest mammals are thought to have lived in the dark floor of the forests of that era and to have most likely been nocturnal (ibid.). Changes in the jaw bones that began in therapsids led to the development of the bones of the middle ear (malleus and incus) evident in the earliest mammal species (ibid.). Audio-vocal communication would have served as a valuable adjunct to vision and olfaction in these circumstances with improved hearing allowing reciprocal interaction via vocal signals, starting with the separation call which "may represent the earliest and most basic mammalian vocalization serving originally to maintain maternal-offspring contact" (ibid.). If this had not been associated with behaviours oriented towards care and protection, this would simply have been a risk for newborn individuals. If, instead, parents were to follow patterns of behaviours exhibited by reptiles, newborns would have been at risk of predation by parent or others. The strategy in reptiles is different – they are born equipped to survive and do not emit vocalizations from birth, silence involving a lower risk.

In non-human primates, complex communicative exchanges are all affect or emotion-based. Indeed, in all mammals, "The primal conscious 'state' . . . is intrinsically affective" (Solms, 2015). This is, nevertheless, consistent with the development of complex hierarchies and social–behavioural systems not dependent on the acquisition of symbolic language or neocortical structures (MacLean, 1985; Panksepp, 2008). In human speech these affective, musically based vocalizations and exchanges are important in relation to motivation to engage socially and hence to *use* language (MacLean, 1985; Panksepp, 2008). The apprehension and expression of feeling give life to language in the process of its instantiation.

In humans input to the prefrontal cortex includes a major projection from the vagus nerve, in contrast to other primates, suggesting an enhanced capacity to utilize embodied emotional feedback from interaction as a source of information regarding self in the environment (MacLean, 1985). This "dual source of information from the internal and external world appears to be necessary for a sense of personal identity and . . . in the case of prefrontal function, visceral feelings may be required for the 'insight' necessary for the foresight to plan for the needs of others as well as the self" (ibid.). The connection between inner and outer worlds is now understood to include feelings of participation mediated through the mirror neurone system while witnessing the actions of others (Gallese et al., 1996).

The main role transformations in human development reflect a growing self in a system of interactional care. The infant develops from being a primary recipient of care with an *emerging* self through gradually increasing intra- and inter-personal levels of coordination. By the age of 3 or 4 the child has consolidated the sense of a separate self with an inner or personal world (Meares, 2005). Over time the child establishes personal and social competence until the individual can *care for him or her-self* when the child becomes an adult. It is not that the child is no more but rather that the adult role assumes care of the "child inside". The emergence into adulthood is often seen as an endpoint of development in the modern world although its primary importance in an evolutionary sense may be as preparation for parenthood, requiring the *capacity to care for others* as well as one's self. It is in the parent-infant dyad that fundamental forms of relatedness and meaning are established. It is in the realization of these roles that a person can be said to have attained first-hand knowledge of life processes. Modern societies often have a heterogeneous relational structure, with a predilection for assertion of individual rights obscuring this basic matrix of relatedness. In simpler communities, the person who has completed these essential life stages (from the community's perspective) may then be looked to as a teacher or mentor, having attained a personal knowledge of life. The sequence of relational significance outlined here places adulthood as an intermediate form in the transition between self-orientation and other-centeredness, understood as the capacity for assuming responsibility for self *and* others.

As an illustration of how asymmetric processes apply across the life span the following account of a parent-child interaction is offered where the parent is aged and the child is now middle-aged:

> *My mother had been in the rehabilitation hospital for three weeks. She was going downhill. The doctors were talking about palliative care and transfer to a nursing home. We all thought she was likely to die. I spent time with her after work. One day I was feeding her, making somewhat desultory conversation. In the main she didn't respond although sometimes there was a monosyllabic answer or attempt at a smile. We were comfortable together despite her bird-like frailty. I was holding her hand. The meal was served. She pushed it away so I fed her as best I could. She attempted to eat a little but her face contorted with the effort involved until soon she refused to open her mouth. It was painful to watch. Her eyes were dull, her body limp. I was at the point of giving up. As a final offering I opened a small tub of ice-cream. Mum accepted a spoonful. Something changed. There was a brightening of her eyes and I sensed that she had enjoyed the sweet coldness of the easy-to-swallow ice-cream. It was a "phoenix from the ashes" moment in which we felt very close. The intimacy made me think of her as a small child. It also seemed a sort of echo, perhaps from an unremembered past. She improved after that. She got well enough to go home and was good for the next two years. It has always seemed to me that was the turning point, when Mum came back to life.*

The discussion has focused on continuous processes that contribute to maintenance and development of significant relationships as part of an evolutionary endowment. The role shifts alluded to, however, also require psychological and behavioural transformations that place emotional demands on individuals. Language, both spoken and internal, plays a significant role in these changes, which is to say "symbolic transformation is a primary need of man" (Hobson, 1985). This involves the engagement of the child in imaginative activities where the carer's capacity to *woo* the child into language play that allows emotional investment in these activities becomes relevant to the child's development (Greenspan & Shankar, 2004). This makes the realization of symbolic play, a peculiarly human form of play, crucial to the future of the individual. All children start from the position of relative smallness and limited capacity so that forward growth potential is always under threat from the sense that next steps may be overwhelming. All cultures deal with this situation through the use of stories and myths that speak to the many hurdles and obstacles encountered in the realization of self.

This dimension of culture was termed *mythos* by the Ancient Greeks, in contrast to *logos*. Both were seen as paths to recognition of truth where mythos was associated with "mystery" and logos with "science" (Jung, 1959). *Mythos* has qualities of timelessness and significance reflecting human emotional states and relatedness where shared understanding requires a symbolic approach employing poetic language, whereas logos is relatively objective, free of emotion, and associated with logical language often taken as a literal description of phenomena. This can be misleading since science is never free of metaphors (Lewontin, 2000) while metaphors often capture actual ('literal') experience better. In the next section of this chapter the notion of significance is discussed from this symbolic perspective.

Significance: a symbolic perspective

Love relations, rivalries, betrayals, jealousies and abandonments that get enacted in triangular human relationships are the stuff of media reports, theatre and community gossip. Understanding the people in these relationships and their sometimes self-defeating behaviours is also the stuff of psychoanalytic theorizing. In psychodynamic therapies one can add consideration of unconscious motivation.

While in politics *metaphorical* attacks and assassinations are more common than literal assaults and assassinations, the consequences of public or, indeed, private humiliation may be severe, sometimes extending to actual death via suicide or murder or less direct impacts on health. Of equal interest are the ways people find to survive and thrive despite experiencing intensely emotional and traumatic circumstances.

The focus so far has been towards dyadic interactions between infant and carer, contrasting the relatively dependent infant with the physically mature carer. However, the dyad does not exist in isolation unrelated to a community. The infant is born into a triadic relational network. The efforts of the mother are initially highly oriented to the infant to an extent made possible by the capacity for care and attention known as *primary maternal preoccupation* (Winnicott, 1960). The situation is not indefinitely sustainable and the infant will have to invest in relationships and skill acquisition in order to survive. Stories are co-created from the beginning of life motivated by the desire to share through communication: "human beings create together because they are motivated from birth to experiment with the exchange of fantasies and to find meaning in them" (Trevarthen, 2008). By some point in adulthood the direction *vis-à-vis* care may be reversed, the parent now requiring care. Relationships with significant others and their transformations form the backdrop for the Oedipus complex.

The Oedipal drama is well known in the modern era because of Freud's famous application of Sophocles' play to patterns of the unconscious. A widely accessible account of the psychoanalytic understanding of familial interactions is quoted:

> [The] **Oedipus complex** denotes the emotions and ideas that the mind keeps in the unconscious, via dynamic repression, that concentrate upon a boy's desire to sexually possess his mother, and kill his father. Sigmund Freud, who coined the term "Oedipus complex", believed that the Oedipus complex is a desire for the mother in both sexes.
>
> In classical, Freudian psychoanalytic theory, the child's identification with the same-sex parent is the successful resolution of the Oedipus complex and of the Electra complex; his and her key psychological experience to developing a mature sexual role and identity.
>
> (http://en.wikipedia.org/wiki/Oedipus_complex)

In this formulation there is a focus of desire on certain fantasied events (kill father; sexually possess mother). There is also emphasis on identification with the same sex parent. However, identification is not simply equivalence. In *actual* development ongoing involvement with parents supports a sense of continuity and a model for learning that depends more on a sense of similarity rather than strict identity.

The Greek myth of Oedipus focuses on a succession of events that make up a narrative that warns of the dangers of breaking the incest taboo, although there are many versions of the story (suggesting many possible resolutions of the "Oedipal drama"):

> *In Euripides' plays on the subject, Jocasta did not kill herself upon learning of Oedipus' birth, and Oedipus was blinded by a servant of Laius. And the blinding of Oedipus does not appear in sources earlier than Aeschylus. Some older sources of the myth, including Homer, state that Oedipus continued to rule Thebes after the revelations and after Jocasta's death.*
>
> (http://en.wikipedia.org/wiki/Oedipus_complex)

Freud's repudiation of his seduction theory led to the Oedipus complex being understood at the level of fantasy. In the original story, however, events are not portrayed as fantasy: "in Oedipus Rex . . . . his (Oedipus') father **did** try to kill him" and Oedipus does kill his father (ibid.). This is to say that the story is one of real trauma rather than a fantasy located in an individual mind. The interpersonal revision of psychoanalysis recognizes the *real* suffering in early relationships with significant others (Levenson, 2017).

The way in which the Oedipus complex was used in psychoanalysis for much of the 20th century led to its somewhat stereotypical application and the use of theory to reinforce standard resolutions, with the result that forms of human sexuality such as homosexuality were seen in pathological terms rather than as normal variants (DSM 1, 1952). This view has become out-dated. There is huge variety within the range of what could be considered healthy development and many paths to identity formation are possible.

The description of the Oedipus complex points towards an event in time involving an effort at killing or at least the idea of eliminating the Oedipal rival. This may apply to metaphoric and emotional efforts at certain stages of development: the phallic stage in classic psychoanalytic theory (Freud, 1905). However, the influence of Oedipus' adoptive family received little consideration by psychoanalysis. Polybus and Merope raised Oedipus as their own and, far from wanting to harm his adoptive father, he leaves the court of Corinth to protect Polybus (his adoptive father), when he hears the prophesy that he is destined to "kill his father" (Lingiardi, 2019). Of course, Oedipus wasn't aware that he had been adopted, reflecting another cultural taboo (talking about adoption).

For self, it is the ongoing nature of relatedness between parent and child that is critical. Metaphoric Oedipal victories or defeats may be associated with a sense of triumph or failure but the sense that builds over time in the child, in relation to his or her capacity to be *like* mother or father, refers more to the sense of "having the potential of", or *similarity to*, rather than "being the same as". The relationship is analogical rather than an equation of identity.

Most psychotherapists continue to recognize Freud's "discovery" of Oedipal rivalry as an important basis of unconscious mental life (Tomkins, 1995). The attribution of the rivalry to sexual drive is more doubtful. The theory has been considered deficient in a relational sense: "Freud's interpretation of the nature of social relationships was crippled by his dependence on the drive theory" (ibid.). Drives, in general, are not dependent upon either affect or language for their fulfilment and hence can operate, as it were, outside the zone of self and meaning. In the case of sexual drive there is undoubtedly, and commonly, a complex affective investment in sexual behaviours and fantasies, although this is elaborated in highly individualized ways that relate to particular selves. Tomkins felt that the emphasis on drive obscured "the family romance" which involves the child's general wish to be like both father and mother, and, in the immature state, "to possess both of them" (ibid.). He also argues social relationships require a quality of tenderness if they are to endure (ibid.). The strongest emotions are linked to intimate relationships where the earliest investment is in the need for relatedness rather than sexuality indicating the "strong biological roots" of attachment theory (Bowlby, 1988). This biological basis for tender relatedness is further highlighted by the identification of a nurturing or "care" system within mammalian neurobiology (Panksepp & Biven, 2012).

From the point of view of normal development, it may be preferable not to overemphasize the role of sexual drive in family relatedness: the Oedipus complex can be seen as a template upon which affectional relationships are placed where the primary need is for relatedness. From the object relations perspective, Fairbairn indicated drive theory had "put the cart before the horse" and the significance of sexuality in relationships was that it provided a natural path towards the achievement of intimate relatedness, rather than intimacy being primarily a means of satisfying the sexual drive (Fairbairn, 1952; Whelan, 2003). The resolution of the child's efforts at overcoming the other lies in the move towards collaboration with parents. This involves a shift from efforts that are directed at control of the other, towards cooperation. The prevailing conditions (e.g. availability; receptiveness) in a given family may favour collaboration with one parent over the other.

Engaged intimacy in the parent-infant dyad involves prioritizing of the relationship for the participants. At a relational level this may mean that, in many cases, the infant *has* supplanted the father in the mother's attentions without inevitable associated conflict, as described:

> In the good enough Oedipus complex – so to speak – the infant has already slept with the mother and enjoyed the fruits of this triumph. This good position emerges from the intimacy of mother and infant holding off the outside world that he represents, and this killing off is a permissible pleasure, which the father supports.
>
> (Bollas, 2011, p. 101)

The pleasure derives from the interaction between infant and carer rather than from sexual drive. The small child needs a degree of protection from the wider world and in good enough circumstances will receive such care. By the age of 4 or so and beyond, the child has developed an inner world or sense of separate self which "puts one substantially out of the reaches of intersubjective knowing even if it simultaneously enhances it" (ibid., p. 105). The contrast between the earlier pre-verbal stage and the emergence of the child as social actor and separate self involves a turning towards the world (ibid.). Conflicts in the self-world arena continue for school-age children, for whom competition tends to be understood as "winning against others". It requires a greater level of abstraction, not present at least before late primary school age, for children to conceive of something like a "win-win" situation.

It has been argued that the way humans experience desire, the centre-point of the Oedipus complex, is that the child knows the direction of his or her desire (that is towards the parents) and, in this sense, "is never lost", because *home* is known and, while parents may be loved or hated, "they are always wanted" (Phillips, 2010). In adult life the individual is expected to leave the home of origin behind and establish a new home. This leads to a situation where adults feel lost, in the sense of not knowing the object of their desire (Phillips, 2010). A new home needs to be found in terms of relationships and place. If this is accomplished, there may eventually be the sense of finding oneself. *Self* may ultimately come to be sensed as a home for the individual, reflecting a capacity for "*alone-togetherness*" where one can be equally at home alone or with others (Hobson, 1985).

The myth of Oedipus relates to the incest taboo, a matter of such shame that drastic actions are taken with terrible consequences. Taboos are associated with powerful affects like shame. Language also plays a role, in that both Laius and Oedipus react defensively to prevent perceived catastrophe, in response to the *prophecies* of soothsayers, sensing the power of hidden affective forces. Taboo points towards an area of risk. The breaking of a taboo does not have to involve risk to life or limb but always risks the status of the person in the eyes of the community. Personal integrity is in question.

As family relationships are enacted, there may be failures of resolution and episodes of conflict. Powerful affects become part of the ongoing fabric of interactional experience, affecting development of self. Of these, shame may be particularly crippling to self. Other strong affects like contempt or hatred are more likely to stimulate a breaking of the relationship, and hence a form of resolution, while shame often is associated with perpetuation of the relationship with a greatly diminished sense of self (Tomkins, 1995).

The Oedipal process speaks to transformations that allow for the inclusion of the child in the family unit with a gradual increase in autonomy. Phillips' discussion of the experience of being *lost* in relation to desire highlights the fact that such transformations do not only occur in childhood. The mode of change is one of symbolic transformation, of change in role and the sense of self rather than a drive-driven biological process. The infinite ways in which feeling can become invested in relationships, activities, stories and images mean that there is a multiplicity of ways in which transformation can occur. In good enough circumstances transitions are likely to be experienced in terms of growing into, and growing out of, new and old roles. In traumatic circumstances there is a tendency to be fixed by the influence of unconscious traumatic memories, so that the attention of the individual remains directed at what has been lost, deficient or traumatic and the sense of growth is attenuated.

The acquisition of language gives additional flexibility to the developing mind through grammatical structure, greatly enhancing the possibilities for symbolic transformation. We can learn old stories and make up new ones. This language-space reflects the material world that the individual observes and the phenomenal world of experience but is not constituted by either (Halliday, 1992). It is an unbounded space with an enormous potential for re-construal (ibid.). When people develop with a sense of safety, this language space becomes integrated into the sense of a *self with mental space*, a mind of her own. In all cases, however, there is a leading edge of experience and the sense of asymmetry with its basis in the reality of the individual being small in the face of a large world. The potential for trauma and helplessness, with an attendant collapsing of mental space, remains throughout life. Trauma can also lead to compensatory hypertrophies in self-importance and tendencies towards domination. Meares refers to "two playrooms", the *playspace* and the *real play room* (Meares, 2005). The real in this case refers to the impinging external reality that often intrudes on the emergent sense of interiority. It is associated with linear, logical thought rather than non-linear, associational thought.

In the developmental context the contrast in size and capacities is writ large in infant-carer relationships. However, even small infants have considerable capacities for attuning to movement and emotional expression in the environment (Trevarthen, 2002). When the infant responds to a facial expression, she is enacting a social intelligence focused on the person of the other, and making use of the "face-heart-brain" connection adapted to social engagement (Porges, 2011). Reciprocally, "for the family of the infant, this baby is already a person, socially aware and capable of considerable power in interactions" (Trevarthen, 2002). The point is that the infant has an active intelligence in the interpersonal environment for which it is adapted (Winnicott, 1960). Contacts with others are constantly evaluated through actions and the responses elicited (ibid.). The intelligence of the infant is absorbent and information-seeking (ibid.).

By the time people seek psychotherapy, circumstances have often become discouraging for the individual. The therapist needs to see the patient as a person first and foremost and to recognize the social intelligence that is the major source of hope for the person's psychological growth and recovery. The ongoing presence of forms of feeling that derive from our familial relationships have a primary significance in terms of inclusion and acceptance as a member of a community and, ultimately, of humanity. Trauma alienates and constricts the self. Recognition of trauma is not sufficient in itself for a therapeutic outcome. A zone of symbolic transformation is also necessary to the psychotherapeutic process.

Modelling communicative complexity

Where affective exchange between self and other occurs within limits felt to be safe, allowing development of an intersubjective field of play, conditions are right for the development of self. Play is engaged in for its own sake rather than for instrumental purposes. Situations of trauma correspond to interpersonal environments where others seek to control or coerce, restricting *self's* affective range and limiting possibilities to specified tasks and *other-determined* ends. In such an environment it would be expected there would be less opportunity for differentiation. While the *default network* cannot be considered equivalent to self, it does seem likely to correlate with realization of self. It is to be anticipated that the DN would display less strength of functional connectivity in traumatic circumstances. In relation to language this would probably be reflected in more linear language used primarily for instrumental purposes, rather than for imaginative and future-oriented speech functions that endow self with the sense of a *life of its own*. In using language humans continually create novelty, "whenever you set out to speak a sentence you haven't spoken before" (Calvin, 1996) involving forms of improvization supported by resonant processes in the brain (ibid.). "Intelligent mental life is a fluctuating view of your inner and outer worlds" where the ability to say something new is crucial (ibid.).

The development of complexity in the default network of the brain seems likely to occur in parallel to the realization of self. Meares has suggested a model of *self* as a self-organizing system. He draws an analogy with the non-linear deterministic equations of Chaos theory, where Mandelbrot's equation states that iterations of a pattern are described by $Z = Z^2 + c$. Meares postulates that if "Z" is the expression of an individual *self*, then Z^2 could be considered the response of the other that contains something recognizable of the "Z" self ("Z^2") but also introduces an element of the self of the other ("c") (Meares, 2005). While speculative, this describes both the potential for change over time and the recurrence of coherent, recognizable patterns of self.

Meares' model is from the perspective of an individual self. The concept of an intersubjective field involves reciprocal influences and reciprocal change in two or more selves. The individual self can't be reduced to a particular dyad and includes multiple interpersonal influences as well as the broader "world" influence. So, for a given self the "c" term itself takes on multiplicity. Such a model does suggest ways in which self acquires complexity with the development of the property of *singularity*. In communicative terms, the conversation of a given self over a lifetime grows in singularity through interaction with multiplicity. In neural terms, this could be consistent with neural networks cohering around "strange attractors" (Edelman, 2000).

We often undervalue talk. Yet, often without knowing it, we grow in conversation. Conversations proceed on the basis of what is *given* and what is *new*. The *call* of the *self* already has both these elements and the *response* of the *other* will proceed by picking up on something *given* and adding in a new element. The model of *given and new* applies both to the affective-expressive level and the verbal level of communication. Indeed, once verbal language is established, the interaction between affect and language is reciprocal. It is by no means the case that one is "trying to find the words for feeling". Often feeling arises through verbal expression. Such realization of affect in speech is taken as a concrete instance of value or conviction. If we manage to balance our lives in the world of social interaction, it will have involved managing feeling and regulating self through integration of relational experience. One attains a singular voice.

Chapter 2

Living language and the resonant self

Overview

The everyday reality with which people are most vitally concerned is mostly intersubjective, involving the shared imagining of experience. Modern science favours objectivity, physicality and its application even to the human sciences. Psychotherapy focuses on understanding and the ways in which people are affected during communicative exchange and in the spaces of internal reverberation. The interpersonal philosophies of Hegel, James, Heidegger and Wittgenstein are seen to provide an underpinning for the discipline of psychotherapy. Language as it is lived in community provides an elastic network of meaning, perhaps mirroring the object-seeking properties of neural systems as they are realized through experiences of significance. From the beginning, humans are participants in a symbolic world that needs to take account of language as a felt experience in relationships where it becomes a regulator of self-experience and emergent personality.

Living language

In the last chapter selves were seen to be shaped by streaming communications, words and images "given and received". An example was given of a session where the patient's expression of vulnerability was experienced positively by both patient and therapist. The moment resonated for both as one of connection. Given the importance of expressed feeling in all communication, it seems likely that there will be the greatest potential for genuine exchanges (and change) when *both* patient and therapist are able to express feeling. A brief account is given of a session where it is the therapist's expression of emotion that seems mutative for the patient:

> *A middle-aged man begins a therapy session with reference to a "really good experience" where, after a period of significant depression, he was starting to get back his old sense of self, "an old feeling . . . remembered". He identifies continuing problems and becomes preoccupied with a sense of deficit in interpersonal situations where he feels at sea in conversation. He pointedly identifies his disadvantage relative to the therapist, saying "I'm not a word*

person like you". *After referring to a sense of paralysis the patient mobilizes himself through an argument he develops over who is in control, characterizing the therapist as "captain of the ship". The therapist is ambivalent, commenting, "Perhaps I'm not a good driver". The patient then delivers a coup de grâce, joking that whatever happens the therapist is the one to get paid. This seems to catch the therapist a little off guard and, after saying "I mean . . . if you find you are wasting your time", his voice wavers with brief but overt expression of vulnerability. The patient responds to this, perhaps feeling both the therapist's humanity and also the removal, in the moment, of the sense of inequality. He comments, ". . . that was good because we did a lot of stuff to get your empathy and . . . responses . . . . . . it was all . . . true reactions".*

The patient had been stuck in a pattern of argument that could have gone on interminably. He seemed unconscious of his effect on the other. This changed with the therapist's spontaneous expression of emotion. There was a humanizing exchange that was immediate and alive, with two selves open to resonant response.

Language is essential to humanity. Human beings live as much in the space of thought and meaning, as in physical space. The capacity to use symbols and the symbolic medium of language "has given the human primate its enormous evolutionary advantage through the creation of culture" (Meares, 2016). The generative potential of language in individual lives begins with the engagement of the infant in the symbolic world through proto-conversation. Deficits in this kind of experience have consequences.

The Emperor Frederick II, an admirer of Albert Magnus and a believer in "observed truth", was said, in the 13th century, to have brought up children in silence, "to settle the question whether they would speak Hebrew, which was the first language, or Greek, or Arabic or at least the language of their parents; but he laboured in vain, for the children all died". (Fernandez-Armesto, 1997). This medieval horror story illustrates the fatal consequences of a linguistically deprived environment for the *actual* development of humans in the material world. In modern times gross neglect or emotional deprivation in infancy have also been shown to have potentially fatal consequences (Spitz, 1946).

Psychotherapists deal with people in whom traumatic disturbances in interpersonal interactions during development have had real consequences for personal growth. There is always potential for relational connection allowing re-engagement in psychological growth. Where talking involves a sense of interpersonal connection, "There can be no semiotic act that leaves the world exactly as it was" (Halliday, 2002). Consider this example of a *semiotic act* that had an impact on the personal world of its "object":

I was three years into an acting course while still working part-time as a doctor. It was tough going at a time in my life when I wasn't sure of my direction. The training was emotionally demanding. One day, while waiting in the foyer with other students and some of the teachers, the principal of the school directed a comment to me. I can't remember the lead-up although it was part of a conversation carried on in plain view of the others. He said, "Nothing is wasted, Tony". It has stayed with me ever since. It seemed to capture and respond to my existential anxieties of the time. Genuine effort is never wasted: that's what I got from it.

The psychotherapist is in the position of engaging with a person seeking some form of enhancement in personal experience. The medium for this process is embodied communicative exchange, based in language and imagery. The natural form for the process is human conversation. The relationship which develops in this medium of exchange is both actual and symbolic. A scientific approach to this field needs to include consideration of *self* and *language* if it is to retain the immediacy of "first-person" experience rather than simply becoming a description of such exchanges (a "third person" account).

Both *self* and *language* present paradoxes for science. *Self*, understood as the flow of private experience, is a whole person concept that can't be defined objectively, yet which has objective correlates in terms of observable behaviour, speech, and accompanying states of the body and brain. *Language* is part of the material world and yet does not correspond to any material "thing". While it is material in its instantiation through speech acts, it also exists independently of any such individual act. When it is instantiated, as it is in psychotherapy, it invariably includes a component of affective expression, a major contributor to the significance and interpersonal meaning attained at any given moment. The concept of mind necessarily involves self, language, feeling and relationship. As such, it is an irreducibly interpersonal phenomenon.

The register of the psychotherapeutic field is that of felt significance and the expression and representation of personal meaning: meaning created together and meaning held alone. This encompasses shared meaning, divided meaning, understanding and misunderstanding, or even lack of meaning. Patients often present with vague dissatisfactions, or painful states of mind, leading to a discomfort with self and incapacity to "see" effective paths of action in life. Personal meaning is never a precise or quantifiable matter. It is a question of approximation and "best fit": of similarity in understanding rather than precise definition. In conversation we strive towards making sense of painful and discordant self-states through the use of language. Analogy and metaphor are central when it comes to communicating personal experience in psychotherapy. The feeling component of speech has resonant properties that build relationship and sustain images. The therapist endeavours to make a response that fits analogically, approximately matching the affect and emphasis in the patient's expression (an *analogical fit*), while also contributing something additional (i.e. not simply imitating).

While the "free association" of the patient was considered the "first instrument for the scientific study of mind" (Strachey, 1962), an *intersubjective* framework requires a shift to "the conversation" as the primary object of study. In therapeutic conversation, when it's going well, there will be a "free associative" flow, although one with two contributors.

Analogical fit

Conversational exchange based on social interest is the predominant function of language at all ages most of the time (Dunbar, 1996). Where social organization and communication in primates is largely based around exchanges involving grooming, gesture and physical display, in humans these interactions are greatly supplemented, and to some extent taken over by, conversation (ibid.). Language is likely to have evolved for more efficient management of increasing social complexity, arguably the major evolutionary force driving increase in relative brain size (ibid.). Language and communication constitute "a fundamentally cooperative enterprise" (Tomasello, 2010) that is prosocial in nature, dependent upon "the ability to create common conceptual ground – joint attention, shared experience, common cultural knowledge" (ibid.). An important element of naturally occurring conversations is the recognition that arises from being able to express and convey the nature of one's experience. This requires a capacity to use analogy and metaphor since there are no words that capture inner experience literally or precisely.

In his formulation of the Conversational Model (CM), Robert Hobson describes the therapeutic process as one of "learning, and learning how to learn, within a personal conversation" (Hobson, 1985). Conversation is the spontaneously occurring form of language that occurs socially between *persons* rather than relating to the description and manipulation of *things* (ibid.). Self emerges in a field of self and other, in the space between feeling and language. The CM conceives of the self as emerging through a process of doubling, originally described by Baldwin as made up of "ego" and "alter", where "the 'alter' is ultimately internalized in a reverberating process . . . . then recreated culminating in the formation of the 'bipolar self'" (Meares, 2000; Baldwin, 1906). The task of therapy can be seen as the "*mutual creation or discovery of a feeling-language*" (Hobson, 1985, p. 15). The personal world of the patient grows through an active process of growth with the therapist, consistent with the notion of the social construction of self. In this view, "perhaps the self can be viewed as more of a verb than a noun – as a process that evolves as we grow and change" (Siegel, 2015).

The sense of self is an everyday experience familiar to everyone yet difficult to define. For the CM *self* is understood, after William James, as the inner flow or "stream" of consciousness with an "I-me" duality, "partly knower and partly known" (James, 1890). A sense of personal being (Meares, 2000, 2005) associated with a level of "body feeling, which is with us all the time . . . To (which) we (usually) pay no attention at all" (Meares, 2000) provides, "**continuity of being**" (Winnicott, 1960). This experience of unity can, at any time, be disrupted. The experience of loss of the contact provided by communication can overwhelm the continuity of being. Its importance for individuals may reflect its importance for the species:

> ... the essential function of language [is] to maintain social contact in the dark. It is doubtful whether man learned to speak in order to convey information or emotion; it was rather that, with the light gone and the comforting visible world with it, he had to convince himself that he was not alone among the possible terrors of the night.
>
> (Burgess, 1970, p. 40)

The emergence of personal selves "from the dark" of isolation, relates to the gaining of personal knowledge acquired through the "vision" that comes from language. Such experiences are rare but when accomplished carry the sense of truth. In therapy, "perhaps – if only for a moment – seeing through the darkness of our fear and envy, we might **share** a gaze, with a new vision" (Hobson, 1985).

The ground of psychotherapy lies in reciprocal communication that seeks resonance with affective life, and finds, using language, an analogical fit with the patient's experience, facilitating emergence of self. Self cannot be separated from language. While individual selves vary in their use of language, it is beyond the individual to change language itself since language is a *social*, not an individual, institution (Saussure, 1959). Hence the sense of self is dependent on language but language is not dependent on self.

Interpersonal fit in the realm of the psyche refers to sufficient similarity in the response to the feeling and need of the individual. Given that self is always linked to feeling the matching required in the developing individual is always of an *analogical* nature rather than being a precise mechanical fit. Forms of feeling are part of the shifting ground of being. For first-person experience we can only speak of "what it is like" to experience rather than define "what it is", as we might with an inanimate object. Hobson draws attention to Buber's distinction between "I-thou" and "I-it": "For the **I** of the primary word **I-thou** is a different **I** from that of the primary word **I-it**" (Hobson, 1985; Buber, 1937). The *I* of the personal "primary word" (also "primary world") is the forerunner of the personal self with its dual form; whereas in the *I-it* configuration the personal sense of self with its duality, is lost" (Hobson, 1985). In normal development the infant and developing child have to negotiate and exist in both of these interpersonal, communicative spaces: one felt to be personal, where play and personal growth occur and one where exigencies of the "real world" interrupt play, requiring the child to adapt and focus on the external world, without the duality of interaction and illusion characteristic of play (Meares, 2005). Throughout life we need to be able to negotiate these two spaces, one relatively impersonal and distanced, one relatively personal and intimate.

There are two nouns corresponding to the adjective *analogical*: analogue, and analogy (Blair, 1982). Each of these has relevance to the phrase *analogical fit*. The self struggles to find words that approximate felt experience. We seek a "best available" analogy or "good enough" fit. This is also characteristic of many biological processes such as immune responses involving a "best available" fit between antigen and antibody (Edelman & Tononi, 2000). The theory of *neuronal group selection* suggests that consciousness is supported by the nervous system in a comparable way (ibid.).

Analogue is defined as "something analogous to something else" (i.e. a relationship of "likeness") (Blair, 1982). *Analogy* is defined as "partial agreement or likeness between two or more things, which forms basis for a comparison" (ibid.). In psychotherapy an "analogue" could be said to be present when an image instantiated in therapy has a likeness to an image from elsewhere (including the past). Analogy, on the other hand, implies a more clearly linguistic process where comparisons are actively made, bringing likenesses into the conversational field.

Physiologically, many vital processes are continuously variable quantities. The term *analogue* is relevant to many such functions: respiration, heartbeat, blood pressure, temperature and so on. This adjective, applied to certain devices and systems of measurement ("*analogue* scales"), describes "measuring or representing by use of a continuously variable quantity" using "a continuously variable display, such as the needle on a car speedometer" (Blair, 1982). This property, of continuous variability, is also true for *feeling*, always present in consciousness, varying both in kind and intensity on a continual basis. However, in contradistinction to physical quantities which can be displayed objectively using techniques such as the electrocardiogram, feeling can only be "measured" through the filter of self. While signs of affect may be perceived by observing another, we rely upon the report of the person subject to feeling to discern what is actually being experienced. We find in doing so that the person often struggles, using linguistic and gestural means to express these states as best they can, by *analogy*.

Physiological variables that can be displayed on an analogue scale, like heartbeat and breathing, are also sensitive to changes in activity within the ANS, influenced by changes in emotional state. They provide an objective correlate to feeling.

Analogical fit in the psychotherapeutic context is necessary to the elaboration of the essentially symbolic processes of language embedded in the material processes of the body as manifest in spoken language.

We live in a simultaneously symbolic and actual world. For humans, the actual includes the symbolic, an environmental stream of the spoken and seen, from the beginning, before the infant becomes skilled in the use of the symbols that surround her. The effects of surrounding symbolic attitudes and the affective ground of the infant's own experience blend into actual bodily consequences in terms of the infant's growth. For the individual infant, the world presents itself already made, with knowledge present, *out there*. For each new life, "In the beginning was the Word" (John, 1:1; KJV). As against this external knowledge that takes many years for a given person to appropriate, partially, into an individual mind, the infant has only its own feeling states to provide a balance of inner, personal knowledge in guiding adaptation to life. These forms of feeling already have some differentiation at birth and constitute a genetic endowment for humans and other species (Panksepp & Biven, 2012). They are also the germ of self, and the beginning of personhood.

The embodied mind: philosophical considerations

Minds that develop in interaction with others are always evolving and embodied. The "flesh and blood" element of mind is the whole person experience of feeling. Minds are works in progress, with a sense of uncertainty and incompleteness. "Unprovability" is applicable to many concepts relevant to everyday life, including *self* (Meares, 2016). Science has its limitations when it comes to the day-to-day decisions that shape lives: "We feel that even when all **possible** scientific questions have been answered, the problems of life remain completely untouched" (Wittgenstein, 1921). Perhaps uncertainty is compensated for by the drive towards relatedness. In the following vignette a patient persists in seeking relationship in response to an internal sense of dysphoria and incompleteness.

> *An adolescent, Geoff, is alienated from his adoptive family. After a brief spell in an institution he realizes that the door has been closed on any return to this family. He finds work in hospitality, working in various countries and finding a sense of family amongst friends made within the industry. While he is able to maintain these friendships for some years, a pattern develops where some dispute or disappointment will spoil things, leading him to feel that he can no longer trust the other. He sees a number of mental health professionals who empathize with his misfortunes and experiences of trauma and loss. He is urged to "let go" of the past but finds it difficult to do so. In his late thirties he succeeds in making contact with his biological mother only to find that she has just been diagnosed with a terminal malignancy. Despite this she welcomes the relationship. Over the next six months leading to her death the two become close. He is introduced to a sibling who also accepts him into the family. While others comment on the pain he has experienced and his continuing losses, Geoff has a sense of finally realizing who he is. It was a step forward.*

Geoff found it unhelpful when therapists focused primarily on trauma and loss. He yearned for recognition of his resilience and capacity to keep seeking. Although the period with his mother involved great loss and considerable emotional pain, it was also felt to have great value. To miss this is to miss who Geoff is.

The problems in living encountered in psychotherapy are legion, taking us beyond answers to be found in any existing science. The conundrums presented by difficulties in defining self-experience, and self-other relationship, have puzzled philosophers for millennia. Because psychotherapy is not yet an established science, it is necessary to consider its philosophical assumptions. A starting point for this discussion is found in the work of Hegel, followed by consideration of the philosophies of James, Heidegger and Wittgenstein.

The *Phenomenology of Spirit* (Hegel, 1807) prefigures aspects of psychodynamic thought. It describes the ontological development of thought in interaction with others. Hegelian *dialectic* speaks to the notion of conversation. A thumbnail sketch of Hegel's *Phenomenology* illustrates the dynamic process of "becoming". Its forward orientation, implying ongoing and evolving experience, with constant efforts, choices, and obstacles to negotiate, highlights *self as process*. A process that derives its significance from an interactive engagement with the world.

The *Phenomenology* begins with desire, oriented towards an "other", who must somehow survive as separate, despite desire's possessive efforts. Interpersonal rivalries are discussed in the ritual of the duel, with its outcomes of hollow victory and pointless defeat. The individual is subject to the possibility of domination, elaborated by Hegel as the *master-slave* dialectic. The *slave*, in this dialectic, gains in skill acquisition, so that the possibility of a more independent life arises. When a sense of separateness and of the separateness of others is achieved, then the individual now engages with the world in a manner where he can make objective distinctions, gaining knowledge of the "facts" of the world. For Hegel this does not amount to a satisfying state, rather it is the *unhappy consciousness* (ibid., pp. 119–138). To develop further, the individual must become vitally engaged in what they are doing in relationships and occupations, in order to gain an intimate, empathically based knowledge of the world. In this quest, guidance may be found in terms of traditions, such as religion, although the individual is in a position where discriminations and discoveries need to be made personally. The scientific attitude is to pursue further knowledge through one's personal strivings, based upon the evidence that can be ascertained in life, rather than being satisfied with what is handed down by tradition.

Such a description is idealized, and individuals may derail, or become fixated, at any stage on the life-journey. Some may be dominated by desire, at the beginning of the Hegelian journey; some may stay in dependent relation to others; some may fixate on the facts (objectivity); others may be content with following traditions. Moreover, all of these possibilities could be consistent with functional personalities. Nevertheless, we see a form of development of the mind that speaks to possibilities for growth of self. The forward orientation of *becoming* contributes to the sense of self growing and seeking, making use of the most basic affective system, the *seeking system* (Panksepp & Biven, 2012).

In psychotherapy the patient endeavours to gain personal knowledge of his or her world through communicative exchange with the therapist. Self is an emergent phenomenon in the manner of "The whole being greater than the sum of the parts" (Aristotle, *Metaphysics*). The part being expressed at any given time has a relation to this whole. In linguistics the relation of the part to the whole is known as *meronymy*, with a *meronym* being "part of a whole", as a finger is to a hand (Oxford, 2011). It is commonplace in scientific writing to equate parts with functions of the whole. For example, certain pictures of brain activity might be taken as equivalent to certain cognitive functions, or affective experience. The ascription of psychological attributes to the brain, or its component parts, has been termed "the mereological fallacy" (Bennett & Hacker, 2007). In understanding something psychologically, it is necessary to utilize communication corresponding to the whole person. The institution that humans use for this is language, although here we also get into problems. In language, descriptions of experience might be taken as equivalent to actual experience. We find a plethora of representations that relate to life but should not be confused with direct experience. In the psychotherapeutic context, *understanding*, in the immediacy of the actual relationship, often reflects a sense of connection and security, rather than specific representation.

William James described consciousness as a "stream". The Jamesian metaphor of stream of consciousness makes it clear that self is a felt process and not a thing: "Thoughts connected as we feel them to be connected are what we mean by personal selves" (James, 1892). His phrase "flights and perchings" (James, 1890) denotes the movements of consciousness, emphasizing both the dynamism that is consciousness, and the human capacity to hold feeling in a way that allows for the possibility of reflection, and clarifies the essential duality of the self as "I" and "me" (James, 1890). Self is both self-modifying and continually adaptive to the external world. A *perching* implies a "chunk" of experience held sufficiently, to become not only an object of awareness in the immediate "grammatical" sense but allowing for "awareness of the awareness", relating to what most consider higher consciousness (Stern, 2004). James was a major influence on the phenomenological and existential schools of the 20th century, acknowledged by Husserl as laying a foundation for phenomenology by "help[ing] him find his way out of psychologism" (Wilshire, 1984).

The world around us becomes affectively invested and familiar during childhood development. James' emphasis on "warmth and familiarity" prioritizes a positively toned felt experience of well-being as conducive to being sensed as *self* rather than alien. James refers to the early process of a "splitting of the whole universe into two halves . . . we . . . call . . . '**me**' and '**not-me**' respectively" (James, 1890, p. 289). The human capacity to sustain felt experience in a mind where succeeding chunks of consciousness have "memory" (though not absolute or everlasting) of preceding chunks, is critical to James' idea that "*thought is itself the thinker*" (James, 1890, p. 401). This insight refers to felt qualities that have a life in the body, reflected in brain maps, invoking a model of consciousness that doesn't require a "centre" of consciousness within the brain. "Mental models" grow in implicit memory systems, helping the mind anticipate its environment (Siegel, 2015). Positive hedonic tone is important in terms of what can be "owned", internally, as "me". This is reflected in a quote James was fond of citing, "to miss the joy is to miss all. In the joy of the actors lies the sense of any action" (James, 1899; Stevenson, 1899).

The existential philosophy of Heidegger brings individual experience into focus by replacing consciousness with *dasein* ("being-there"), emphasizing the inseparability of human experience from the environment, and demonstrating the irreducibly temporal qualities of human life (Heidegger, 1927). We always find ourselves in a situation. The subject-object distinction is seen as a development in human thought, but not the primary state of affairs. *Dasein* has a past, present and future, and is a "being with possibilities" (that is, inclined to a future), not simply a materially defined, fixed being (ibid.). Heidegger rejects questions such as "what is a man?" as unanswerable, and asks instead questions of the form of "what does it mean to be a man?" (Gelven, 1989).

Such a view opens up possibilities for a self that creatively contributes to life rather than being externally defined, shifting the ground of inquiry to the realm of first-person experience, posing the question of what dynamic first-person experience is like, requiring understanding at a human level. This kind of understanding, "*verstehen*" ("perception of meaning"), relies upon empathic apprehension. It is contrasted with "*erklaren*" ("perception of causal connection"), relating to knowledge about facts, or "*static*" understanding (Jaspers, 1963). Communication of *verstehen* involves analogy and metaphor or *analogical fit*. Self is understood through "knowledge of acquaintance" rather than "knowledge about" (the objective facts) (James, 1890).

In *Being and Time*, Heidegger considers the world as experienced by the individual, not as objectively defined. What is experienced includes resistance and self, coming into awareness in relation to this resistance (Heidegger, 1927). Meaning in life comes to centre on the relational concept of *care*, although *awareness* of care occurs first in relation to its *lack*. This is part of a general human tendency to notice matters only when they go wrong or can't be taken for granted. By implication this may follow a time where care has been present but outside of awareness, felt simply as part of the natural order. For Heidegger the realm of psychic life, what we *mean* by "having a life", is understood as a dynamism, i.e. necessarily unfolding in time. Mental *space* is, after all, time.

Heidegger highlights the relationship of *Being*, and thought, to language:

> In thinking being comes to language. Thinking accomplishes the relation of Being to the essence of man. It does not make or cause the relation. Thinking brings this relation to Being solely as something handed over to it from Being. Such offering consists in the fact that in thinking Being comes to language. Language is the house of Being. In its home man dwells. Those who think and those who create with words are the guardians of this home.
> (Heidegger, 1977, p. 239)

Heidegger's emphasis is on thought deriving from and being directed to *whole persons*: "beings". The kind of language to which he refers, is seen as having a relation to the core of affective life, represented in the modern world by "poetic creation" (Heidegger, 1977). It may be that Heidegger, while acknowledging the centrality of language to the experience of *being*, may have underestimated the role of others and interpersonal responsibility in the development of self (Orange, 2010). One might say the role of *communicative exchange*. Overemphasis on *self* may lead to a one-sided view of personal development. Selves develop in milieus of "self and other", "self and world" and "self and language". In each case, emergence of an autonomous self would imply a balance in these oppositions, reflected in development of the capacity to resonate and reciprocate rather than being subject to domination.

While James can be said to have made the concept of *feeling* philosophically respectable, he was met with derision by philosophers such as Russell who considered James' pragmatic doctrine one of convenience where truth is defined as "what works" (Goodman, 2002). Russell was more attracted to mathematical notions of identity as defining truth, in a way that suggested an objective definition of language. His student, Ludwig Wittgenstein, came to philosophy from a background of education in logic and mathematics. In contrast to Russell, Wittgenstein was attracted both to James' humanity and his appeal to everyday experience. There is a famous contrast between the early and late work of Wittgenstein. He initially attempted to employ the formalistic approach of Russell to language, reducing it to algebraic forms and propositions (i.e. to statements that are held to be generally true) (Wittgenstein, 1921). Later, Wittgenstein came to see language as always embodied, locally defined in the particular case, and itself defining of what humans mean by "having a life" (i.e. a non-reductionist position) (Wittgenstein, 1958). In the final line of his earlier work, perhaps marking the transition in his thinking, Wittgenstein states that "what we cannot speak about we must pass over in silence" (Wittgenstein, 1921), pointing to those aspects of existence beyond objective definition.

Wittgenstein succeeds in demonstrating limits in the extent to which anything in the human world of experience can be objectively defined. Using the tool of sceptical argument, he highlights the possibility of non-standard explanations for any given event, undermining the degree to which any rule can be seen as fixed, or irrevocable. Other rules could always be imagined that would also give a plausible, if often unlikely, explanation for phenomena (Kripke, 1982). Rules and concepts, for Wittgenstein, can only be understood in the context of human language and, in turn, language cannot be conceived of in isolation: it is an interpersonal and cultural phenomenon. Rules are a product of life in communities rather than logic. When he says, "to imagine a language means to imagine a form of life" (Wittgenstein, 1958, PI, 19), he implies language gives rise to particular forms in human life. Ways of life (e.g. "being a Catholic") are "language games" (ibid.). The reference point for his use of the term is the ways in which humans naturally express themselves. There are sufficient commonalities here that languages are always capable of comprehension, ultimately, to other people. Such a definition encompasses the range of natural emotional expression in humans, not simply the words that are spoken. Through such forms of life "the adult human subject emerges slowly, as its life becomes structured through the acquisition of new and more complex language-games" (McGinn, 1997, p. 52).

Use of language is also seen by Wittgenstein as a development of customary action, only ever to be understood as it applies in a particular context. Any given statement is seen as part of a "lifelong conversation". Hence, Wittgenstein locates language in an embodied, relational, and spatially particular way as a *text in progress*, where others make a contribution.

There is no such thing, for Wittgenstein, as private meaning. He rejects the idea of an internal world, or of an internal "private" language, on the basis that "everything lies open to view" (Wittgenstein, 1958). Language is a mode of expression learnt in conjunction with others, not something developed in isolation. Wittgenstein came to see philosophy as a kind of therapy, a clearing away of the misconceptions and misunderstandings induced in individuals through their development in a "fog" of complex linguistic interactions. Similarly, Hobson considered that "Learning how to correct misunderstandings is one (and, perhaps, **the**) most important therapeutic factor" in psychotherapy (Hobson, 1985, p. 16).

Wittgenstein's private language argument developed in response to James' notion of an "ideal psychological language" arrived at by introspection of privately "felt" states of consciousness, without reference to externalities (James, 1890; Goodman, 2002). Wittgenstein considers that we don't *know* sensations as something that *belongs* only to oneself (Wittgenstein, 1958, PI 275). Rather one *has* sensations and states (ibid.). The way we express ourselves will vary depending upon our stage of development, starting, for example with the cry as an expression of pain that tends to be replaced by verbal linguistic expression as we learn *language games*. There is no "hidden" language. Even when thinking to oneself, thought is in the mother tongue, not a private language.

When it comes to the level of the unseen, including the level of background feeling, Wittgenstein believed efforts at fixed definition would always fail. Rather, he points to a level of experience beyond verbal definition. In a psychotherapeutic sense this may inform the issue of provision of fixed meaning through interpretation, as opposed to approaching personal experience through analogy. It also is a reminder that no single approach, philosophical, religious or scientific, can claim a monopoly on the truth or even on what constitutes the facts. Many modern "realities", such as systems of government, corporations and human rights, are intersubjective creations rather than naturally occurring "objective" facts (Harari, 2011). A *language game* not based on objectivity or logic may be as effective as one that is. Sometimes, at least in some ways, such organizations of life may be more effective when it comes to matters such as social cohesion, stability and sustainability of environmental provision. It is not difficult, for instance, to imagine a pre-scientific tribal culture being more inclusive and cohesive than complex modern societies.

The philosophical progression that has been traced here might be seen as providing a concrete, grounded position for self in relation to feeling and language. Hegel places the emergence of self in interaction and conversation with others. James' self is based in experience-near phenomenology that is highly individualized: no two selves are identical. James and Heidegger emphasize process and a temporal animation of self, inseparable from the world, irreducible to temporally frozen objective description. Wittgenstein helps us see that any life is locally and contextually defined. Selves arise in living relationships, at the intersection of language and feeling. Self cannot be objectively defined outside learned language games. It is, therefore, not separable from language.

This helps us understand why the project of psychotherapy, in one form or another, is necessary. Things just won't do. People need people. However, psychotherapy needs to be seen as pluralistic, and locally defined to fit the particular context, not a universal method where "one size fits all" (Korner, 2008). The emphasis on language should not be seen as undermining the significance of other material aspects of reality. Material contingencies are inescapable and not all aspects of being human are encompassed by self and language. Historically there has been tension between materialist and idealist positions philosophically. The account presented, however, does not require any "non-material" element to reality. Rather it takes language seriously as part of inter-subjective material reality (Korner, 2008).

The response of the materialist to the idealist can be characterized as *show me*, don't take the route of referring to evidence that has its basis in the *unseen*. The tension between these positions has always been difficult to resolve. Hegelian dialectic sees it as reflecting two *moments* in thought, each with an area of validity, but by itself, "*deprived of life*" (Hegel, 1807). Wittgenstein would see the situation in terms of different language games, each with its place, but frequently leading to confusion. While encouraging staying with observable phenomena ("don't think, look!") (Anderson & Shotter, 2006), he also demonstrates the limitations of scientific searches for fixed meaning in the domain of human interaction and mental phenomena.

From a psychoanalytic perspective, "the mind alone knows what it feels like to be itself . . . in the case of the human mind, it can provide a verbal report about this subjective state of being" (Solms, 2015, p. 42). However, work is required in communication for understanding and growth. Experience acquires meaning "not only by being ordered chronologically but also by being rated on a scale of biological value. This is the primary function of 'emotion'" (ibid.). Life is brought to experience through feeling.

In formulating a current neuroscientific model of consciousness, philosophic assumptions are spelt out (Edelman & Tononi, 2000) (commentary added in brackets):

1 "Being comes first, describing second" (describing can never capture first-person experience).
2 "Doing generally precedes understanding" (language and other actions need to be performed before understanding is possible).
3 "Selectionism precedes logic" (differentiation comes about through selection, not logic).

Summarizing their position on higher forms of consciousness, they say, "we emphatically do not identify consciousness in its full range as arising solely in the brain, since we believe that higher brain functions require interactions both with the world and with other persons" (Edelman & Tononi, 2000, p. xii). The interactions referred to clearly include the exchanges of language that form the basis of personal thought.

In the context of the present discussion, it does not make sense to say that brain and mind are one, although this is a position commonly taken (e.g. Detre, 1987). We do better to say they are inseparable. Brain, mind and language live together, inseparable in lively co-dependency. From a logical perspective it makes sense to say, of relationships between mind, brain and environment that:

1 Mind and brain cannot be separated.
2 Mind cannot be separated from the objects of perception.
3 The embodied human brain is a necessary but not sufficient condition for human minds.
4 The (peopled) environment is a necessary but not sufficient condition for human minds.

(Korner, 2008)

In noting these relations, the point can also be made that *mind* is a whole person concept relating to a particular self, whereas *brain* is not (rather it is part of the body). When we consider *whole* relations through concepts involving mind and meaning, we see many perspectives are possible. Even as logical statements are made, we should remember that such assertions are just one type of language game, one *form of life*.

Wittgenstein was inclined to view life in three *phases*: the world of objective definition characterized by fixed meaning where "it is either this or that"; the world of moving but observable phenomena where meaning could be "this, that or the other" and finally the world of unseen phenomena, characterized as "neither this nor that" (Anderson & Shotter, 2006). We shouldn't take ourselves too seriously or attempt to be authorities when it comes to the personal meaning of events. Adopting a flexible position assists the therapist in allowing meaning to develop.

Early mentality: the liveliness of being

Over the last half century relational developments in psychoanalytic thought, informed by the growth of a developmental psychology focused on normal development, have seen a movement away from a predominantly intra-psychic, drive-based psychodynamic model. The shift towards a relational orientation has taken various forms. For example, Winnicott emphasized environmental provision with focus on the maternal relationship and the development of the capacity for play. In contrast, Lacan refers to the unconscious relationship of the individual to language, highlighting not only personal relationships but also broader conditions to which an individual life is subject (Luepnitz, 2009). Recognition of the role of early development on adult personality has led to greater emphasis on understanding the pre-verbal world of the infant (e.g. Stern, 1985; Emde, 1983).

Freud saw the infant as motivated primarily by pleasure-seeking curbed by external constraints (Freud, 1911). Concepts such as pleasure and pain, reward and punishment, do have great importance in understanding mental functioning. However, they are ultimately based upon a "good – bad" organization that is divisive rather than unifying in terms of mental functioning, and probably not appropriate to the earliest levels of development (Korner, 2000). In contrast, shared experience, reflected in moments of connection (dyadic intersubjective states), is associated with increased well-being and "an expansion of (the) state of consciousness" (Tronick, 1998). Implicit relational knowing in infancy involves procedural and perceptual memory, and *moments of meeting*, co-constructed with carer (Lyons-Ruth, 1998). *Moments of meeting* are considered crucial to the psychotherapeutic process (ibid.). In psychotherapy one way in which such shared moments may be manifest is in the development of a particular language (i.e. characteristic phrases and stories) that identifies a specific therapeutic dyad.

With understanding of the modular way in which the brain handles perception, it is no longer tenable to consider minds as composed of fully formed contents or perceptions (Stern, 2006). Although it remains problematic to attempt characterization of the pre-verbal world of infancy, it seems likely that early experience, shaped by rhythmic interactions with the environment in the form of vitality affects (Stern, 1985), might correspond to a sense of aliveness or "liveliness" (Ogden, 1995; Korner, 2000). This is consistent with the account of primordial feelings being associated with the sense of existence (Damasio, 2012). It has been argued that "the sense of aliveness and deadness of the transference-countertransference is . . . the single most important measure of the analytic process on a moment-to moment basis" (Ogden, 2005), suggesting an ongoing importance in shaping experience. Psychotherapists' efforts need to be directed at linking to what is most alive for the patient (Meares, 2005).

An enlivening-deadening axis of experience might encompass basic principles of mental functioning in a way that allows a revision of Freud's *pleasure* and *reality* principles (Freud, 1911). The *pleasure principle* might be restated as "a tendency to seek or continue experiences of liveliness and to seek escape from, or foreshorten, deadening experiences". The reality principle becomes "the tendency to seek conditions that allow for a sustainable experience of liveliness" (Korner, 2000). Recognition of a primary "seeking system", associated with strivings towards the environment (Panksepp & Biven, 2012), overcomes some of the apparent conflict between the reality and pleasure principles. The sense of liveliness is largely engendered in ongoing strivings to work, relate and play rather than through the episodic satisfactions of consummatory pleasure.

The concept of liveliness is somewhat fuzzy, perhaps appropriate to an intersubjective model, with indistinct boundaries. The liveliness of the infant, for instance, is felt by the mother. The two principles, as restated, include recognition of the environment's role in shaping learning. The conditions sought include language and relationship. Where liveliness is engendered in interaction between people, the emphasis is more on the resonance and harmony that fosters complexity (Siegel, 2015), and less on mastery or dominance, more likely to arise under traumatic conditions. Rather than seeing *id* and *primary process* as impediments to integration, we see a primary form of mental functioning that allows creative engagement with others and the environment. It has a typically non-linear, *associative* form determined by unconscious selections based on patterns of emotional resonance that go back to the earliest forms of mental life. The fate of this element of experience is to be integrated with, rather than supplanted by, a distinct secondary process.

Personality and the embodied text

We look at an infant and speak of his or her *personality*. Human beings are highly attuned to person: in some ways it is what we know best. An individual's voice, face and movement are highly identifiable, and become more differentiated over the trajectory of a lifetime. In the case of the infant we see someone whose personality is not fully formed. The *personality* we speak of in this context is at least partially an endowment from the caring *other*. The view from *inside* is different, with access to feeling states but without the full view of face seen by others (Merleau-Ponty, 1945).

Various dictionary definitions of *personality* include: "personal existence or identity", "lively, engaging qualities", "the combination of characteristics or qualities that form an individual's distinctive character" (Oxford, 2011). For the present purpose, this last definition is most relevant. Personality is identified with being: "Personality is what one **is** rather than what one **has**" (PDM Task Force, 2006).

In everyday discourse, the positive connotation of "distinctiveness" is present when we refer to someone *having personality*. In psychiatric discourse this may be clouded by concepts that have the effect of defining a person in terms of disorder, an inherently stigmatizing process. Classification in psychiatry is continually evolving. In the DSM-5 (2013) there are two alternative classifications for personality. One remains categorical, in keeping with earlier versions. The alternative is dimensional, with emphasis on relatedness and the psychological concepts of self, empathy and intimacy (DSM-5, 2013). Also significant in DSM-5 is the conflation of "personality disorder" with other mental disorders (no longer distinguished on a separate "axis"), perhaps increasing the tendency to see these disorders as "things": "diseases" that "afflict" people, rather than disturbances of self, modifiable through collaborative work. Ironically, in current classificatory systems individuality tends to be depersonalized: neither authors, nor the subjects of authorship, are evident to the reader as persons (Kriss, 2013).

In contrast, James saw "the personal self . . . as the immediate datum in psychology . . . . The worst a psychology can do is so to interpret the nature of these selves as to rob them of their worth" (James, 1890, p. 226). From the objective perspective, personality dysfunction is what stands out in assessment and diagnosis. For psychotherapy, however, there needs to be recognition that the "personal self" at any given time reflects the individual's best effort at adaptation in a complex world and, as such, is an achievement of value. Although James states that "No psychology . . . can question the **existence** of personal selves" (ibid.), classificatory systems that objectify people may do just that.

The relation of self and value is crucial, reflecting the intimate connection between self and feeling. Differential processing of positive and negative affect greatly influences development of self, with the traumatic range of affective experience associated with developmental arrest and a constricted, "adualistic" sense of self (Meares & Lichtenberg, 1995; Meares, 1999a). In contrast, familiarity and warmth in personal experience facilitate individual development and differentiation at both psychological and neurological levels. The inner stream of consciousness is an essentially private experience, although it develops in the public space of personal relationships (Meares, 2005). From early in life, the child develops a repertoire of responses adapted to fit different relational configurations, seen by others as the individual's identity, while simultaneously there is an emerging private experience, that of self (Meares, 2005). Personality consists of both identity and self.

James defines personal experience in a way that includes environment and others: "a conscious field plus its object as felt or thought of plus an attitude towards the object plus the sense of a self to whom the attitude belongs . . . such a concrete piece of personal experience may be a small bit but it is a solid bit as long as it lasts" (James, 1902, p. 385) (i.e. we experience consciousness in "chunks" that include feeling, an attitude to the object of our attention and a simultaneous awareness of self). There is a relation here between the chunk of experience, the state of the body and nervous system of its experiencer. This complex formulation of mental states including feeling, thought and attitude, can be compared to the notion of the *present moment* (Stern, 2004) or Janet's concept of *présentification* (Ellenberger, 1981). For therapists, this reflects the moment to moment presentation of the patient requiring attention. James' description is of a state of *self* at any given time. In keeping with James' view, Whitehead saw self as based upon meaningful "drops of experience, complex and interdependent" (Whitehead, 1978), providing a thread of continuity (Smith, 2010). His "organic" philosophy prioritizes the temporal development of the subject, shifting emphasis from the individual as *mere* subject: "for the philosophy of organism, the subject emerges from the world – a **superject** rather than a **subject**" (Whitehead, 1978, p. 88). To become meaningful these "drops of experience" need to be seen as part of a larger whole, that of the personal narrative.

A human life is properly *considered* as a text. While a life can never be *reduced* to a defined text, it cannot be understood psychologically in any other way. Indeed, in any case beyond the cross-sectional fact of "being alive or dead", consideration and understanding of people's lives *are* carried out in terms of texts: biographies, stories, reports and histories. The term "text" tends to be identified with the written word. However, in relation to psychotherapeutic practice (and indeed most life contexts), such a definition misses what is essential. In practice, each person is an *embodied text*, where the spoken word, or sometimes non-verbal bodily forms of expression, predominate. In psychotherapy the patient presents embodying a partially expressed text. The task of the therapist becomes one of collaborating in development of the text so it can be more fully expressed and appropriated by its author, the patient. The therapist seeks immersion in the patient's world, following the agenda of the text (Meares et al., 2012).

Personal selves and early investment in significance

Patterns of self-organization become established early in life. These *internal working models* (Bowlby, 1984; Holmes, 1993) are not accessible to conscious awareness, yet structure the individual's perception of the world. Internalized models of relatedness are an unconscious influence in the mind, although also part of *felt reality* in development. Such models are held in implicit memory systems (Schore, 2012; Wachtel, 2008). These are sensed as *the way the relational world is*, part of a *worldview* that assumes these models as facts rather than recognizing their relationship to personal context (Korner, 2011). The *internal working model* is manifest in the way adults use language, as demonstrated by the reliability of the Adult Attachment Interview (AAI) in identifying early attachment patterns. If a person hasn't had a secure experience in early life, as an adult they will have difficulty talking coherently about their childhood. In the case of those with early disorganized attachment experiences, life narratives typically become markedly incoherent. In adults the AAI is primarily a measure of coherence of linguistic expression (Main et al., 1985).

A level of feeling is always present in consciousness but is not synonymous with emotion. Concepts such as *vitality affect* (Stern, 1985), *background ("barely detectable") feeling* (Meares, 2005) and *primary emotion* (Siegel, 2015) have been employed to capture the range of states that cannot be equated with specific emotions. Feeling is intimately related to the concept of self, since the individual can never entirely separate self from feeling. The capacities to sustain feeling for relatively long periods, and for feeling to endure, linked to memory, are characteristic of human consciousness (Korner, 2002). Such capacities are probably prerequisites for a sense of innerness and for the dualistic form of consciousness that gives rise to the sense of self dynamically participating in the world.

The prolonged developmental dependence of humans ensures great emotional investment in communication. Affective investment in communication precedes conceptual learning and is thought to be mediated by the right hemisphere (Schore, 2012).

Each individual develops a distinct repertoire of feeling and emotional states. Feeling constitutes an important dimension of language. The majority of meaning in verbal exchange is conveyed by the combination of affect and context, rather than by conventional semantic meaning (Goleman, 1995; Stern, 2004). Affect refers to dynamic processes unfolding over time in a living context. While we are born with affect systems, it is mistaken to see affect as purely innate. Each person begins life with *potential* access to the range of human feeling and emotions. How that is realized, and in what combination, or sequence, is uncertain at the outset. The situation is comparable to language: each infant begins (normally) with the *potential* to attain mastery of the mother tongue. The form and style of verbal expression and the extent to which the full capacity for linguistic expression is realized, will vary as a result of experience, environmental affordance and innate factors (*nature and nurture*). With affects the particular constellations and combinations experienced and expressed in relation to life events constitute an *emotional fractal* (McWilliams, 2010) or set of kaleidoscopic responses unique for that individual: something like an "affective fingerprint". Affect sequencing is distinctive for the individual (Brandchaft, 2012).

Observational mother-infant research has highlighted the delicate reciprocal interplay between infant and carer crucial to the developing infant (Trevarthen, 1974; Schore, 1994). The infant is a *communicant*, with whom carers interact, rather than merely an object to be acted upon (Brazelton, 1979). The disturbances of attachment described by Bowlby have been identified as a central aspect of human development although potentially subject to later modification given more favourable attachment opportunities. Broadly speaking there appears to be a relationship between attachment style and dominant adaptive strategy ("flight", "fight" and "freeze" being mammalian defence strategies that bear some relation to "avoidant", "ambivalent" and "disorganized" styles of attachment). In the phase of dyadic, inter-subjective engagement, it is typically the mother that takes responsibility for providing language and specific meaning, in interplay with the infant. Provided the carer effectively facilitates fields of care and play, both mother and infant become active contributors to the sense of significance in interaction. This is why we refer to familiar intimate others as *significant* others.

Highlighting the infant's dependency in some ways obscures the infant's competence in areas significant for language development. These include the capacity to cry, and in so doing, to *call* to the carer to respond. Apart from the cry, other forms of expression involving vocal and visual images of well-being, such as the smile or laughter, are crucial, from an early stage, in establishing interactions upon which development of self will rest. "The foundation for interpersonal communication is 'there' at birth", including capacities for engagement in vocal and gestural exchange, for pointing and sustaining attention in these relational contexts, using musical qualities of the voice and gestural expressiveness (Trevarthen, 1975). Turn-taking in vocalizing and engagement in periodic vocal activity, has the "narrative" quality of "beginning, middle (climax), and ending", with both parties contributing (Malloch & Trevarthen, 2009). Communicative exchanges of social significance for both parties occur virtually from the outset in mother-infant exchanges (Brazelton, 1979; Bullowa, 1979; Malloch & Trevarthen, 2009). Such rewarding exchanges have implications for the extent to which communication will become pleasurable and fulfilling for any given person.

Personal selves and whole-body autonomic response

In terms of bodily responsiveness to the environment, it is clear the ANS plays an important evaluating role, placing autonomic response in the position of being a prime marker of shifting dynamic states for each individual. While the sympathetic nervous system plays a crucial role in the organism's stress response, current evidence highlights the role of the parasympathetic nervous system, through its more recently evolved division, the myelinated vagus, as crucial for regulation of social engagement and mediation of relaxed and pleasurable states of mind (Porges, 2011).

Both constitutional factors and environmental circumstances influence the ANS and associated bodily emotional responses. The traumatic range of experience, particularly when this is the ongoing relational reality, tends to be associated with increased, often chronic, sympathetic activation, and sometimes activation of the more primitive, defensive components of the archaic (unmyelinated) division of the vagal nerve (Porges, 2011; Williams & Gordon, 2007; Lyons-Ruth et al., 2006). Adequate care promotes vagally mediated autonomic states providing opportunities for play and fostering infant capacities for enjoyment in seeking and exploring in relation to the environment (Panksepp & Biven, 2012; Williams & Gordon, 2007).

The failure to establish dyadic interplay and a linguistically stimulating environment could be a predictor of deficiency in parasympathetic responsiveness (social reward) in communicative interaction (Austin et al., 2007). Elucidating the nature of these inter-relations between bodily response and semiotic interaction may be central to development of knowledge of personality substrates in infancy, before the notion of individual as a *self-organizing system* can be said to be present.

Preliminary physiological evidence suggests that established therapeutic couples, with high patient ratings of therapist empathy, have high levels of autonomic concordance (synchrony), as measured by skin conductance (Marci et al., 2007). Models of emotional processing related to "a spectrum from 'mismatches', signifying potential danger, to 'matches', signifying safety", may contribute to understanding the development of neuropsychiatric disorders (Williams & Gordon, 2007, p. 349). For example, parasympathetic responsiveness has been found to be differentially processed in patients with Borderline Personality Disorder, suggesting lesser support for social engagement behaviours (Austin et al., 2007).

The ANS coordinates a whole-body interface with the environment with great significance for phenomenal awareness throughout life. This is manifest in literature, such as the writing of James Joyce, who saw his most famous novel, *Ulysses*, as "the epic of the human body" (Budgen, 1972). Ulysses can be seen as "blue print for knowledge that is not based on intellect" (Mason, 2008; Beckett, 1929). In a celebration of Joyce's work, his writing on the phenomenal awareness of everyday bodily functions was related to the ANS, taking the vagus nerve as exemplar, a coordinator of human bodily function "from the ear to the rear"

(Mason, 2008). For Joyce, "trouble and bustle always finds its way into the bosom of my stomach" (Joyce, 1966, p. 213). At the time Joyce was writing there were significant developments in neurology, and the emerging discipline of psycho-analysis. It may be no accident that, while science was beginning to place an emphasis on the significance of the peripheral nervous system through concepts such as "the abdominal brain" and psycho-analysis was describing pre-verbal stages of development in bodily terms (oral, anal, phallic, genital), there emerged a new form of literature highlighting the continuing role of the whole body in phenomenal awareness: "if they had no body they would have no mind, it's all one" (Budgen, 1972).

Locating the person

Language is both embedded in the body, and the interpersonal worlds we inhabit. Language is a manifestation of life that streams around us, impinges upon us and takes root within us, ultimately giving rise to the individual voice with which we navigate our way through life. The individual person needs to be located within this stream. *Person* and *self* are language-dependent concepts. Persons require definition in terms of roles, responsibilities and meaningful action in a network of relationships, as well as through delineation of objective characteristics.

Whereas an object can be located in physical space, a person needs to be located in a relational network and within linguistic space. Self and personality are better understood as processes rather than "things". This shifts the ground of inquiry to one where we seek to understand the person through "knowledge of acquaintance" (James, 1890).

Each person finds him- or herself at two interfaces:

1 An interface with the larger world presented in the form of environment and the language, cultural practice and behaviour of those around him or her.
2 An interface with the body and its cellular functions and organ systems operating in a continuous way both in and beyond phenomenal awareness.

Hence the individual emerges constituted both by material phenomena outside the organism, and within the organism. These phenomena include the cultural beliefs and values manifest in interpersonal behaviour and speech. There are three levels to the dynamic, open system described in points 1 and 2 (Thibault, 2004): the potential knowledge and opportunities for interaction afforded by the environment, the particular capacities afforded by the individual's biology and the present moment where these capacities and opportunities are negotiated and realized. The present moment will contain many and varied interactions within the unfolding process of navigating life constituting a unique trajectory of life for a given individual.

When applied to the human world, these levels suggest a source of knowledge "coming from within" and another that derives from being "part of a community". Knowledge that becomes familiar includes that based upon symbolic expression, constituting a major part of the dynamic human environment. We need to locate people within the symbolic world as well as within the physical environment.

The exchanges through which people transact experience in the environment are underpinned by two communicative systems. One is the human range of feeling (in expressive and receptive forms), including associated propensities for the formation and valuation of affectional bonds, the capacity to sustain attention and memory and to resonate with other individuals. This *communicative musicality* allows the infant to become intimately related to carers before the mother tongue is acquired (Malloch & Trevarthen, 2009). Throughout life the affect system remains the primary motivational system (Tomkins, 1995), the primary internal value system and a central aspect of communication. The second communicative system is conventional language. This is language in the sense described by Saussure as a social institution, composed of arbitrary conventional signs, serving as a network for the discrimination of value (Saussure, 1959).

It is the acquisition of *symbolic* language as lived and expressed that most differentiates the human world from those of other species. It is a game-changer. For other species the world is presumably experienced within the framework of objects and actions within a natural environment. Communicative capacities are part of such worlds but are embedded in systems indexically tied to the present. They are pre-symbolic, and hence pre-linguistic, in the conventional sense (Deutscher, 2005).

By contrast, symbolic language takes on a life of its own and brings into consciousness a present, past and future, greatly expanding the environmental and conceptual matrix into which humans are born. The more purely linguistic aspects of communication, involving conventional signs and syntax are thought to be "culturally constructed and passed along by individual linguistic communities" (Tomasello, 2010, p. 11). The acquisition of syntax structures our experience, helping us become *mental time travellers* (Siegel, 2015).

Early immersion in the symbolic world

Language in humans has been thought of as developing in a linear way from a pre-symbolic phase to the symbolic stage in humans. The contrast between *infant* (from Latin, *unable to speak*) and *child* (with language), suggests this transition from the pre-symbolic to the symbolic. Various formulations in psychoanalysis highlight this distinction. Freud thought of the earliest part of life as "autistic" in nature (Freud, 1895, 1911). Mahler thought of the "psychological birth" of the infant as not being synonymous with actual birth because of physiological immaturity (Mahler et al., 1975). Stolorow and Atwood drew a sharp distinction between "attunements communicated in the sensorimotor dialogue with caregivers", with the shift to the capacity to use symbolic language at about 18 months: "By the middle of the second year, the child is able to use symbols, making language possible . . . . mak[ing] possible 'a sharing of mutually created meanings about personal experiences'" (Stolorow & Atwood, 1992).

However, it seems likely that these views are in error. An alternative view of language development is that the infant is immersed in the human world of symbolic meaning from the beginning. The relationship is interpenetrated in the same sense that *breathing the air* is an interpenetrated relationship with the environment. Capacities for interaction and turn-taking in vocal exchange are evident from the neonatal period (Malloch & Trevarthen, 2009). The infant's face and gestures (and those of the carer for the infant) become symbolic in an *iconic* sense in these exchanges. Although not expressed initially with intent or self-awareness, the infant is contributing to symbolic communication in an active way. Indeed, *iconicity* relates to the sense of timelessness that become the stuff of myth-making and story-telling. The infant could be said to have a *proto-symbolic* capacity, even at this stage. The powerful images of infant and carer will remain psychologically active throughout life albeit often unconsciously.

By the period of 9–18 months there is substantial evidence the infant has developed a more complex form of communication reaching up to 50 concepts or representations (vocal or gestural) shared with the carer. The nature of this *proto-language* is that, in a symbolic sense, it is *indexical*, i.e. tied to the present. This form of communicative interaction reflects the closeness that develops (usually) between infant and carer. Affective expression is a major element of such exchanges, although there are also recognizable and reproducible signs known between infant and carer (Halliday, 1975). This form of *proto-language* lacks grammar and does not represent a conventional system of signs as we understand a mature language. Nevertheless, it represents an enhanced symbolic capacity, relative to the earlier phase where the infant's contributions are understood as largely *iconic*.

Being, individual, self, person: a dynamic progression

The following progression is relevant to an understanding of personality: *being, individual, self* and *person*. **Human being** is a term applicable to any stage of development of *homo sapiens*, at least once a foetal stage has been reached. What is implied is an organism capable of feeling and responding. In the relatively protected uterine environment there is limited opportunity for differentiation in response to environment. In the neonatal period these opportunities are greatly expanded in the specific environment that pertains for a given infant. While a rudimentary *proto-self* operates in relation to body image and kinaesthetic experience (Damasio, 2000), the sense of being is both easily disrupted and restored.

Infants are adapted to develop preferential knowledge of a primary caregiver. With biological maturation and exposure to a "good enough" caregiver, the infant–caregiver dyad will develop unique patterns of stimulation and response that become increasingly meaningful within the dyadic system. A *proto-language* develops that remains bound to present interaction. This will be associated with development of individualized characteristics. The term "individual" may be thought of as the "indivisible duality of self and other". Other mammals also individuate through such interactive processes. Indeed, we refer to the *individual* in relation to humans and other species. We see the increasing emergence of externally identifiable characteristics.

With the acquisition of the mother tongue, the individual emerges into a greatly expanded conceptual universe and cultural context. The syntax of language facilitates the grasping of concepts that begin to be accessible for utilization and, later, reflection. This confers spatiality to the mind, allowing emerging awareness of past, present, future, cultural context and engagement in the symbolic world, differentiating human minds from those of other mammals.

The spatiality of language provides a locus within the individual for the development of self-relationship, over and beyond self-other relationships. Once language has been mastered to the extent that it is realized inner speech is not accessible to others, there are the grounds for a reflective space that takes on the lively sense of a separate *self*. There is evidence for the emergence of this sense of *innerness* around the age of 3–4 years (e.g. Meares & Orlay, 1988). Internalization of language follows a period of "symbolic play" where the young child chatters to him- or herself while playing with toys and manipulating objects in the external world (Meares, 2005; Vygotsky, 1934). Autobiographical memory also becomes established, leading to consolidation of personal associations (Siegel, 2015).

This associative stream of self-talk, developed in a context of generally positive hedonic tone, becomes the basis of an inner or personal world. With the development of a sense of interiority, *self* emerges as an object of self-awareness and reflection rather than simply a point of reference. In this way language provides possibilities for self-realization. Inner "talk" (verbal thought), however, always faces the challenge of reconciling itself with the bodily based signs of the feeling system.

The further journey of self, towards the mature *person*, occurs over a longer time-scale, involving acquisition of skills, development of expressive capacities, formation of relationships and the finding of a "voice" capable of navigating a path through the complex demands of adulthood and parenthood. This arises through coordination of the publicly recognizable identity of an individual, with the internal direction of a private self, such that it is reasonable to speak of a relatively autonomous "self-organizing system". The introduction of syntax into the human situation allows us to analyse the situation of self in terms of grammatical as well as spatial location. Commonly this is thought of in terms of whether one is *subject* or *object* in a given context. This can be misleading insofar as confusion is common in relation to what is meant by "object". It is common to mistake the term as synonym for "thing". What is meant, generally, in the developmental or psychotherapeutic context, is closer to a *dynamic focus of attention* i.e. a *grammatical object*. Ultimately finding one's voice, generally following considerable receptive experience in tandem with a developing range of expressive action, means becoming a *player* in the larger community. The voice referred to here is the "true voice of feeling" (Hobson, 1985), denoting genuine engagement with life.

In terms of biological and neurological maturation, personality is not established fully until well into adulthood. Social integration takes longer. Mature personality implies the capacity to negotiate a way through complex social environments with a sense of self-awareness and responsibility, becoming both *agent* (MacMurray, 1961) and *author* of one's life (Benjamin, 1998). Emergence from dependence on caregiver occurs through the realization of self in language. In turn, the development of personality occurs through the organization of self in relation to others through skill acquisition and the emergence of expressive capacities.

The trajectory of self through iconic, indexical and symbolic levels of exchange: the emergence of self-states

The first-person perspective can be seen as moment-to-moment phenomenal awareness. However, there is a big difference between having basic awareness and capacities for reflection or structuring narratives of self. This involves integration of language and the creation of higher order self-states.

Phenomenal awareness, in the sense of being able to perceive separate events, occurs in humans over very short time frames, from as little as 20 milliseconds (ms) (Stern, 2004). The presence of the psychological refractory period means that humans can't make a discrimination until the last one is completed – at least 100–150ms (Edelman & Tononi, 2000). Phenomenal awareness consists in a flow of conscious states each of which has a limited duration (20–150ms). It is associated with a sense of unity, in that each conscious state cannot be further divided (ibid.). In recent work using a stimulus-response paradigm, the conscious recognition of feeling took 500ms (Damasio, 2012, p. 122). Processing a concept takes longer still – about 800ms (ibid.).

In response to environmental stimuli the organism automatically organizes its attentional resources with rapid selection of a response (Edelman & Tononi, 2000), based upon its experience of similar circumstances, and innate capacities. This form of consciousness has been termed *primary consciousness*, shared with other species (ibid.). Choices are not based upon reflection and the selection process is not accessible to conscious awareness. These are non-conscious, neurally based processes. For phenomenal awareness, the implication is of a kaleidoscopic flow of scenes "out there", a moving world projected through the lens of the individual organism, with digital (time-limited) characteristics.

For higher consciousness, language is required. Therefore, understanding of the phenomena of higher consciousness cannot be confined to mechanisms within the individual organism. Inner speech is "linguistically realized thinking", leading to the claim that "inner speech just **is** higher-order or symbolic thought" (Thibault, 2004, p. 273). Language is a living and embodied phenomenon, not an abstraction isolated from individuals and societies in which it is spoken and written (ibid.).

Participation in communicative exchange is evident from the outset. There is a level of communication embedded in the here-and-now that tends to be interpreted by the carer as a "mood sign" (Bateson, 1954). This is to say the infant is a participant in interaction that includes proto-symbolic exchange, from birth. The infant is *an iconic symbol in the minds of significant others* in addition to being an actual presence, even though the infant does not begin with self-awareness of this iconicity. The actuality of the infant-carer dyad has *felt significance for both*. This level of "felt significance" in interaction continues throughout life endowing language, communication and relationships with a sense of liveliness.

In taking the infant's *cry* as communication, we see it is a *sign* for the mother. The concept of "sign" is fundamental to linguistics and the human sciences (Innis, 1985). C. S. Peirce emphasized that signs are *not* to be understood as a "name" for a "thing". Language is not a code. In Peirce's terms, the sign is a "representamen", which "stands to somebody for something in some respect or capacity" (Peirce, 1897, p. 5), connected to an "object" (in this case, the crying infant) by an "interpretant" (mother) (Peirce, 1897, p. 5). The cry is only a sign when there is a responding other capable of "reading" it.

Taken as a two-person system Peirce's tripartite semiotic structure is of *firstness* (representamen), *secondness* (object) and *thirdness* (interpretant). The need for living participation in language is emphasized. While the mother is usually capable of receiving the infant's cry and holding its relation to the infant as object of her attention, then "reading" and responding, the infant is not capable of "reading" the sign or holding it as an object of attention – hence the infant lacks *thirdness* in Peirce's terms. The participation in communication is carried out unconsciously by the infant in a whole-body, imagistic sense. This early period of development involves differentiation of systems of memory, contributing to pre-conceptual knowledge stored in implicit perceptual and procedural memory systems. The infant comes to know movements through repetition and to recognize faces, expressions and gestures through repetition of presentations. Early immersion in communication also occurs at an iconic level for the infant on the receptive, as well as the expressive, side of communication. Although unreflective, these forms of knowledge are constantly being utilized throughout life as we move, speak and perceive. They become part of the individual's continuity of being, colouring and shaping the emerging personality.

Communication is social, for the infant, before it is conceptual (Vygotsky, 1934). Within this relationship, the infant is able to participate in and even initiate vocal exchanges (Malloch & Trevarthen, 2009). Gestures and vocal expressions come to acquire distinctiveness, becoming points of reference within the particular, increasingly differentiated, dyad. From about 6–8 months communication becomes *indexical* in terms of communicative exchange (Thibault, 2004; Halliday, 1975). That is to say the infant has acquired the capacity, at this point, to *consciously* use signs with specificity in a particular context of time, place and person and is not restricted to natural modes of expression. The infant appears to gain a conscious awareness of being an active partner in relationship. At this stage the infant's communicative function involves participation at both *iconic* and *indexical* levels.

Finally, the infant becomes a child, acquiring competence in the shared language of the community. The child is now a participant at *iconic, indexical* and *symbolic* levels. She has now acquired "thirdness" in Peirce's system. Realization of a mature self requires the *symbolic* level of participation, providing the child with maximum communicative flexibility. The way is prepared for this kind of involvement in the human world by the child's engagement in *symbolic play* which follows on from the dyadic engagement of the proto-conversation and becomes characteristic of the child's solitary play from about 18 months to the age of 4 or so (Meares, 2005).

> *My four-year old granddaughter had an array of soft toys, all of whom she had given names. There were two favourites, Abi and Wolfie. She spent hours happily talking and playing with these toys, engaging them in games and sometimes chiding them, reminding them of what Mummy had said. When she had had enough, she'd put them all back in their original places. She was upset if anyone moved them. It was **her** world.*

Here the child will often relate to toys as if they were personified others, talking out loud in a non-linear associative way corresponding to later "inner talk". One of the values of symbolic play is that the child represents his, or her, personal experience, allowing emergence of a sense of distinctness. Experiences that occur in play are not abstract: they are real for the child, having the quality of being both real and not-real simultaneously (Bateson, 1954, pp. 132–133). Entry into participation in communication at the symbolic level is a practical matter in a world of intersubjective realities and intellectual possibilities.

A different form of play (rough and tumble) is also of social importance. While it may serve a practical preparatory function for later adult behaviour, it also engenders positive affect, significant in helping infants and children support a broad affective range (Panksepp & Biven, 2012, pp. 351–352). The development of a capacity to encompass, and utilize, a broad range of affect is important in fostering a sense of vital engagement with life, allowing for affective investment in symbolic play and the movement beyond the indexical present.

A huge range of concepts become potentially available and learnable, within the temporo-spatial flexibility provided by the lexicon and syntax of language. A new trajectory is created through internal resonance and reflection on the stories of self, other and the world. The learning and application of concepts will be the work of a lifetime for each self. This process occurs on a different time scale, *proceeding at a much slower rate, closely related to the rhythms and memorization of language itself, rather than the constant flux of environmental images.* This time frame is properly thought of as the *trajectory of self* in that higher consciousness, as opposed to unreflective primary consciousness, is operant. The trajectory of self relates to episodes of personal significance, accessible to declarative memory and linguistic representation. These can be thought of as *self-states*, rather than states of passing phenomenal awareness.

It should now be clear that *conscious state* and *self-state* are not synonymous. *Conscious states* are required, however, for *self-states* to develop. In principle measurement of *self-state* needs to involve recognition by the individual of images and language as objects of reflection. It requires representation in meaningful language since this is the primary means that self has of reporting reflective experience. In Chapter 5 a methodology and some preliminary results for measurement of self-state are put forward.

Processes of self-realization, and self-understanding occur over the life span, episodically rather than continuously. The earlier forms of continuous, moment-to-moment exchange still occur, embedding language in bodily processes. Just as language is effected through the body, so the body is affected by language. In particular the ANS, linked to the brainstem and hypothalamus with an array of central projections that, at a whole organism level, is thought to provide a continuously operating value system, strongly influencing perception and behaviour (Edelman & Tononi, 2000). Self-realization necessarily involves processes of reconciling this continuous stream of feeling states with the conceptual knowledge being appropriated from the external social institution of language, so that knowledge can be "owned" and incorporated by self.

Flexibility and transformation in the "zone of proximal development"

Flexibility is generally considered a hallmark of a mature personality. The human brain and nervous system provide a complex interface with the environment supporting an internal value system, while language provides us with an instrument that can be gradually appropriated to provide a medium for shared understanding with our fellows and understanding of the external value system of the community. With maturity humans are held increasingly accountable for their behaviour, considered by the community as both agents and authors of their own lives.

In much scientific writing, a bottom-up form of causality is espoused. Hence the activity of neurons, and cells, are said to "cause" movement, speech and so on. Such forms of causal relation bear little resemblance to forms of causality that we speak about in our personal lives where we say things like: "*he committed a crime*"; "*she looks after her children well*"; "*I hit him because he hit me*". Everyday notions of responsibility are very much based in the notion of individuals as causal agents.

When higher order consciousness is under consideration, it has been argued that language has a constitutive significance. Conscious states, as already discussed, tend to reach phenomenal awareness as unified scenes of the world *out there*, somewhat in the manner of a moving picture. While receptive capacities in humans, and other animals, tend to be oriented out to the world, they are always also attached to kinaesthetic images of the body and feeling. Feeling is the phenomenal side of trans-modal perception, constituting an animating principle central to subjectivity and self.

In his paper "On a Certain Blindness in Human Beings" James argues that the incapacity to imagine what might be *felt* to be of most significance to others is often missed, particularly in scientific accounts (James, 1899). Similarly, if language is to be accorded its role as constitutive of both higher order consciousness and self, it is crucial for this lived dimension of feeling to be included in the account of language. Language as expressed, under the influence of emotion and bodily systems, will show shadings of inflection, disruptions of grammar, hesitancies and silences, musicality with shifts in pitch and tone, all reflecting the life of the person: a very particular *form of life*.

The flexibility and plasticity of the brain have been increasingly recognized in recent decades. Edelman describes the property of *degeneracy* in selectional neural systems as accounting for considerable flexibility in the system: "there are typically many different ways, *not necessarily structurally identical*, by which a particular output occurs" (Edelman & Tononi, 2000, p. 86), i.e. different pathways can yield similar results. While this capacity is present in other species, in humans, with highly developed cerebral cortices, the quantity of potentially available pathways is greatly increased.

Just as the evidence of brain plasticity that has accumulated in recent decades challenges old notions of fixity in neural systems, the study of structure in language also faces the challenge of variability (Butt, 2005). Halliday's description of language and its emergence from strict dependence on here-and-now phenomenal experience, through the acquisition of grammar and a common system of meaning, refers to the inherent *redundancy* in linguistic systems (Halliday, 1992). This is to say there are many ways of conveying a message: "collective human consciousness created a semiotic space which is truly elastic, in that it can expand in any number of dimensions" (ibid., p. 356). This emphasizes the tremendous flexibility of the language system. The principle of redundancy is not that, "(i) meaning is realized by wording and wording is realized by sound", emphasizing precise one-to-one correspondences with little flexibility, but that "(ii) meaning is realized by the realization of wording in sound", emphasizing the unique instantiation of meaning in local conditions, particularly meaning **arising as we speak** (ibid., p. 357).

Linguistics is a science of relations across strata, describing a *realizational model of meaning*, where special conditions apply to semiotic processes. Semiosis depends upon the prior working of a social order, itself dependent upon biological levels of organization and the primary level of expression through the physical stratum (Butt, 2005). These special conditions optimally include responsive carers who constitute an environment that is a *zone of proximal development* for the child (Vygotsky, 1934, p. 187). This reflects cooperative engagement, where the child is learning through participation: "In learning to speak. . . . What the child can do in cooperation today he can do alone tomorrow" (ibid.).

Flexibility in meaning-making depends upon the *symbolic attitude* (Jung, 1923; Hobson, 1985). Where this is present there are infinite possibilities for the realization of meaning in psychotherapeutic and other interpersonal contexts.

Once the child enters the "speech fellowship" by learning the mother tongue, there is an ongoing relationship with language. An important determinant of this relationship is the initial affective conditions under which it was learnt. Myriad idiosyncratic pronunciations and meanings compete with conventional and contextually appropriate meanings, within the individual. This personal, inner language has been termed *language underground* (Baum, 1977). It is seen as the basis of linguistic expression in works such as *Alice in Wonderland* involving wordplay, humour and imagination. The extent to which the individual is able to play internally with meaning in this way may have significant implications for the way in which reality is perceived. For some people there will be little play and language is perceived as only having conventional meaning, so that at any given time one is either "correct", or not. Where inner play is lively, there is flexibility, and the creation of personal worlds, with dream-like characteristics contributing creative potential to the wider world. Here meaning can be "this, that or the other", depending on creative input at the time! The flexible use of language enhances the capacity for shared meaning-in-interaction. Where there is little capacity to play with language, one is left with a restricted, stereotypical view.

Each person has his or her own store of *language underground*. The inner speech of adults has its function as "speech for oneself" (Vygotsky, 1934, p. 32). Although this doesn't always coincide with language the person uses in actual interpersonal exchanges, it does constitute a hidden resource that may be expressed in the psychotherapeutic context. This includes unconscious elements that may only be realized under certain circumstances, such as in a therapeutic "zone of proximal development". If accessed there is potential for growth.

In the preceding discussion of conscious states, mention has been made of the nervous system's capacity to recall configurations (global mappings) of past experience, utilizing them unconsciously as a reference system for action in the present (Edelman & Tononi, 2000). This occurs in the context of ongoing interaction with the environment and continual modification by re-entrant activity in the nervous system that modifies the global mappings. This is applicable to both conscious and non-conscious memorial processes and explains why memory is not replicative, but rather creatively modified by new experience and behaviour (ibid.).

Neural degeneracy and memory provide a substantial basis for the flexibility, adaptability and ontologically evolving characteristics of *self*. The parallels with symbolic linguistic systems that have flexibility provided by redundancy, and evolutionary potential provided by the freeing, through grammatical structure, from immediate phenomenal contingencies, have led various authors to consider that living linguistic systems mirror neural-organic properties (Lamb, 1999; Halliday, 1995; Lemke, 2000). Humans live in interaction and cannot help but experience meaning in interaction, even if it is at the level of automatic selections linked to non-conscious feeling valuations, or at the levels of iconicity or internal relational models, rather than meaning in the sense of well-defined, conscious meaning. Selections are always *motivated*, both at the level of the nervous system and the level of language (Butt, 2008; Butt & Lukin, 2009, pp. 4–6). The intrinsic system of valuation (feeling) is motivating insofar as it is a system that involves experiences of reward and punishment with a continuous reinforcing influence on behaviour, experience and their neurological correlates. The felt sense of significance, rather than conceptual meaning, is the most fluid and dynamic aspect of self at all levels, including the evolving nervous system. However, without language and gesture to give it effective expression, feeling is constricted, leaving the person with a sense of entrapment and limitation.

Under conditions of early trauma and neglect, there are often failures to develop the sense of interiority required for the emergence of an autonomous self. This may manifest as chronic stress. Such conditions may involve chronic sympathetic overdrive, narrowing of consciousness and reduced flexibility, leading to psychological manifestations such as hyper-vigilance or stimulus entrapment (being dependent upon external stimulation for a sense of continuing existence) (Meares, 2005, pp. 88–96). Inner language may also be deficient or inaccessible to the person through processes such as dissociation. This does not mean there are no potentials within the traumatized person. It means that such potentials may be hidden, with change requiring engagement in a creative psychotherapeutic process or other nurturing relationship, with establishment of a new zone of proximal development.

Growth in psychotherapy only occurs if the person is emotionally engaged, without being overwhelmed. Change is sought in areas of felt significance. Change, if it occurs, will be in the personal use of language, in new affective investments and in new perspectives and orderings of the person's worldview. Even apart from psychotherapy, the world is replete with stories of transformation associated with a changed view of the world that may arise dramatically, as in an epiphany, or more gradually, as in *The Ugly Duckling*.

Psychotherapy has potential to bring about change in the direction of greater understanding and realization of humanity. Such a process necessarily involves language. It has been said that, "Given the intricacy of human meaning making – an intricacy which is both a function of its longevity and centrality in the evolution of human beings . . . . it is language which created humans, rather than humans language" (Butt, 1990, p. 346). This refers to the *humanizing* of *homo sapiens* into social, cooperative groups rather than the fact of biological creation. Such is the aspiration for psychotherapy. Self is realized as an expressed and developing text, involving creative and reflective processes. To apply the description of redundancy in language systems (Halliday, 1992) to self, one might say, it is not that (1) the person is realized by self and self is realized by language (which would imply some sort of formula in language), but rather, (2) the person is realized by the realization of self through language.

Chapter 3

Heart and soul: the feeling body

Overview

Therapists usually enter into the field with a wish to work wholeheartedly with their patients. Similarly, infants come into the world with the desire for social connection and relationship underpinned by neural systems that support the experience of feeling in interaction. Bodily rhythms of vitality, such as found in breathing, are backdrops to the living rhythms of exchange in communication. Language as lived through the utterances of speech, listening to it and even thinking with it has a prosody, beginning with the musicality of the exchanges between infant and carer. A normative model of emotional experience is useful to psychotherapeutic care. Such a model is substantially informed by Porges' Polyvagal Theory which holds that social engagement of vital functions has had a central role in human evolution and culture. It highlights a principle of whole-body, whole-person engagement in communication of purposes and feelings. This chapter forms a background to an intersubjective approach to research that recognizes both the privacy of self and the centrality of relationship to embodied mental lives, while maintaining awareness of the objective interests that may inform understanding of the living process.

Working with heart

A young woman, Helena, is admitted to hospital after a suicide attempt. She is highly emotional and distressed and, despite a number of attempts to discharge her to community care, she continues to self-harm and attempt suicide. She spends the better part of a year in hospital over multiple admissions. A number of pharmacological measures are tried and attempts are made at psychological work. The level of perceived risk results in her being confined to a locked area for long periods of time. She attracts various diagnoses including Depression and Borderline Personality Disorder. After many months she confides a background of sexual abuse at the hands of a relative. She has never disclosed this within the family. She is now prepared to do so and a meeting with her mother is arranged at which she finds the mother unexpectedly receptive and supportive. Within a week or so Helena is successfully discharged from hospital with arrangements for further counselling. A year or so later I see her by chance in the hospital cafeteria. She has a baby and is there with her partner. She comes over to say hello and seems pleased to see me, telling me that she has been well and had come off medication when she became pregnant.

This kind of story will be familiar to people working in the field of mental health. It illustrates how unexpressed feelings can dysregulate the whole person. A problem that is an aspect of mind, a secret associated with strong emotions, is resolved by being expressed and responded to in a sensitive, humane way. It would be an oversimplification to say the secret was Helena's sole problem. However, the intervention around disclosure proved decisive in her recovery. In many cases disclosures are not associated with rapid resolution, and there can be many complexities that mitigate against resolution, which may only be achieved after prolonged periods of psychotherapeutic work. The point being made is that the experience of meaning is intimately connected to bodily physiology and autonomic dysregulation, which was pronounced in this case.

The practice of psychotherapy is an embodied interaction, requiring sensitive attention to affective states, and awareness of bodily responses. The sense of significance in the interaction is very often *felt* rather than experienced in a conceptually clear way, particularly when it comes to experience that is conflicted, or on the margins of the patient's (or therapist's) established comfort zone, as evident in the case of Helena. The therapist works with the immediate phenomena of first-person experience, that of both patient and therapist. The work requires resonance, effective emotional connection and an intellectual grasp of the situation.

In everyday language "heart" and "soul" are used to convey notions such as "with all one's being", "with feeling for another", "with generosity towards another" and so forth. Expressions like "my heart is pounding", "my heart skipped a beat", "I couldn't breathe" or "my heart stood still" are descriptive of a range of emotional experience, commonly encountered in clinical contexts. They also illustrate the connection of meaning and bodily response. Complex feeling states and their associated sense of significance and bodily participation is captured by the term *forms of feeling*. The quest in psychotherapy is to find words that relate to these complex states:

> Metaphors which carry experience forward are those which disclose a meaning which is beyond, or prior to conceptual thoughts and formulated words. The significance is "felt in the blood, and felt along the heart".
>
> (Hobson, 1985)

In this chapter, connections between emotional expression and basic physiological functions, such as breathing and heartbeat, are considered. The Polyvagal Theory (Porges, 2011), a physiological model based upon recognition of biological factors underpinning emotional and social interaction, is found to have implications for the conceptualization of emotional life that are different from the dominant models of the 20th century.

Traditional notions of breath, life and spirit

Traditionally, "breath . . . was ever the original of 'spirit'" (James, 1904). In the pre-technological era *soul* (*psyche*) was seen as closely tied to breathing, as in the biblical verse, Genesis, 2:7 (KJV), "And the Lord God formed man of the dust of the ground, and breathed into his nostrils the breath of life; and man became a living soul."

The soul is considered present in the breathing individual and to have "left" when breathing ceases, at death. This remains a reasonable definition of the journey of life as a separate being, at least as far as the common-sense view is concerned. Life begins with the first breath and ends when we breathe our last.

An Ancient Greek definition of *psyche* describes it as synonymous with being alive: "anything which possesses my psyche is the very same living thing as I am" (Gregory, 1987). Contrary to later notions of immateriality, the psyche is here tied to the material processes of life, arguably to the forms of feeling that have become engraved in the embodied text of each individual life.

In contrast, there is a tendency in modern psychology, psychiatry and science, to dismiss the notion of *soul* as unscientific or unexplainable. This is paradoxical for sciences named after the *psyche* (*soul*). The traditional relationship of breathing to *psyche*, *spirit* and *soul* serves to emphasize the *temporal* dimension of these concepts. In other words, for something to have value for the organism, and therefore to be constitutive of the psyche, there has to be a rhythm and flow of exchange with the environment that occurs over time. The ebb and flow and cyclic re-iterative patterns of breathing follow a path of regularity, with irregularities, that tracks mental life. The modern scientific tendency to objectify effectively freezes the body into *breathless stases* that lack life. It then endeavours to re-animate bodies with mechanizing theories.

A common element to creation myths is the *spark* of fire. Forms of feeling, encompassing affect, emotion and context can be seen as the source of the metaphorical *spark* in the psyche. The myth of Prometheus involves *stealing from the gods*, giving man the *divine spark* that vitalizes him, motivating individuation and differentiation. However, even with breath, body and feeling, the psyche would be impoverished without communication, recognition and the provision of a speaking environment. Conversely, without the feeling of human connection and the comfort of human relatedness, language is empty, insufficient for fulfilment. In Mary Shelley's allegorical tale *Frankenstein, or The Modern Prometheus*, the new 19th century technology of electricity is portrayed as the Promethean *spark*. The story illustrates the implications of "scientific creation of life" outside a context of care. The creature is mistreated, as an object, with failure to take into account its psychological needs (Shelley, 1818). *Psychological* existence, for humans, involves communication and significance. We don't survive as pure isolates.

Breathing and consciousness

William James' descriptions of the stream of consciousness are still considered, in a phenomenological sense, definitive of our current understanding of consciousness. James also had a sense of humour. He was being ironic when he said,

> I am as confident as I am of anything that, in myself, the stream of thinking (which I recognize emphatically as a phenomenon) is only a careless name for what, when scrutinized, reveals itself to consist chiefly of the stream of my breathing. The "I think" which Kant said must be able to accompany all my objects, is the "I breathe" which actually does accompany them.
> (James, 1904, p. 178)

However, it is also characteristic of James' use of introspection to illustrate the limitations of what can be directly experienced and known. In a similar vein he subjects his own spontaneous thought processes to an "introspective glance" and finds, "all [I] can ever feel distinctly is some bodily process, for the most part taking place in the head" (James, 1890, p. 300). While James uses humour, he doesn't speak carelessly. The point of his reference to breathing is not to question the existence of thinking or the reality of experience. Rather, James states, "I mean only to deny that the word [consciousness] stands for an entity, but to insist most emphatically that it does stand for a function" (James, 1904, p. 163). Consciousness is a process not a thing, while breathing is an accompaniment present in consciousness.

During meditation one may focus on thoughts, sensations, feelings, *objectless awareness*, movements or, most commonly, the breath. As James suggests, it is breathing that is ever-present, in its ebb and flow. Usually in the background of awareness, accessible to conscious control, although most often continuing in unconsciously driven cycles and rhythms, the breath is something of a barometer of our mental states, part of the rhythmic background feeling of life. For example, over-breathing is well known as an accompaniment to anxiety. Expressions such as "catching one's breath", "waiting breathlessly" or "panting in anticipation" are markers of a variety of affective conditions.

Unlike other visceral functions, the breath remains part of consciousness in a manner similar to feeling, ever-present to consciousness. Both contribute to the sense of continuity for self. Both mediate our response to the environment. Properties that are continuous in consciousness provide the individual with something akin to an analogue scale containing re-iterative, self-relational information. However, this information is not in a simple one-to-one relationship with different emotional states (Kreibig, 2010). In relation to thought and breathing James' comment suggests an analogy between the two phenomena: the *ebb and flow* of breathing (breathing in and out) might be compared to the processes of *taking in* (information) and *expressing* (one's mental state) that constitute the basis of thought. The stream of thought in its adult verbal form develops as a stream of language. In turn, language has its ontogenetic beginnings in vocal interactions with carers, for which breath is the vehicle.

Feeling, breathing, apperception and self-states

While breath and feeling share continuity in consciousness, they have very distinct functions. The affective experience of human beings works as an inbuilt value system (Panksepp & Biven, 2012; Solms, 2015), inseparable from body, providing sensitively nuanced information to self in relation to both environment and the state of the body. Breathing clearly has a primary metabolic function, although it also serves a self-regulatory function. Breathing and heart rate vary with autonomic response, and so provide, amongst other bodily systems, continual feedback variably present to consciousness. These are intrinsic contributions to consciousness, against which conceptual thought is continually being gauged.

The area of feeling is intensely personal: "we feel as though they (emotions) were in the soul itself" (Descartes, in Stocker, 1996, p. 19). Hence, personal selves experience life in terms of its affective qualities of reward, punishment and more nuanced feelings which motivate social engagement and growth (Porges, 2011; Meares, 2016).

Feeling is an integration of cross-modal sensory and contextual information, translated into the "language" of affect, involving deep structures of the limbic cortex. There has been interest in the role of the amygdala in relation to the experience of affect. While the role of the amygdala in mediating fear has been well-studied (LeDoux, 2000), it is also important in facial recognition, social responsiveness and appraisal of the valence of situations, thereby "updating representations of value" (Morrison & Salzman, 2010). This suggests a role in the process of apperception, in relation to the environment. However, the amygdala does not generate affect by itself. While important in the detection of environmental dangers, its role in the "generation of affect . . . . has been vastly exaggerated" (Panksepp, 2008, p. 48).

The capacity of humans (and other species) to **apperceive** refers to the "ability to understand perceptions in their context; to interpret them appropriately; to connect them with each other and form associations; and to incorporate them into total experience" (Sims, 1988, p. 41). Feeling, in imbuing value to perception, is central to this capacity. Affective appraisal systems "connect stimuli with their intrinsic or learned affective value" (Niedtfeld & Schmahl, 2009). Feeling tones are experienced cross-modally. This means, for example, the same feeling aroused by rhythmic touch, could also be produced by an action pattern, with a similar rhythm and intensity, in a different modality, such as a sound stimulus. So, while feeling is always in the body in the sense of being embodied, it reflects a whole person experience rather than a localized sensation. Hence, feeling is reflective of the experience of self as a whole: "I consider affect to be psychic, not just bodily" (Stocker, 1996, pp. 18–19). One is reminded of forms of feeling as a total organization of experience rooted simultaneously in body and mind (Hobson, 1985).

In saying, "If the passing thought be the directly verifiable existent which no school has hitherto doubted it to be, then that thought is itself the thinker", William James refers to a "chunking" of consciousness into states which have a rise and fall and contain memory of the preceding state (James, 1890, p. 401). While he uses the term "thought", he is referring to states that are continuous from the beginning of life, preceding verbal thought. These states have early organization around an *affective core* (Emde, 1983) and, even earlier, around the emergent perceptual and procedural patterns of interactive experience (Stern, 1985). Early organization of the mind through feeling and image patterns is now thought to be more dependent upon the right cerebral hemisphere than the left (Schore, 2012). The role of the right hemisphere, in conjunction with the right vagal nerve, in regulating homeostasis and emotion, and processing aspects of social engagement, like facial recognition, continues throughout life (Porges et al., 1994). The overlap between mental states, provided by memory and feeling, allows for the experience of continuity in consciousness, necessary to the emerging experience of self.

Chunks of consciousness sufficient to be psychologically meaningful and reflectively accessible are elaborated within *the present moment* (Stern, 2004). While humans can "perceive" separate events in a sequence that lasts as little as 20 milliseconds, such ultra-brief experiences "do not make life meaningful" (Stern, 2004). He argues the present moment of experience is determined by "the duration of a phrase" (ibid., p. 42), generally of the order of 2–10 seconds. This is consistent with the theory of Systemic Functional Linguistics where the clause which provides context as well as content, is seen as the basic unit of language (Halliday & Matthiessen, 2004; Butt et al., 2000). In an interpersonal context, Stern also relates meaningful experience to turn-taking, involving exchanges in cycles of 2–3 seconds, between two speakers. Ultimately, these cycles, the timings of the clauses of language, are related to breathing, given that one cycle of inspiration and expiration takes about 3 seconds, on average.

Stern also refers to flexible neuronal encoding of meaningful chunks of experience, via the *re-entry* loop described by Edelman (Edelman & Tononi, 2000). Stabilization of the re-entry loop requires that events in experience be sufficiently salient (that is, have sufficient significance as "measured" by the feeling accompaniment of the experience). "The present moment is the time it takes for such a loop to be sufficiently stabilized to give rise to consciousness" (Stern, 2004, p. 53). Here Stern is referring to not just a bare awareness of the environment, but awareness of that awareness, i.e. self-awareness.

The periods of time that support reflective consciousness are the time scales of breathing and vocalization. These are the conditions that allow for feeling, and thought, to be "seen" by the mind. Early on this relates to the spans of time required for emotional, gestural and vocal reception and expression and later to the timings of language, related to the breath and clause structures.

The experiential regulation of feeling through narrative

Psychological understanding necessarily encompasses feeling, the intrinsic human value system and motivator. It also requires language, the system underpinning verbal thought (Thibault, 2004). Tomkins' account of *General Images* of Affect (Tomkins, 1995) helps show how selectional processes shape individual selves. It is made clear that humans are self-organizing systems even before integration of verbal language:

> In the case of the human being, the fact that he is innately endowed with positive and negative affects which are inherently rewarding and punishing and the fact that he is innately endowed with a mechanism which automatically registers all his conscious experience in memory, and the fact that he is innately endowed with receptor, motor, and analyser mechanisms organized as a feedback circuit, together make it all but inevitable that he will develop the following General Images: (1) Positive affect should be maximized; (2) Negative affect should be minimized; (3) Affect inhibition should be minimized; (4) Power to maximize positive affect, to minimize negative affect, to minimize affect inhibition should be maximized.
>
> (ibid., p. 67)

While points (1) and (2) look like a simple version of behaviourism, this isn't necessarily the case when one considers that affects interact and one may inhibit another. Hence, although positive affect is reinforcing, it may, for example, be chronically inhibited by fear or moral convictions about what is socially acceptable, e.g. shame may make a great range of behaviours seem unacceptable. Nevertheless, at an individual level, these first two principles directly reflect *reward* and *punishment*. The third principle, that "affect inhibition should be minimized" relates to *expression* of affect: "inhibition of the overt expression of affect will ordinarily produce a residual form of the affect which is at once heightened, distorted, and chronic and which is severely punitive" (ibid., p. 69). While this is obvious in the case of negative affect, Tomkins points out that it is also the case for positive affect: "chronic inhibited positive affect is also painful since it leads to distress or anger by the fact of inhibition, or to chronic fear, shame or self-contempt at the ever-present danger of disinhibition" (ibid., p. 69). This principle speaks to the *need for affective expression*, highlighting the need for reciprocal communicative engagement with others in order to maintain a state of affective balance.

The fourth *general image* in conceived of, by Tomkins, in terms of *power*. He refers to coordination of the first three principles. While it *is* likely that effective coordination will maximize personal efficacy and, in that sense, be associated with a sense of empowerment, power tends to imply domination in interpersonal terms. In my view, this principle refers to *coordination* and *organization* of affective life, serving the purpose of sustaining lively engagement with the world. As such, this coordination involves the organizing principles or mental models that shape relational life and, over time, the emerging personality. Once verbal language is established, all of these *general images* require coordination and integration through verbal exchange.

Affects are inherently brief, requiring amplification and coordination, in order to become part of a meaningful fabric of experience for the individual. Experience is organized into scenes, "the basic element of life as it is lived" (ibid.). Scenes form the basis of "script theory" (ibid.). Scripts are developed on the basis of two principles: that of *variants* and *analogues* (ibid., p. 184). **Variants**, which involve recognition of "changes in something which in its core remains the same", are most relevant to elaboration of positive affect as illustrated by the example: "if one's wife is wearing a new dress, one does not say to her, 'you look very similar to my wife' but rather, 'I like the new dress you're wearing'" (ibid., p. 184). According to the Conversational Model (CM), positive affect is enhanced through amplification that builds upon *self*, something which "in its core remains the same".

Analogues may be applied to either positive or negative affect. They are particularly powerful in "dealing with negative affect scenes" (ibid., p. 185). Depending upon the way an individual has organized her internal working models, such analogic constructions, termed by Tomkins as "nuclear scripts", can "become the major mechanism whereby a negative affect scene is endlessly encountered and endlessly defeats the individual when the ratio of positive to negative affect becomes predominantly negative" (ibid., p. 185). This is clinically relevant to situations where trauma has dominated early, pre-verbal development. This is a situation where internal working models have become organized outside the awareness of declarative memory systems, around negative feeling.

This form of analogue may become problematic for the individual. Transformation of such a "script" requires analogical intervention. The impact of trauma, and the ways that narratives become organized into scripts in these circumstances, is important in terms of clinical interaction, and understanding the level of response required. A traumatic script "is made in isolation and shut off from the domain of discourse. No discrepant information can enter into it. It is a system of 'facts'" (Meares, 2000, p. 83). Confronting, or directly challenging, such a system will be ineffective and may be traumatizing or lead to fragmentation. It is governed by "invariant organizing principles" that Meares' terms "the impinging narrative". This is not only internally impinging, but also leaves the person in the position of susceptibility to further external impingement (Meares, 1995).

> *A man in his sixties seeks therapy. He declares that his problem is that he's "stupid . . . really just a fool". He had a background of severe neglect with*

older parents, a father who abused alcohol and was periodically violent to a mother who was depressed. He had a younger brother who was favoured by his father. Pointing out the considerable evidence that demonstrated the man was no fool had no effect. It was necessary to engage with the impoverished script by which the man defined himself. With time devoted to the many shame-filled illustrations he could give of his "stupidity" a more complex and interesting narrative began to emerge.

The ways in which trauma may be reflected in language have also been described as *scripts, chronicles* and *narratives* (Meares, 1998). These are organized in relation to implicit memory systems in the case of scripts and chronicles, and episodic (autobiographical) memory, in the case of narratives (ibid.). Meares' use of script corresponds roughly to Tomkins' use of *nuclear script* based around negative affect. A main reason for the form of the traumatic script is the impact of intense, *vehement* emotions which have the effect of disorganizing conscious states, leading to fragmentation, having a dis-coordinating effect that over-rides the natural synthetic effects of attention and apperception (Meares, 2012, pp. 114–118).

In conversation, the form of scripts may be broken up by the conversation itself, conversational form being different from recitation of a story, having bits of narrative, interspersed with the concerns of the relational engagement. However, fragments of *script*, with their traumatic basis, get incorporated into therapeutic conversation. There is an ongoing re-calibration of the conversation by both patient and therapist as the traumatic narrative comes to be understood. This can be identified and modification in conversational form can be used as a measure of progress (Henderson-Brooks, 2006).

Language, the cardio-respiratory apparatus and the feeling body

Communication between living creatures is transmitted through various sense modalities. In humans, the modality of sound has become highly developed through language. Communication between people can be understood developmentally as a resonating social exchange with increasing semiotic differentiation, before it becomes expanded in scope by the complex conceptual network of the mother tongue. Humans respond in an embodied way to significance, affectively and through action, before they understand, specifically, what experience *means*. All responses involve the ANS and the cardio-respiratory apparatus (CRA).

For example, the newborn cries without knowing the reason or questioning why such an outlay of effort has been made. The CRA can be seen as one functional unit, with a primary function of metabolic regulation. It is closely integrated with the ANS, which, in turn, is integrated with the central nervous system "at all levels of nervous activity" (Kreibig, 2010). Moment-to-moment cardio-respiratory regulation is largely mediated through vagal regulation of the CRA under normal conditions because only vagal mediation occurs with sufficient rapidity to correspond to breathing cycles in the timings of the present moment, as described previously: the parasympathetic nervous system (PNS) exerts a peak effect on the CRA over 0.5s, with a return to baseline functioning over 1s, whereas the sympathetic nervous system (SNS) takes 4s for peak effect and 20s to return to baseline (Appelhans & Luecken, 2006, p. 230).

The ANS is a major mediator of feeling, being particularly responsive to situations that relate to the sense of safety for self in the environment. As such, it recognizes that variations within the bodily self (organism) are an important intervening variable in the response to environmental stimuli. In humans, language and the sense of significance get entwined into this intervening response. The ANS provides a neurophysiological basis for understanding how body and mind participate variably in the process of stimulus-organism-response (SOR) (Porges, 2017). Relative to "stimulus-response" (SR) paradigms that seek to demonstrate correspondence between brain response and environmental stimuli, the SOR paradigm makes clear the role of body and mind in shaping experience and response. The brain is part of the feeling body.

Vocalization begins in humans, and other mammals, with the *cry* that occurs at birth. While this occurs unconsciously, it is not without significance. It is meaningful in its interpersonal context. While often seen as a sign of distress, the cry also serves a communicative function, referred to as the *separation call*. This makes the infant an effective participant in communication. This evolutionary development relates to modifications to the respiratory and auditory apparatuses across mammalian species. In people, these modifications have allowed the development of complex vocal expression. At least in its manifestation as physically produced sound, speech is a complex modification of breathing. The first breath also signals transition from the relatively passive relation to the environment *in utero* to an active one. Breathing requires inspiratory effort which must continue if the infant is to survive. The separation call is of evolutionary significance for all mammals. It highlights the fundamental need for newborn mammals to be accepted and included into the family of their birth.

Beyond the direct connection between speech and breath, there is an analogical relationship between breathing and language. Both are *interpenetrated* relationships connecting individual and environment. Just as we are born into a world surrounded by air that we must take into, and let out of, our bodies for survival, so we are also surrounded by a peopled, communicating environment where we must also "take in" (hear, listen), and "let out" (express, speak) to survive as effective social participants. While respiration is essential to our physical survival, effective communication is essential to psychic survival and the growth of self. It also contributes to metabolic regulation.

We are participants in communicative exchange before we develop symbolic language. Narrative form is also evident in the vocalizing exchanges between infant and carer, occurring in the neonatal period (Malloch & Trevarthen, 2009). These exchanges typically have a musical quality such that we "sing before we speak". Resonating capacities are evident in social exchanges from the outset. Their role in modulating affect is evident from this early period. Interactions with carers engage the autonomic networks of the infant, with moment-to-moment regulation of feeling being modulated through the parasympathetic system, also thought to modulate the CRA during ongoing social engagement throughout life (Porges, 2011).

Developing hearts and minds

The heartbeat is another bodily rhythm sometimes present to consciousness, more intermittently so than breathing. Even *in utero* the rhythms of heartbeat, both of self and mother, may at times be present sensations to the developing foetus. In relation to language it may be of note that *sound units* of speech (phonemes) correspond approximately to the range of intervals of the human heart-beat, while *meaning units* (clauses) correspond to the range of human breathing. After birth, variation of heartbeat occurs continually in relation to breathing through the phenomenon known as Respiratory Sinus Arrhythmia (RSA). Heart rate increases as we breathe in and decreases as we breathe out. Variability of heart rate is of greater amplitude when the individual is in a non-stressed condition under predominant parasympathetic influence (Porges, 2011). Heart Rate Variability (HRV) is a vagally mediated phenomenon thought to be important in optimal metabolic regulation under conditions of perceived safety.

Variability in heart rate occurring in relation to breathing was first recognized and measured in the 1733 by Stephen Hales, reflecting the increased availability of accurate timepieces (Hales, 1773; Kenwright et al., 2008). HRV has been shown to have implications for health. Reduced HRV is associated with increased cardiac and mental morbidity as well as reduced life expectancy (Billman, 2011; Kemp et al., 2010). Specifically, depression that doesn't improve with antidepressant treatment, associated with higher cardiovascular morbidity, has been shown to correlate with reduced HRV (Kemp et al., 2010; Schwerdtfeger & Friedrich-Mai, 2009). Reduced HRV also occurs in the early stages of bereavement, suggesting a possible mechanism for increased cardiovascular morbidity in this period (Buckley et al., 2012). Slowing of the breath through meditative techniques (Rubia, 2009) or using biofeedback (Gevirtz, 2003) has been shown to increase HRV. Conversely increasing respiratory rate has been shown to decrease HRV (Hirsch & Bishop, 1981). HRV is also reduced by the stress of an attention-demanding task requiring sustained mental effort and increased when people were not engaged in such tasks (Porges, 2017). These findings raise questions regarding the possible effect of speech on breathing and, in turn, on HRV.

This functional relationship, between breathing and heart rate, can also be seen in analogical terms that have communicative, as well as metabolic, significance. The infant is born and takes its first inspiration, involving effort. With the first expiration, the infant cries; in crying, the infant makes an unconscious communication. This communication is understood to facilitate social inclusion across mammalian species. There is a creative analogy to be made between the physical act of inspiration, necessary for animation of the body, and the psychological experience of inspiration. Similarly, the experience of expiration as "relaxation", or letting go, bears similarity to the emotional process of *letting go*. When the expiration is oriented to communication, through speech or emotional expression, there is an expiratory, communicative effort, subserving the same function as the original cry of the infant. That function is to enhance social connection in the human social world.

The associated physiology reflects these functions: when we inspire there is a temporary *gate* on vagal influence, functionally meaning a relative preparedness for activation or mobilization; while with expiration there is reinstatement of vagal influence, consistent with relaxation and receptive function (Appelhans & Luecken, 2006). Under non-stressed conditions these influences are small. Vocalization increases the effort of expiration and is associated with a shortened RR interval, but does not, in itself, exert a significant influence on RSA (Kotani et al., 2007). (The RR interval is the interval between successive R waves on electrocardiogram recordings.) This is consistent with vocalization and speech being activities compatible with a sense of social safety. In the context of an emotionally engaged psychotherapy, conversations occur that will, at times, have significant emotional content. This can put participants in the position of experiencing significant mobilization of the ANS and CRA. Indeed, these areas of emotional significance are likely to be important to the process of change (Schore, 2012). For both patient and therapist management of these states is crucial to the outcome of the therapy.

Measurement of RSA as an index of vagal tone relating to activity of the myelinated division of the vagus is thought to be a clinically relevant measure of autonomic and emotional state: "I had the vision that monitoring physiological state would be a helpful guide to the therapist during the clinical interaction" (Porges, 2011). Higher RSA values reflect a greater range of HRV with positive implications for health and well-being.

Vocalization itself plays a part in the maturation of the respiratory apparatus, and is thought to contribute to the strengthening of the chest muscles, allowing the infant to shift from paradoxical breathing, to coordinated movements, involving chest and diaphragmatic musculature (Reilly & Moore, 2009). In turn, this coordination is required, for the support of more complex vocalizations. The spoken word from carers and the infant's vocalizations provide opportunities for resonance, important to the sense of social connection, long before the infant acquires language. As mentioned, initially vocalization is primarily social. Spoken language *continues* throughout life to serve a primarily social function. Notions of scientific, legal or cultural "truths" come later and, even then, serve social functions additional, in the case of scientific truth, to any status as "fact".

"Measuring" hearts and minds

> *Humans are the measure of all things: of things which are, that they are, and of things which are not, that they are not.*
>
> Protagoras, c. 440BC

The sense of *measure* here is primarily relative to individual phenomenal experience (Audi, 1995). That is, to knowledge acquired privately rather than distanced forms of knowledge, such as forms of measurement utilized in objective description of a thing involving numerical or instrumental measures. Phenomenal "measures" include the sense of *liveliness* attached to experience, essentially a felt quality. It is the investment of the objects of the world with feeling that is central to the sense of connection with the world (Greenspan & Shankar, 2004). Protagoras also encompasses "*things which are not*", and hence allows space for *negative* qualities. This element of human experience is missing in a philosophically positivist account. By negative or absent, one is referring to "that which isn't seen or sensed". From an intersubjective viewpoint, however, much of what isn't seen can be accounted for by a restriction of the view, implicit in the observation of the individual in isolation. In the experience of relatedness that forms the basis of meaning in human life, it is what happens *in relationship* that is of primary importance.

In his work on *interpersonal neurobiology* Siegel makes the claim that the brain and mind can't be understood without an additional member of the mental triad, *relationships* (Siegel, 2015). In this view brain is part of a larger system: "When we add to this that the brain is a 'social organ' . . . . . we can see that viewing the 'brain' as limited to the skull makes no biological sense. It is 'bio-illogical' to view component elements of a whole as isolated from one another" (ibid., p. 27).

Interaction between people will be sensed as meaningful even when there is no explicit statement of meaning (no words spoken). The phenomenon of *primary consciousness* arguably involves an *automatic selection* of the past experience of *best fit*, assisting in immediate contextual evaluation (Edelman & Tononi, 2000). Although it makes use of implicit memory, this is a non-conscious operation. The development of automatic processes of selection is efficient and seems to be characteristic of most day to day behaviour and communication, leaving available mental resources for new challenges and interests that concern the individual (ibid; Bargh & Chartrand, 1999).

In developing the concept of *neuronal selection* as a model of brain function, an analogy is made to operation of the immune system, where it has been demonstrated that the antibody response to antigens is recruited not on the basis of a precise fit but rather on the basis of *best fit*, given the individual's *prior* exposure to antigens (Edelman & Tononi, 2000). From an experience-near perspective, the mode of primary consciousness is thought to be similar: *past* experience gets recruited with elements of implicit readiness, helping to orientate the individual to the present moment, conferring an anticipatory advantage, without the individual's awareness of these operations. The presence of feeling in experience confers a sense of value, with positive, negative or neutral valence, such that behavioural repertoires will be activated in a manner optimal for the individual in a given context.

Such patterns may relate to experiences of knowing, connection, orientation and familiarity, sensed rather than conceptually defined. Where feeling-based evaluation is not operating optimally, the individual's "measure" of situations, and consequent response, may be deficient or maladaptive. A concomitant of humans being affectively attuned to environment is that situations are experienced in terms of matches and mismatches primed by past expectations. Danger-related mismatches are often processed over short time periods, with obvious value in terms of immediate survival (Williams & Gordon, 2007). However, it is the matches associated with reward-related stimuli that "may be considered relatively more important to safety and survival at a longer time scale" (Williams & Gordon, 2007). Rewarding experience is central to the development of a mature self. Emotional processing seems to occur with greater rapidity in the right hemisphere than the left throughout life (Schore, 2012). Response to emotional cues and images also comes into conceptual awareness (left brain processing) *via* the right hemisphere (Schore, 2012; McGilchrist, 2009).

Higher order consciousness, arguably the defining characteristic of the human world, is not possible without language (Edelman & Tononi, 2000). The involvement of language, a property of speech fellowships, in higher consciousness means the full realization of mental capabilities arises from an intrinsically interpersonal field, *a priori* relative to the developing infant. The individual must learn the mother tongue before language can take on a life of its own within, bringing reflective consciousness into being. Verbal choices made in conversation will also be influenced by a similar selection process to that outlined for primary consciousness.

In the 21st century there has been a growing move away from the view of life as mechanism, towards the "contemporary concept of life forms as self-modifying beings", coinciding with the shift from "a mechanistic to informatics view of living organisms" (Shapiro, 2011, p. 4). This view emphasizes the capacity of organisms, from single cell level to complex life forms, to sense the environment and actively transform themselves on the basis of this information, even at basic levels such as DNA structure and protein production (Shapiro, 2011). The ebb and flow of the relationship with the environment, as exemplified by breathing and feeling-in-relatedness, is constitutive of an interpenetrated *living* relationship, not simply mechanistic processing. In Freudian theory, pleasure is conceived of in relation to accumulation of "unpleasurable tension" followed by efforts towards "lowering of that tension" (Freud, 1920, p. 275). Unpleasure "corresponds to an *increase* in the quantity of excitation" and "pleasure to a *diminution*" (Freud, 1920). The *pleasure principle* was seen as central to motivation (Freud, 1911) even though pleasure was defined negatively (relief of tension).

In contrast the CM argues for pleasure as positive well-being experienced through the sense of connection, warmth, play and cooperative action with others that is primary to development of self (Meares, 2005). Tension and relief speak of mechanisms within a solitary organism, conceived as a machine. Ebb and flow imply reciprocal exchange. For humans this is largely carried on through communicative exchange.

Measurement in psychotherapy

The task of finding measures that illuminate therapeutic process in psychotherapy is complex. Measures need to be meaningful at both individual and interpersonal levels. Methods that chart "the movements of inner life,. . . . indirectly, through the study of language, . . . can discern shifts in the flux of personal being" which, coupled with direct measures of autonomic responsiveness, could inform the study of therapeutic change (Meares et al., 2005b). Statistical approaches that objectify experience do not inform us directly about an individual or a particular relationship. Modern tendencies to standardize and objectify lead to a distancing from experience and a de-contextualization of the individual: "a push to 'de-world' the patient, transforming experience through the lived body into an objective body fully perceptible from the third person perspective" (Frenkel, 2008). One is left with a body in isolation. Such measures may help categorize people but they do so at a cost, with loss of specific, affectively based information.

The embodiment of communication means that language as expressed and received cannot be considered separate to whole-person experience (Stocker, 1996). Psychic equilibrium as well as physiological homeostasis are maintained by self-regulatory tendencies constantly in play. These tendencies have characteristics of flexibility and "non-stationarity", i.e. "variable regularity" rather than fixed pattern. It is not the case that language provides us with a symbolic medium in which symbols can be manipulated in the mind without attendant bodily changes. Rather, "language cuts to the quick" (Butt et al., 2007/10), accounting for what can at times be radical physiological shifts in short periods of present experience. The parasympathetic component of the ANS is implicated in this kind of rapid response, the sensing of "something not right", mediating orientation to safety and threat from within (Goehler, 2006; Porges, 2011).

For objective data to be psychologically meaningful in psychotherapeutic terms, it would be desirable not only to demonstrate shifts in experience and state in the patient. Rather, both participants in the conversation need to be considered. This is particularly so since many psychodynamic theories are now based upon a relational rather than intrapsychic paradigm. Growth in the therapeutic relationship is thought to precede growth of self (Meares & Jones, 2009; Schore, 2012), analogous to early development, where experience occurs *between* infant and carer before a secure sense of *internal relationship* is acquired. The form of matching required between patient and therapist is not exact imitation or perfect fit but rather one involving recognition, similarity and *good enough fit* (Meares & Jones, 2009).

Scientific research in both the physical and human sciences has relied considerably on probability theory. Probability theory rests upon assumptions of an *all or nothing* relationship: either one is or has a certain characteristic, or not. Statistical methods answer the question of the likelihood of such "set membership" in a particular case. Philosophically it answers the question, "Is this object a member of set y?" In contrast, *fuzzy logic* allows "partial set membership" and "partial truth values", more closely resembling human control logic (Kaehler, 1998). This allows development of control systems that operate on the basis of approximate values. In a sense, variables can be treated in a way analogous to the intuitive measure of feeling, where an experience may be "a bit too much", "far too much" or "not enough", etc.

The fuzzy logic of human control systems is based in language, rather than numerical measurement. Instructions are based upon an *"if . . . . . and . . . . . then . . . . ."* linguistic structure, applicable to various systems, such as temperature regulation. *"If* the process is too cool, *and* the process is getting colder, *then* add heat to the process" can be applied as a regulating instruction to machines, in ways that are intuitively closer to the way a person would regulate temperature in a situation such as *having a shower* (Kaehler, 1998). Fuzzy logic, when applied to control systems, has the characteristic of providing successively better approximations with further iterations of recognition and "measurement" of the ongoing process in question. This allows for emergence of smoother functioning with greater automaticity.

Many living processes involve iterative surveillance and adjustment with gradual achievement of greater precision, even at a cellular level: "the most applicable cybernetic models are **fuzzy logic** control systems. In such systems, accurate regulation occurs by overlaying multiple imprecise ('fuzzy') feedback controls arranged so each successive event results in greater precision" (Shapiro, 2011, p. 14). This may provide an approach relevant to the ongoing processing of emotional interaction in psychotherapy as reflected in ANS variables, measured concomitantly with the language of the psychotherapeutic conversation where repeated iterations of emotional configurations are to be expected. It is also consistent with the views of Wittgenstein and Sapir that much human behaviour, including habitual forms of communication and expression, are deeply embedded in language, social networks and culture (Sapir, 1951; Wittgenstein, 1958). Complex behaviour cannot be understood at purely objective or quantitative levels.

The notion of approximate responses that have a positive relational intent is well known in psychotherapy. Positive therapeutic intent was emphasized by Winnicott, who made the analogy to the mother with caring intent who generally proves *good enough* for her infant (Winnicott, 1965). Following Winnicott, it has become common to speak of the *good enough* therapist. In psychotherapy, the patient is participant in an emerging relational experience, subject to continual "measurement" of an approximate, affective kind that includes the apperception of safety. Given that conversation is a clear focus of attention in psychotherapy, it would be expected that changes in the sense of self would occur around emotionally salient moments of conversation, and that this would be reflected in shifts in the ANS, reflected in variables such as heart and respiratory rate, HRV and skin conductance. These shifts would be expected not only in the patient but also in the therapist. It is possible that some degree of co-variance may be identifiable.

Manifestations of the ANS are generally seen as non-conscious psychophysiological phenomena. Hence the development of techniques allowing their measurement could provide a window into "unconscious" interactions. A key issue, in terms of collecting data relevant to psychotherapy process, is to be able to identify changes that occur on the scale of the *present moment* (2–10s). This time scale represents a unit of experience accessible to self. Many current methods rely upon measures taken over significantly longer periods of time, making assumptions about the steadiness of rhythmic waveforms, like heart rate. In fact, signals like heart rate are not highly regular. Indeed, the irregularity of heart rate is a matter of clinical interest, given the implications of HRV for health.

A methodology and some preliminary results for the application of ANS variables to the psychotherapeutic setting will be discussed in the Chapter 5. The relevance of the ANS to social function and in relation to spoken language is considered next.

The Polyvagal Theory

The Polyvagal Theory (PVT), developed by Stephen Porges, is one of two major current psycho-physiological theories of autonomic function (Appelhans & Luecken, 2006). It relates autonomic flexibility in social interaction to a division of the vagal nerve providing fine-grained regulation of metabolic and emotional response (ibid.). The theory is based upon an evolutionary understanding of the development of the ANS with emphasis on mammalian patterns of social engagement, whereas the other major theory takes a dynamical systems perspective with emphasis on the role of the central autonomic network (ibid.). The PVT entails a significant revision of the understanding of emotional life, away from a focus on sympathetic arousal and towards recognition of the regulation of feeling and metabolism in everyday social life, mediated by the evolutionarily recent, myelinated division of the vagus nerve. Effectively it also provides a model linking brain to both body and environment allowing an understanding of the brain as a complex interface for reciprocal interaction with the environment rather than as a central control system.

The 20th century view of emotion, related to sympathetic arousal, cast emotional life in primarily *defensive* terms with frequent reference to activation of the hypothalamic-pituitary-adrenal axis: "The sympathetic nervous system has long been associated with emotion and stress. The label sympathetic reflects the historical identity of this system as a nervous system with feelings and contrasts it with the parasympathetic nervous system, a label that reflects a nervous system that guards against feelings" (Porges, 2001, p. 131). This may be appropriate to stressful, traumatic effects on the individual, but fails to capture the nuance of affective life.

Porges argues that the polyvagal theory provides "a bidirectional brain-body model that interprets the brain regulation of peripheral physiology . . . as providing a neural platform for emergent adaptive social and defensive behaviours" (Porges, 2011, p. 3). The emphasis is first on what is social and normative rather than on defence. The lynchpin of the polyvagal theory is the *orienting* response, i.e. the orientation of the individual to perceived safety in the environment. This allows people to deploy attention and behaviour in manners appropriate to the circumstances. The orienting response is present from birth, often referred to as the *startle* response during infancy. From this standpoint, the system of feeling becomes understood primarily as an *evaluative* system rather than a defence system, allowing flexible allocation of metabolic and attentional resources to situations of social engagement or to varying levels of challenge and threat.

The theory posits an evolutionarily based hierarchy of autonomic function (ibid.). This hierarchy consists of: (1) the evolutionarily recent, myelinated *smart* vagus subserving a function of social engagement; (2) the evolutionarily older sympathetic nervous system described as a *mobilization* system, adapted to activate efforts in the face of threat or challenge; and, (3) the evolutionarily ancient unmyelinated vagal system subserving a primarily defensive function activated in response to the sense of *life threat* initiating a relative metabolic shutdown. The *smart vagus*, so-named by Porges, consists of myelinated nerve fibres, with a distinct central nucleus in the brainstem, the Nucleus Ambiguus (NA). This part of the vagal nerve has a distribution involving organs and muscles above the diaphragm. The unmyelinated vagus has as its central nucleus the Dorsal Motor Nucleus of the Vagus (DMNV) in the brainstem with a distribution to viscera below the diaphragm.

Porges refers to the capacity of *neuroception* as the detection of conditions of safety, danger and life threat in the environment (ibid.). This concept seems related to *apperception*, discussed earlier although it is more specifically a non-conscious, automatic function. The interpersonal environment is critical since the presence of a *safe other* makes a major difference to the likely perception of safety, consistent with many developmental theories in psychology (e.g. Bowlby, 1988). While threat may sometimes be overt, such as when a person is subject to imminent attack by a predator, it is important to note that, for humans, much of the sense of safety or danger, is *communicated* in everyday interactions involving feeling and language. Given that response is to *sensed* significance in relation to *self*, it is quite possible for spoken language to have a devastating significance for self in the absence of explicit threat to life and limb. Indeed, such situations are more common than direct threats to life itself. Sometimes the autonomic implications may be similar.

Under conditions of *chronic* threat, as may be seen when there is ongoing abuse or neglect, there are important changes in bodily regulation with re-setting of homeostatic mechanisms away from *smart vagal* regulation towards "a state that supports chronic defense responses", with associated changes in RSA and HRV (Kolasz & Porges, 2018). This is thought to have implications for pain regulation because normally vagal regulation contributes to inhibition of nociceptive spinal neurones (ibid.). This may be an important mechanism in relation to central sensitization to pain and the chronic pain syndromes commonly seen in clinical practice.

In an evolutionary sense these developments in the ANS are shared with other mammals, for whom characteristic nurturing bonds between parent (usually mother) and newborn are critical to survival (Porges, 2011; Panksepp & Biven, 2012). Mammals, particularly humans, have also developed needs for physical and psychological closeness, with a behavioural repertoire that requires a degree of immobilization in the presence of others. Sexual intercourse, breast feeding and relational intimacy are examples. Porges postulates that unmyelinated vagal circuits subserving the defensive function of metabolic shutdown via *freeze* or *death-feigning* behaviours in many species, have come to be co-opted, in humans and some other species, under the influence of the neuropeptide oxytocin, to allow, in safe conditions, the experience of *immobilization without fear*, necessary to the formation of strong pair bonds (Porges, 2011, p. 178). More generally, recent research suggests that the coordination of oxytocin activity with serotonin, in the central nervous system, is required, for the reinforcing, rewarding properties of social interaction to be evident (Dolen et al., 2013).

The brainstem area regulating the myelinated vagus is involved in regulating voluntary and involuntary muscles of the face and neck, in conjunction with the closely associated pathways of the facial, trigeminal, accessory and glossopharyngeal nerves. Phylogenetically, these structures have a common origin in the branchial ("gill") arches (Porges, 2011). While they have developed into the musculature and organs of social engagement, the ancient evolutionary role in metabolic regulation is not altogether lost: "even when the gill arches evolve into the branchiomeric muscles common to all mammals, oxygenation of the blood through a coordination of breathing and heart rate during interactions with the environment remains a primary functional objective" (Porges, 2011, p. 38). These structures are responsible, not only for facial expression, but also for orientation and disposition of attention through head-turning, prosody of the voice, sound production, coordination of feeding and swallowing. The *smart vagus* has direct regulatory effects on the CRA with its area of control extending to the carotid body, directly involved in metabolic regulation with chemosensitivity to oxygen and carbon dioxide.

Homeostasis

The PVT posits homeostasis as a self-regulatory system guided by *interoception* and linked to higher order social interaction (Porges, 2011). In both physiological and psychological senses *homeostasis* is to be understood as a dynamic concept. Interoception is identified as operating on four levels:

> Level I involves physiological systems regulating internal organs with bidirectional sensory and motor pathways between brain and organs. This is a level of operation "not seen" either by self or other.
> Level II involves "the integration of interoceptive responses with other sensory modalities and psychological processes", requiring conscious and often motivated influences on brainstem regulation of homeostasis (ibid., p. 78). This level of operation may to some extent be present in the feeling of self but is not seen by others.

Level III processes are observable behaviours that can be evaluated in terms of quantity, quality and appropriateness of motor behaviour (ibid.). Here we are dealing with what can be seen both by self and other.

Level IV which reflects the coordination of behaviour, emotional tone and bodily state to successfully negotiate social interactions (ibid.). This level is seen and felt but also **requires shared social understanding**.

It is thought that during the first three months of life, infants master homeostasis relating to Levels I and II. Relevant to understanding this process is the fact that the vagus has a strong component of *sensory* afferent neurones as well as motor efferents (up to 80% of vagal neurones are afferent) (ibid., p. 82). This early period of life is thought to involve recognition and coordination of perceptual patterns and memory as well as early motor skills. At three months infants have developed to the point of establishing organization at the level of a primary affective core (Emde, 1983) with a concomitant growth in the capacity to act as a relational agent.

In order to explain ANS regulation during social engagement, the *vagal brake* is postulated as a key functional mechanism (Porges, 2011). The myelinated vagal nerve fosters calm behavioural states by inhibiting the influence of the sympathetic nervous system on the heart: this action is termed the *vagal brake* (ibid.). When an orienting response occurs, there is a transient release of this influence (i.e. down-regulation of vagal activity), resulting in *relative* enhancement of the sympathetic influence, without actual, costly sympathetic up-regulation, putting the individual into a state of readiness. If safety is perceived then vagal tone is again enhanced, social engagement proceeds and attention can be directed freely, with continuing cardiovascular regulation of metabolic needs via the vagus (ibid.). A degree of mobilization of self can be facilitated in this way without the dissociation that characterizes full deployment of defence systems.

> *At a first meeting, an anxious patient is frequently seeking clarification and checks the intent of the therapist's comments. Through the therapist showing interest and being able to connect to the things the patients says, the conversation gradually develops a narrative flow and the patient starts to feel more confident in disclosing concerns.*

Where challenge is sufficient to be perceived as *a threat to be overcome*, the individual proceeds to greater engagement of the SNS, potentially up to the level of full flight or fight response. Blood is diverted away from the brain, and attention becomes narrowed, shifting consciousness away from an associative form of engagement, towards a goal-oriented, linear focus. If the threat is sensed as serious (imminent life-threat), defensive regulation may go further, engaging the *freeze* or *death-feigning* unmyelinated vagal system. Blood is diverted from the brain and there is general metabolic down-regulation, impairing attentional systems (ibid.). In extreme cases this may present a threat to life itself: "dying of fright" is thought to be mediated through such vagal effects.

Another patient displays initial confidence and gives a coherent account of recent events. When the conversation moves to an inquiry about the patient's family of origin, there are more overt displays of emotion. When the therapist enquires about the patient's father, there is a marked display of autonomic arousal, with shaking and a fearful expression, despite protestations that the father was "a good man". The patient comes to a point of distress and leaves the room.

These variations in consciousness and response do not rely upon higher cortical or conscious appraisal but rather operate on the basis of coordination of the *smart vagus* with phylogenetically older parts of the nervous system.

A social species is one "where animals regulate one another's fundamental physiological processes", also know as *allostasis* (Atzil et al., 2018). In most mammals and birds there is evidence of this kind of regulation at least early in life. Allostasis accounts for change in response to the environment in the service of balance and stability. For humans, with prolonged dependency and continuing reliance on social networks throughout life, it is an important property over the lifespan. Social competencies are learned, driven by the need to predict social patterns and are associated with the gradual development of associational cortices and cortico-cortical connections that underpin communicative, social capacities (ibid.). When capacities for shared attention and bodily synchrony are fostered by early interactional life, the ground is laid for sculpting of the brain, for shared understanding that becomes enhanced by a shared language, characteristic of *level IV* homeostasis and for the potentially generative spiral of growth that nurtures self.

Physiological correlates of self and feeling in psychotherapy process

Feeling, as the element in mental life providing continual measures of value, is central to the sense of self and the prospective experience of relatedness. Since feeling can't be directly measured but only expressed in approximate, metaphorical ways, psychotherapeutic research struggles to find objective methods to help define this dynamic aspect of mental life. The positive re-appraisal of the role of affect and emotion provided by the PVT leads to consideration of markers of autonomic response as potential physiological correlates of self. The activity of the myelinated *smart vagus* may be a physiological marker of social engagement, a key to affective life. Both breathing and HRV are physiological parameters continually varying, in context-sensitive ways, throughout life. As continuous variables correlated with autonomic function via vagal pathways, they are promising markers of changes in relatedness that occur in psychotherapy contexts.

The complexities of emotional responsiveness and interaction between people in social contexts attest to the inter-relation of mind and body. While the attention of each person is typically focused on the meaning of interactions and the sense of self in relation to other, there is much happening at an unconscious level in terms of physiological, autonomic and CNS activity. Investigation of such phenomena may require a two-person paradigm. A sole focus on the responses of the patient leaves out half of the relational equation.

Interaction involving language is only meaningful in terms of the network that language provides. The exchange of meaning can never be precise or externally defined. Emotional cues and triggers are personalized, often highly specific to a particular individual and unpredictable in the context of intense emotional exchanges, such as may occur in psychotherapy. The extent to which autonomic responses can be contained and kept within limits that allow processing and eventual reflection, is likely to be closely related to outcome in psychotherapy (Schore, 2012, pp. 79–95). The PVT informs us that attention needs to be paid to autonomic regulation between people. Language may itself serve this function, as evidenced by work showing vagal tone can be maintained during conversation (Kotani et al., 2007), and supported by work which demonstrates slowing of respiratory rates during speech (Korner, 2015). However, for some people, particularly those prone to trigger into traumatic states of hyper- or hypo-arousal (Schore, 2012), additional work relating to enhancement of vagal tone, perhaps involving meditation, biofeedback or other modalities, may facilitate optimal care.

We develop with both *active* and *passive* pathways capable of down-regulating defence (Porges & Dana, 2018). Early in life *passive* environmental support for the infant is provided to a large extent by the sound, the melodic intonation and prosodic quality of the mother's voice. In therapy this also applies to the "therapist's vocalizations, and music modulated across frequency bands that overlap with vocal signals of safety used by a mother to calm her infant" (ibid., p. 66). Provision of environmental sound that utilizes this kind of "music", known as the Safe and Sound protocol, deploys the *passive* social engagement pathway and has been shown to be beneficial in the treatment of autism (Porges & Dana, 2014). When we seek to understand what has evolutionary value, we need to consider what allows for the experience of safety. Porges cites Dobzhansky (1962) in this regard, with reference to what we mean by "the fittest": "the fittest may also be the gentlest, because survival often requires mutual help and cooperation" (Dobzhansky, 1962).

Since humans respond to meaning, psycho-physiological measures might need to relate both to the language of the conversation and the private sense of self of each participant in order to enhance the possibility of correlating physiological variables with psychologically meaningful experience. A trial methodology is discussed in Chapter 5.

It has already been stated that breathing provides continuity in consciousness in a manner comparable to feeling. Respiration is driven largely although not entirely by non-conscious central nervous system centres in the brainstem (Cole,

1975). In a quiet state, breathing is likely to be regular, although there is considerable variability in relation to body movement and psychological state. The setting of psychotherapy is a situation where it is anticipated that breathing rate and form are influenced by a variety of factors including posture, bodily movement and most significantly emotional state. It is a situation where there are generally two participants, and it would therefore be expected there may be some relationship between the two participants, in a number of ways. Therapists quite frequently note synchronies, or mirroring, of physical movements and posture in therapy. This kind of synchrony is likely to be seen as open to conscious, willed motives. Similarities between bodily functions whose control is largely via central or autonomic regulation, such as breathing and heart rate, would suggest unconscious influences at play between the two participants.

The cultural evaluation of emotional life in human experience may be changing, perhaps, amongst other things, reflecting the influence of the polyvagal theory. Beyond this theory, there has been increasing recognition, in recent years, of the importance of feeling to the development of self. This is thought to relate to fundamental differences between emotional (Right Brain) and conceptual (Left Brain) processes (Schore, 2012; McGilchrist, 2009). If feeling is integral to what is meaningful in human lives, with a central role in evaluation crucial to the growth of self, then psychotherapists may be encouraged to respond genuinely, rather than defensively (i.e. affectively as well as intellectually), to the expression of emotion by patients.

Fuzzy ending

To conclude this chapter on a slightly, light-hearted, *fuzzy logic* note, perhaps the 20th century view of emotion could be characterized as, "*If* I notice a feeling or emotion *and* it gets stronger *then* I better hide it or escape, or even shutdown completely", whereas an emerging 21st century "fuzzy" view might be "*If* I notice a feeling or emotion *and* there is no threat that can be seen, *then* I am free to express myself or direct my attention as I please . . . . ."

On a more serious note, these *fuzzy scripts* might be considered illustrative of how the language we select can affect our apperception of basic psycho-physiological phenomena. In turn, this may influence the experience of these same phenomena. If we don't see emotion as something to be avoided, we will be able to participate more fully in social engagement.

In the 20th century view the emphasis was on emotion relating to arousal, signalling danger or defence, while safety was identified, at least to some extent, with a lack of emotion impinging upon the mental state. In the 21st century view there is a more positive evaluation of feeling, with its correlation to the sense of liveliness and social engagement, under conditions of perceived safety. This makes feeling a marker of personal value guiding interest and attention, necessary for the development of a positive sense of self, while maintaining appropriate recognition of a variety of challenges that might require the individual to mobilize or mount a full defensive response. The language of emotion in this vision is more normalizing than has typically been the case in the past.

Chapter 4

Making meaning together: the realization of value

Overview

We grow in shared communication involving language and language grows within us. The need for personal language grows within an integrated self-with-other-consciousness. The notion of *synchrony* refers to the growth of language held within self-awareness that seeks association. The principle of communicative exchange is embodied and concrete. Stories develop through enactment and embodiment in moving. They are generated and influenced by the felt accompaniments of communication, in part mediated through the ANS. For psychotherapy, conversation can be understood in terms of *narrative units* which serve the purpose of enriching the patient's text of personal vitality. In linguistic terms, the affective component of language, present in the lived transactions of conversation, provides the warrant for messages that constitute something new in the patient's experience. Conversation has messages that are "given" and "new", carrying potential for growth. Such change involves transformation of the personal story from restricted and restricting traumatic forms to living, optimistic narratives that can grow and be shared in companionship.

Growing in a symbolic milieu

Self is defined, for the CM, in terms of flow of experience in the stream of consciousness. Self is realized in a network of relationships, both in the actual relationships of experience and the language we use to relate to each other and within ourselves. Although self is a private dimension of experience it is inseparable from, and dependent on, feeling, relationship and language. The growth of self occurs "in a relationship in which the other represents the essence of our experience by means of a 'picturing' capacity, which is usually verbal but may be visual or auditory" (Meares, 2016). This requires use of metaphor and analogy whereby likenesses may be seen even in dissimilar things, providing a basis for the sense of human connection and the expression of subtle and complex feeling (ibid.).

In the previous chapter it was acknowledged that a change in our conceptual understanding of feeling doesn't alter basic physiology, but may alter the way we understand and enact emotion. For example, if we see crying as a healthy form of expression rather than as a sign of weakness, we may be less inclined to inhibit it. Such movement is possible at an individual level, reflecting change in an underlying *script* or *internal working model*. For each person, self is an essentially private process that, paradoxically, develops in a public space (Meares, 2005). Growth occurs in relation to the development of personal stories and myths at both conscious and unconscious levels. An infant is subject to the story-making of significant others that shapes consciousness even at a pre-verbal level.

Synchrony and diachrony: language as resource and manifestation

> *We are such stuff as dreams are made on; and our little life is rounded with a sleep.*
> Shakespeare, *The Tempest*, Act 4, Scene 1

Ferdinand de Saussure was a seminal figure in modern linguistics: "the impact of Saussure's theory of the linguistic sign has been such that modern linguists and their theories have since been positioned by reference to him: they are known as pre-Saussurean, Saussurean, anti-Saussurean, post-Saussurean, or non-Saussure" (Hasan, 2011). Saussurean influence extends to many academic disciplines including psychoanalysis. In the modern world, "Language is no longer regarded as peripheral to our grasp of the world we live in, but as central to it" (Harris, 1988). Some of the central tenets of Saussure's *Course in General Linguistics* (Saussure, 1959) are discussed.

Saussure contrasts what he terms "static linguistics" with "evolutionary linguistics" on the basis of the effect of "the intervention of the factor of time", creating "difficulties peculiar to linguistics" (Saussure, 1959). He highlights two axes relevant to the understanding of linguistic phenomena: the Axis of Simultaneities, standing for "the relations of coexisting things and from which the intervention of time is excluded", and the Axis of Successions, where "only one thing can be considered at a time but upon which are located all the things on the first axis together with their changes" (ibid.). Subsequently he frequently refers to the axis of simultaneities as *synchrony* while the axis of successions is referred to as *diachrony*.

In order to illustrate these concepts, one might consider the language of a play. There is one line after another, carrying the action and describing scenes. The sequencing and direction of language is structured and fixed, where only one utterance is spoken at a time. This corresponds to the Axis of Successions where "one thing can be considered at a time". However, actors will also speak of the lines having a sub-text, which is to say there is more than meets the eye in the words that are written. In order to bring the play to life, actors will also bring personal associations that contribute vitality and emotional authenticity to the action. These associational resources exist in the text and in the actors who play the parts, reflecting the whole play and the whole person of each actor. They aren't defined by their sequence in time and could be thought of as occurring on the Axis of Simultaneities.

For the therapeutic situation one might think of the complexity of the person's associational world held *synchronously and simultaneously* within, representing much more than is seen at any given moment. In clinical settings access to this resource may be limited by dissociative processes. The actual words spoken (the Axis of Successions) may be relatively impoverished. It is, however, useful to think of the patient as having a potential resource within, understood as her personal language held in the Axis of Simultaneities.

Language is a "a system of pure values" determined in a network of language relationships. Words and phrases are not determined in a positive sense but take on meaning *because* of the contrast with other value terms in the language network (Saussure, 1959). When it comes to actual speech, both speaker and observer are confronted with a state. The speaker is concerned with *expression of a state*. The observer is in the position of observing language outside himself (although may also be actively engaged in the exchange). This is closer to the position of the linguist who observes language from an external position. Saussure saw contemporary linguists prior to his work, as being "completely absorbed in diachrony" (ibid.), i.e. with the process of change and the history and development of language, rather than with instances of expression. He considered it essential to examine both axes in the study of linguistics. For the individual, in the instantiation of speech acts, one is always dealing with a state rather than an evolution (ibid.).

In Lacan's application of Saussure to psychoanalysis he contrasts Saussure's description of *langue* as "the social and collective institution of language as a system of signs possessing certain values and beyond the conscious control of the individual", with *parole*, "the individual act of combination and actualization of speech", seen as, "an essentially conscious use of unconsciously determined structures" (Lacan, 1968, p. 204). He refers to synchrony having the quality of timelessness.

When we refer to *states* in the way described we are clearly not referring to a situation outside of time. Speech acts still require time for their utterance. In Saussure's discussion of static and evolutionary language he speaks in a relative way. In the case of the synchronic dimension language, its internal network of relations constitutes the object of study. In the diachronic dimension it is change in language over time that is of interest.

A given language or cultural group may be relatively "static" (i.e. the language and customs relatively unchanging) over long periods of time or, as in many modern communities, the pace of change can be such that attention is drawn to the evolutionary changes of language and culture. When there are clashes of language state between cultures, the stability of relatively static language-culture groups may break down. For example, an Australian Indigenous elder speaks of "*the end of the Jukurrpa*" ('The Dreaming') for Indigenous Australians, with the arrival of a technologically dominant colonizing group (Napaljarri & Cataldi,

2003). Since that time, although "The Dreaming" continues as cultural reality, it can no longer be all-encompassing in the sense of a total worldview but rather has become interpenetrated with other languages and views introduced by the colonizers (Korner, 2011).

It is evident that there has been a historical trend towards larger and more complex societies requiring development of institutions, bureaucracies, separation of powers, and other measures in order to overcome corrupting influences stemming, in more ancient communal organizations, from familial ties and personal connections associated with favouritism (Fukuyama, 2011). The net result for individuals is a world of increasing psychological complexity with ever-increasing rates of change, where it becomes more difficult to find one's place and purpose, relative to communities that are small and culturally homogeneous, with limited role expectations, such as in tribal life. While we may subscribe to the idea of progress, there is little evidence that modern societies are associated with greater happiness or improved mental health for individual members.

Urbanization has led to the situation where children develop greater familiarity with images and language abstracted from immediate environmental experience. In modern urban communities, for example, it is far more common for infants to be familiar with "pictures of horses in books" than with actual horses. This results from changing patterns of education and acculturation, rather than increased intelligence (Hasan, 2005). In everyday language this translates to more people in developed communities living life on the basis of mental operations rather than living through the development of concrete physical skills. We are also increasingly confronted with a wealth of linear language emanating from institutional systems that often seem to lack personal relevance to individuals.

The concept of state, at an individual level, refers to the growth of representable experience over time: the synchronous expansion of associations and images present simultaneously as each person develops. In the CM, Meares contrasts two communicative (thought) spaces: one essentially non-linear, associational and personal in form, corresponding to poetic language; and one that is linear, logical, goal-directed and essentially impersonal in form, corresponding to the language of objectivity and adaptation (Meares, 2005). The first form is that of play, closely related to the sense of self, while the latter linear form is related to instrumental action and public manifestations of language, such as the laws that apply impartially and impersonally to all. In adult life both of these forms of language are mixed up, experienced in ways largely unconscious to the individuals concerned.

The dynamic, language-like nature of personal states, with their entwining of feeling and verbal elements, may be illustrated by the following anecdote:

I remember a time in my late twenties when I felt somewhat afflicted by what I can only describe as an ache in the heart. I wasn't concerned about my physical well-being but did have a sense that my body was speaking to me. A need for closeness was part of it. My life had been busy and involved responsibility and service to others. Perhaps it felt insufficiently shared. Out of balance. A new relationship raised hopes although I'd had other partners and no strong reason to think this would be more than a temporary balm. Driving home one night I became intensely emotional. Out of this emerged the conviction that I could commit to this woman. The sense of having this choice was something of a revelation. My bodily feeling shouting at me.

When Shakespeare says, "*We are such stuff as dreams are made on; and our little life is rounded with a sleep*", the *little life* referred to could represent the personal self with timeless, dream-like qualities. The particular self with individuated values and associations born of life in communicative exchange with the environment can be seen largely as a resource contained in the *synchronic* dimension of language. Personal expression, feeling exchange, play and intimacy are phenomena that shape the sense of value for individuals, held within this axis of simultaneities. On the other hand, linear language is more in keeping with the *diachronic* dimension of language, describing the world of external appearances and unfolding events. This impersonal, logical and goal-directed language has instrumental value, particularly in relation to the development of ways of utilizing the environment. This is language in the public domain reflecting the larger society, in contrast to the *little life*. This contrast is accentuated by the sheer scale of the world that each individual confronts in the global era. Linear language describes observable characteristics and external identity rather than the private world of self.

Signs and symbols in the psychotherapeutic context

In psychotherapy, what is felt can only be approached analogically as a matter of similarity or likeness rather than one of precise definition. The therapist requires the medium of language to approach the private self of the patient, seeking understanding of her personal world. Language was defined by Saussure as a system of conventional and arbitrary signs providing a network of value discriminations. In practice, humans live in a world where language provides a medium that is both symbolic and literal, where the task of sorting the symbolic from the actual is not straightforward since both forms of communication affect us in embodied ways. Therapists find that certain gestures or communications evoke unexpected responses in patients, suggesting the person of the therapist becomes a *symbol* to the patient, over and above any semantic content in the verbal exchange.

The distinction of three fundamental relationships between a sign and its object (Peirce, 1897) is relevant to understanding the emergence of communicative capacities. These are (1) the *indexical* relationship, denoting a physical or existential relationship between the sign and its object, meaning that such signs are tied to an "indexical present", *e.g. if a car is scratched, this sign is locked to a particular moment in time and is an index of that moment*; (2) the *iconic* relationship where there is a resemblance between sign and object, *e.g. a drawing of a tree is an iconic representation of a real tree*; (3) *symbols* where the relationship is without motivation, rather based upon convention and rules *e.g. a crown is a symbol of power*.

Jung also refers to the symbolic in communication as "the best possible formulation of a relatively unknown factor which cannot be more clearly or characteristically represented, is **symbolic**. . . . The symbol is alive only insofar as it is pregnant with meaning" (Jung, 1923, p. 344). This is closer to what is conveyed in poetic or mythic forms of language requiring understanding through the *symbolic attitude* (Jung, 1923). Its application to the psychotherapeutic setting fosters metaphorical exploration. It is the language of feeling rather than literal or technical description.

Ricoeur emphasizes the role of metaphor more generally in language, in creating vivid expression with new meaning: "If to 'metaphorize well' is to possess mastery of **resemblances** then without this power we would be unable to grasp any hitherto unknown relations between things. Therefore, far from being a divergence from the ordinary operation of language, it is the 'omnipresent principle of all of its free action'" (Ricoeur, 1977, p. 92).

For a particular therapeutic couple certain metaphors may be found to *fit* experience, changing and growing over time: "a moving metaphor opens up depths of experiencing 'where silence reigns'. It is one kind of living symbol" (Hobson, 1985, p. 61).

Saussure asserts that we cannot study both the diachronic and synchronic simultaneously. At any given time, we can focus on one or the other. Arguably, this prefigures Heisenberg's Uncertainty Principle, relating to measurement in physics: "The more precisely the position is determined, the less precisely the momentum is known in this instant, and vice versa" (Heisenberg, 1927). This deals with the influence of the observer on the observed, now considered essential to an understanding of quantum physics and its contrast with classical physics. As commonly understood quantum physics refers to the world and its objects, either in terms of *wave* properties or *particle* properties but cannot do both at once. This is despite the paradox that either perspective would have validity at a given moment. Taking this quantum perspective as a metaphor for linguistics, it could be said that diachrony refers to man as communicative object ("particle"), experiencing one thing after another, at the level of individual-environment interaction, whereas synchrony refers to the resonating, felt ("wave") quality of that experience and how it is realized cumulatively in embodied communications and associations.

Language is made real psychologically by felt processes of resonance and recognition, understanding that any given state reflects a personal reality and context. The role of psychotherapy is to assist with elaboration of the complexity of the personal, allowing a broadening of consciousness and enhanced affective engagement with the world. For the CM, as well as for Saussure and Systemic Functional Linguistics (SFL), **conversation** is the natural form of language. When a therapeutic conversation becomes lively and engaged, it will engender growth in associational complexity and the sense of self.

In the processes of psychotherapeutic assessment and intervention, the development of narrative form through formulation is important. This involves emergence of a *story* rather than simply a recitation of facts. As such, it requires use of language that is personally meaningful and expressive of the emotional life of the person, rather than a dry recounting of events (Korner et al., 2010). It has symbolic value. Units of conversation with interpersonal significance are likely to have potential in the ongoing development of personal narrative. An effective formulation involves rendering of a state into a dynamic (*emotionally moving*) form, with the sense of an evolving story implying future growth of self.

Consider the response to Joe, a man who presents in a suicidal state after the death of his cat. This man was feeling fragmented but still gave attention to expressing his state to the therapist. After having attention focused on Joe, the therapist collects his thoughts and offers a tentative formulation, trying to communicate an initial understanding that may provide a starting point for further work:

> *I don't know if this is right, but it seems to me that it is no wonder that you were inconsolable when your cat died, as she was the only thing that you could safely talk to. Because your dad was unsafe when you were a kid, and your mum was distant, you never felt that anyone really cared for you, and you learnt that when things go bad, like your parents separating, you just have to look after yourself. At first your wife was like a breath of fresh air, but when the children came, you seem to have lost the feeling of closeness with her. The only person that seemed to matter was your good mate, which probably made his death doubly painful. You lost him, and there was no one to talk to about your sadness. I guess you dealt with this by pulling away from everybody, spending a bit of time with your cat, and just following a routine of work and sleep. The situation got worse after you were assaulted, particularly as the lack of concern from management seem to have dovetailed with that feeling that nobody cares, which you have lived with all your life.*
>
> (Korner et al., 2010)

The patient felt sufficiently encouraged that someone had understood that a basis for therapeutic conversation was established. There was a reciprocal exchange.

Communicative beginnings: the principle of exchange through play

Proto-conversation precedes proto-language. Proto-conversation is the responsive interplay between infant and carer, fostering the infant's capacity for play (Trevarthen, 1974). It establishes a flow of associations, images, shared feeling and a zone of proximal development for the infant.

From the beginning the infant has "an instinct to the word, that is, as the impulse to be present with others in a world of streaming communication, of an image given and received" (Buber, 1947). The iconic exchange of images becomes organized into a flow of experience. The infant or developing child gradually locates himself within this flux of living symbols. "Symbolical transformation is a primary need of man. It goes on all the time throughout life, within and beyond awareness. It is the mind's recreation and its re-creation" (Hobson, 1985).

Symbolical transformation refers to the basic need of people to find meaning, not only for its own sake but also for the sake of organizing themselves as effective participants in the social world. Symbolical transformation occurs primarily through the medium of conversation that occurs first at a proto-symbolic level in the infant-carer dyad before flowering into an inner life (Meares, 2005). It may be realized in therapy where a *symbolic attitude* prevails (Jung, 1923).

At birth, physical separation from mother marks the start of a long journey of growth mediated through the infant's network of relationships, beginning with primary carers. This network carries significance throughout life, both for the infant and others with whom the infant is connected. Physical immaturity at birth and the prolonged period of relative dependency during development accentuate the need for sustained personal bonds facilitated through the symbolic medium of language. An adequate early environment is one where the responses of carers approximately match the communications and needs of the infant. In contrast, a traumatic environment is characterized by:

1 Impingement that exceeds the infant's capacity to receive or respond.
2 Neglect that leaves the infant isolated.
3 Failure to provide the field of play necessary to growth of the child's imagination and self.

While discrete traumatic events occur only too often, the process of development will be most significantly affected by ongoing relational conditions that constitute forms of trauma not necessarily remembered as specific events (Meares, 2005, 2019). In the early environment images such as facial expressions and vocalizations, gestures and movements are the initial contents of the flow of experience and become iconic for the emerging self. Where affect is too intense for the infant, the capacity to experience flow is likely to be impaired. There is disruption to the sense of "going on being" (Meares, 2005). In circumstances of severe neglect there may be insufficient exchange for an effective flow to be initiated.

While almost all children acquire the mother tongue, it is clear that early circumstances influence the manner of language acquisition and hence the individual's internal relationship to language, manifested in speech behaviours. The experiential dimension of life isn't either objective or subjective in any pure sense. The "place where we live" (Winnicott, 1971) has elements of both that are manifest in the communicative exchanges between infant and carer.

The world as it presents itself to infants is the world of persons, initially the person of the carer. It is the area of personal existence that concerns us in psychotherapeutic practice. The initial conditions of experience play a significant role in determining how the world is sensed and the *worldview* that individuals form, based on the pre-reflective, pre-conceptual experience of the world into which they have been born. This worldview is typically taken, although mistakenly, to represent "the facts" of the larger relational world (Korner, 2011). Conditions that are of a sufficiently "holding" environment accompanied by maternal absorption and emotional availability to the infant (Winnicott, 1956) provide a *necessary illusion* of safety, allowing psychological growth, attainment of trust and confidence in relationships and exploration of the world (Winnicott, 1971).

In contrast to Freud, who saw "the ego pitted against two tyrants: instinctual wishes and external reality. . . . Winnicott . . . accepted **reality** as the ally of the maturational process in the infant and examined . . . the character of the environmental (maternal) provisions towards the personalisation of the infant's . . . psychic potential into selfhood" (Khan, 1975, p. xxxvii). Perhaps it can be seen that the creation of an environment that is safe and encouraging involves a complex coordination with a number of players, a feat that is always imperfectly realized.

The sequence that occurs at birth has been taken as representative of cycles that occur between infant and carers at a communicative level. The infant is born and with the first breath *cries*, paradigmatic as a *mood sign* (Bateson, 1954). Although not aware of doing anything in an intentional sense, the infant unconsciously makes a communication which has significance. For the listening carer the cry is at the forefront of consciousness. It is an "image given and received". Distress and well-being are effectively two different systems handled in distinct communicative ways (Meares & Lichtenberg, 1995). Apart from the cry, the *smile* is paradigmatic as a *mood sign* representing the system of well-being. The *cry*, nevertheless, is the first act of the infant as communicant (Brazelton, 1979).

The notion of *mood signs*, as described by Bateson, refers to increasing differentiation of signs occurring in particular relationships, as the mother gets to know more specific signals the infant is making and the infant develops an increasingly specific repertoire. Once it is understood that signs are not invariably linked to real danger, signals become recognized as "only signals" and therefore as having communicative significance (Bateson, 1954). There is an emergence of communicative space and differentiation of the actual from play. Carers typically contribute to communicative interaction by "marking" their responses to infants (Fonagy et al., 2002), demonstrating playfulness, the absence of danger and the sense of interest in the well-being of the infant.

Marking typically involves exaggerated facial responses and vocalizations, with emphasis and amplification relating to the intonations of spoken language characteristic of the mother tongue to which the infant is acclimatizing. It injects an element of fun into the interaction for both parties. In highlighting things beyond objective description, it can be seen as part of the infant's induction into the world of symbolic exchange. Many of these interactions proceed without conscious intentionality, being forms natural to the circumstance. If an atmosphere of play is sustained, there will be a sense of safety with an element of revocability: that which occurs isn't associated with threat. Within such an environment, the infant's tolerance of affect is likely to be broadened. Without such an experience of play even apparently minor interactions, like a raised voice, may be felt as a blow carrying the sense of irrevocability that inhibits growth of self.

Marked responses draw the attention of the infant, conveying something new or funny that can be received. Even before words are understood, the principle of exchange develops with anticipation that the carer's tone will herald new information in an affective sense. The infant is extremely sensitive to vocal stimuli and responds to the musicality of the voice (Meares, 2016). Although the face is another main way of recognizing feeling, there is evidence of greater differential responsiveness at the age of five months to "positive and negative vocal expressions, suggesting the voice is more powerful than the face as a social stimulus" (Fernald, 1992). This principle will continue once verbalization is established through the tonal emphases, rhythms and musicality of language. Iconic tonal, melodic and narrative forms structure the exchanges of the proto-conversation.

Much of the knowledge of mood signs that develops in relationships is implicit knowledge, thought to be mediated through right hemispheric processes, of dominant importance relative to left hemispheric processes in the first two years of life (Schore, 2012). These processes are inaccessible to declarative consciousness. Hence, conscious intent is often not relevant and should not be so attributed. In the current state of knowledge of "voluntary" action (i.e. involving "voluntary" muscles), Bennett comments "it is patently absurd to claim that before each voluntary act there is a separate act of willing" (Bennett, 2009, p. 294). Interaction with carer involves the infant's brainstem and diencephalic structures, well developed by birth, allowing coordination with the ANS and body generally, given that some of these nuclei (locus coeruleus; serotonergic raphe nuclei; dopaminergic nuclei; cholinergic; and histaminergic, nuclei), "project diffusely to huge portions of the brain . . . [leading us to designate] them collectively as **value systems**" (Edelman & Tononi, 2000, p. 46).

The importance of mood signs (affective expression) is increasingly recognized as crucial to the development of language (Panksepp, 2008; Shanahan, 2007). Where a capacity for play has developed adequately, it will be more possible for individuals to process stimuli at an "as if" level (i.e. "within the brain", bypassing high degrees of bodily arousal) which is economical in terms of energy expenditure (Damasio, 2000). In contrast, individuals with traumatic backgrounds experience stimuli, including linguistic stimuli, as more likely to recruit bodily defence systems.

These types of communicative interaction contribute to the development of a field of safety where the infant's instinct to play can be realized (Freud, 1915; Meares, 1990). While play is a form of interaction we share with other mammals, in humans the capacity for *symbolic* play greatly augments the range of participation in play. Even in other mammalian species it is evident that there are implicit rules. In the rough and tumble play of monkeys, for instance, both parties understand that *play combat* is not *real combat* or that a "playful nip" is not a "real bite" in the sense that it is "not meant to harm" (Bateson, 1954, p. 133). The development of a field of play leads to a situation where actions are understood as "not serious" or "not fully meant", although they retain the sense of "*standing for*" something that could be meant seriously, or require a defensive response (ibid.). Play fosters duality in the mind, where the real and "not real" can co-exist.

Where development proceeds in good conditions infants show flexibility in switching between the world of play, imagination and pretence and the world of actual events. A parent is observed playing with a child who is eating an "alphabet soup", communicatively *marking* the "bits" in the soup as *horseys* in a way that engages the toddler in a game. The child is not confused that these bits are *real horseys* and proceeds to eat them as part of the game, retaining a grasp on reality (Emde et al., 1997). There is an element of pleasure in the exchange. In all cases there may be times when play spills over or switches into "serious" interaction with sudden loss of the sense of safety. Analogously, psychotherapy felt to be significant by the participants, also has some sense of risk: people will feel themselves to be working on the edge, on occasions, of what can be tolerated. If negotiated successfully, the effect is a broadening of affective range.

In most animals, perceptions are responded to by movement and action without significant delay. Where a human infant perceives the other without taking action, she is left with a "freestanding image" which becomes "seasoned with more and more emotional experiences", an experience "on its way to becoming an internal symbol" (Greenspan & Shankar, 2004, p. 27). This illustrates how significant others take on iconicity in early development, as does the infant for carers. This creates a situation at the same time actual and symbolic. The type of emotional signalling engendering of self includes warmth: "the baby needs to have been wooed into a warm pleasurable relationship . . . so that there is another human being towards whom he experiences deep emotions and, therefore, with whom he wants to communicate" (ibid.).

Under less than adequate conditions, parents are less emotionally available and will tend towards a more primary focus on necessary actions such as doing something when the child is distressed, making sure that the child is fed, etc. Under severely traumatic conditions even these actions may be compromised and the field of play will be grossly deficient or absent. However, in all relationally inadequate situations there is attenuation of play and the positive regard required for playful exchange. Traumatic consciousness is *asymbolic*, limiting the capacity for symbolic play and development (Meares, 2012). The result may be that the experience of language and communication is more closely related to actual events that take place, with less opportunity for social pleasure through communication and development of imaginative capacities.

The growth of complexity in the play of feeling

There is an innate endowment of affect and the neural systems that support its expression (Tomkins, 1995; Panksepp & Biven, 2012; Solms, 2015). Engagement in feeling language takes the therapeutic dyad beyond the constraining indexicality of the present emotional state towards the symbolic resources of language. The need for a play-space in therapy is informed by an understanding of forms of feeling as they develop from infancy onwards, contributing greatly to the complexity and differentiation of experience. The following is an outline of the development of feeling elaborated from *The Poet's Voice in the Making of Mind* (Meares, 2016).

Subtle feelings for which there may be no words are characteristic of mature human consciousness. They have been termed "little emotions" (Wood Jones, 1931) and may often be overlooked or neglected: "Unless they have some means of representation they will wither and sink to the bottom of consciousness" (Meares, 2016). They encompass what is sometimes referred to as the tender emotions. Their representation requires a "picturing function" found in poetic expression. One shouldn't assume that this means their representation necessarily requires great intellectual sophistication since, "Creators of single words or phrases are by far the largest class of poets. Many ignore all other poetry" (from *Infinite Anthology*) (Murray, 2010).

Meares discerns seven stages in the emerging complexity of feeling (Meares, 2016). In the earliest phase (0–3 months) the experience and expression of feeling typically relates to single stimuli. The carer provides a "picturing function" that enriches the communicative exchange (ibid.). At a second stage, around 3 months, infants begin manifesting frustration and anger in relation to more complex situations that disrupt the flow of activity (ibid.). The third stage, around 7–8 months, is heralded by separation anxiety and the concomitant awareness of the infant holds of the other as a distinct entity. By 18 months or so, a fourth stage involves the emergence of "social emotions" such as shame, guilt and embarrassment, dependent "upon the child's awareness of herself as a person in relation to others" (ibid.). At this stage there is still no reflective consciousness. For the child, experience just happens.

Of particular interest in relation to the emergence of "little emotions" and the sense of self is the fifth stage, from 3–4 years of age, associated with the emergence of autobiographical memory and the beginnings of a sense of innerness and "I-me" duality. "With this development, feeling states may seem almost entirely 'inner' and can be triggered by inner events alone" (ibid., p. 72). The child can now represent herself, a reversal of the original situation where the carer took on the "picturing" function (ibid.), a crucial milestone in terms of agency.

However, the child's consciousness is still immature in relation to time and the sense of past and future (ibid.). The awareness of the passage of time and the simultaneous experience of something past in the present, such as memory of a childhood scene replete with pleasurable sensation, is more typical of more mature consciousness (ibid.). This kind of "double" experience doesn't usually emerge at least until adolescence. There is also a lack of awareness of the future in childhood. A consciousness where "our perception of time is a duration with a bow and a stern, as it were – a rearward and a forward-looking end" (James, 1890) is also characteristic of maturity. These appreciations of the "movement of time" constitute the sixth stage in the development of complexity of feeling (Meares, 2016).

Taking into account the factor of time and the frailties and idiosyncratic pleasures experienced in a complex web of relationships, the complex "little emotions" or feelings portrayed in poetry place experience in the context of the larger human condition, although with a sense of interiority that is particular. It may reflect a capacity to integrate positive and negative feeling, contributing to the overall resilience of the individual (ibid.).

Finally, there is reference to a seventh stage, "the sense of spirit", often not achieved (ibid.). When it is, it tends to be experienced transiently as oceanic feelings or a sense of at-oneness with the world.

Perhaps the biggest single leap in this hierarchy of consciousness is the fifth stage, where acquisition of autobiographical memory brings reflective consciousness into play. Now the child understands that secrets can be kept and that parents and others can't automatically tell what is in the child's mind. Lies can be told and sometimes the child will succeed in deception. This brings into play a more complex internal relationship with truth and ambivalence in relation to truth-telling. Often the child says what she thinks the parent wants to hear. Capacities to deceive and transgress aren't necessarily maladaptive. There may be an evolutionary advantage for duplicity in relation to individuation, relating to avoidance of subjugation by more powerful others, at least in the short term. The phrase *evolutionary duplicity* captures this sense of temporary advantage. Options of misleading, lying, avoiding, conforming, pretending or dissembling make for a great number of "grey areas" for the child in relation to forms of feeling and their relationship to truth. What is disapproved on in one arena (e.g. stealing from parents) may gain kudos for the child in another arena, such as the peer group (seen as a display of daring and getting the better of authority). Moral agency gets forged in the tension between feeling *for self* and feeling *for others*.

Proto-language and indexical exchange

In the detailed observation of communicative patterns that developed between a male infant and his mother, Halliday noted the development of what he termed *proto-language* in the child between the ages of 9–18 months (Halliday, 1975). This corresponds roughly to the period of development of the third stage in the notional hierarchy of consciousness in the preceding section. At this stage there is an increased sense of intersubjectivity (Stern, 1985). It is well after the establishment of the *proto-conversation* which can be observed to some extent from birth and is well-established by 3 months. Halliday observed that this *proto-language* is not specifically related to the mother tongue. While functional in specific contexts, it lacks grammar. Hence it is to be understood as an *indexical* form of communication, tied to the present, that nevertheless serves a variety of functions. Halliday enumerated these, in the particular case as,

1   Instrumental (glossed as, "I want that")
2   Regulatory ("do that")

3   Interactional ("hello, pleased to see you")
4   Personal ("here I come")
5   Heuristic ("tell me why")
6   Imaginative ("let's pretend")

(Halliday, 1975, pp. 19–20)

Of these the first two are to be understood as primarily practical or pragmatic in function, whereas the next two are primarily social and the last two would seem to be related to the development of exploratory, differentiating and imaginative capacities. The first to develop, under what appeared to be adequate conditions of care, were the "interactional and personal" functions. It might be expected that under traumatic conditions it is likely the less social "pragmatic" functions would be first to develop. This would entail less opportunity for play, less space for the separation of object and action and for development of reflective function.

At the level of proto-language specific meanings are differentiated although remain bound to present experience in the infant-carer dyad. The players in this communication are subjects of each other's attention in the immediate context. However, the infant hasn't become a grammatical subject, capable of locating himself in the broader conceptual world of the speech fellowship. Although a participant at *iconic* and *indexical* levels, the infant is still an "unknowing" actor in the symbolic medium of language. The acquisition of grammar, as the infant begins using the mother tongue, marks initiation into "knowing" engagement with the conceptual world. Although competence with the mother tongue involves the child as active participant in a symbolic medium, it is not equivalent to development of a symbolic mode of thinking.

The linguistics of exchange

For most people the notion of *subject* is thought to be a unitary concept. For simple clauses this will often hold true. For example, if I say *I ran away*, it will be understood that I am the person who is the actor, who does the act that constitutes the subject matter ('running away') and who, as the speaker, conveys the sense of conviction by which the clause will be taken as truthful or not. However, often clauses are more complex and have a divided function when it comes to "subject". These "resolve themselves into three broad categories . . . summarized as follows:

i   that which is the concern of the message
ii that of which something is being predicated (that is on which rests the truth of the argument)
iii the doer of the action."

(Halliday & Matthiessen, 2004, p. 55)

A newspaper headline reads "State Ignores Fish Kill Warning" (SMH 14.1.19). Here the subject, as the concern of the message, is the "state" and it is also the doer of the action ("members of government ignore"). However, the truth of the statement is predicated upon the author of the article and the conviction contained in the report, the "warning" that was available. If we change the sentence to, "Fish kill warning provided by experts ignored by state", the concern of the message is now the warning, the logical doer of the action is the state and the truth is predicated upon the report of the experts. In practice the different functions of subject get enacted in various combinations of these three functions.

Systemic *Functional* Linguistics (SFL) divides the notion of subject into these three parts: *theme (psychological subject), subject (grammatical subject)* and *actor (logical subject, doer of action)* (Halliday & Matthiessen, 2004, p. 57). In turn these distinctions are used as the basis for identifying three dimensions of functional meaning that are always present in language: *theme* corresponds to *clause as message, subject* to *clause as exchange* and *actor* to *clause as representation* (ibid., pp. 58–59).

Broadly speaking these can be understood as the function of imparting information (*message*, "what the speaker had in mind"), the "interactional doing" of language and its affective accompaniments (the conviction of the *exchange*, providing a "warrant" for the truth-value of what is being said) and the concept meant and received (*representation*, reflecting the semantic meaning of the statement) (ibid.). Representation is seen as corresponding more closely to discrete concepts or chunks of meaning, termed a "segmental organization", while message is seen in terms of "*culminative*" patterns of communication that have personal narrative form relevant to the development of coherence (ibid.).

The exchange characteristics of language, on the other hand, are most evident in the prosody and affective qualities of linguistic interaction, sensed as continuous, rather than discrete, forms of expression, contributing to the sense of continuity of self. The more personal dimensions of language, more closely related to development of self, are *clause as message*, and *clause as exchange*; whereas *clause as representation* is more related to language as a system of value discriminations with existence independent of any given individual.

In turn these three dimensions of the clause relate to what SFL terms *metafunctions* (ibid.). These invariant properties of language consist of four basic functions: the *experiential metafunction* which involves "*construing a model of experience*", the *interpersonal* which involves "*enacting social relationships*", the *textual* which involves "*creating relevance to context*" and the "*logical*" involving "*constructing logical relations*" (ibid., p. 61). The first three of these are related to the three clause functions in the preceding paragraph: the *experiential* corresponds to the clause as representation, the *interpersonal* to the clause as exchange and the *textual* to the clause as message. The fourth is often grouped together with the *experiential* as the *Ideational Metafunction* (Butt et al., 2000). It relates to constructions that increase in complexity as growth proceeds, depending upon "iterative structures" rather than culminative, discrete or continuous structures (Halliday & Matthiessen, 2004, p. 61).

The *interpersonal metafunction* is of particular interest to the significance of action and interaction in psychotherapy: the "doing" of therapy. In interpersonal terms, reflecting speech roles, all linguistic communications can be reduced to having properties of the "giving", or "demanding", of either "goods and services", or "information" (ibid.). Table 4.1 illustrates a 2 × 2 range of possibilities for any given communication.

The process of exchange is already present in the proto-conversation. Giving and demanding shape personality. Where the environment is not sufficiently responsive the infant may try escalating demands, which, if successful, may become an established strategy. Alternatively, if the environment remains unresponsive, the infant may become withdrawn and apathetic, superficially "undemanding". The anxious or immature parent may perceive ordinary gestures as demanding and have difficulty seeing the infant's behaviour as having any "giving" component (all that seems to be given is the demand). A well-adjusted parent, on the other hand, may delight in the expressions the infant "gives", or in her vigour and contentment: "new" experiences that relate to this new relationship. For psychotherapy, the "goods and services" or "offer" of the therapist is of attention and relative warmth in affective exchange, while the "command" relates to the limits and conditions of the therapeutic relationship. On the "information" side, it is clear in Table 4.1 that information in the form of statements is likely to be experienced as "giving" something, while questions are often found to be "demanding".

The *giving* and *demanding* of "information" occur more at the mental-relational level whereas "goods and services" often implies material exchange. Much that occurs at the informational level is not strictly seen or observed, particularly by those external to the interaction, who lack access to the same body of referents that make sense to the participants. Even within the conversational dyad much that goes on at this level is unconscious, related to "mood signs" and gestures, not directly encoded in verbal language. Conversational analysts see "the basic unit of language as the turn constructional unit" (Schumann, 2007), which is to say that conversation is basic to language, constituting the interaction from which "grammar is an emergent property" (ibid., p. 281).

Language provides resources for organizing the flow of discourse: grammatical units on the one hand and units of text on the other. Texts vary greatly but usually have narrative qualities. Intonation, rhythm and emphasis in spoken language divide expressions into marked segments that don't necessarily correspond to clauses or grammatical structures. This marking, or tone group, will be taken

Table 4.1 Transactions in the interpersonal linguistic realm

	Goods and services	Information
Giving	Offer	Statement
Demanding	Command	Question

Source: after Halliday & Matthiessen, 2004, p. 107

to denote significance regardless of the grammar, with the segment so marked being considered a "unit" by the listener. Narrative form, apart from its grammar, may be evidenced in these units by melody and pitch contour denoting a musical phrase with a beginning, middle and end. Halliday refers to these non-grammatical textual resources as "information units" where he considers the basic informational unit as involving "an obligatory New element" and "an optional Given" (Halliday & Matthiessen, 2004, p. 89). One is the focal point of the communication and the other reflects a matter "already known". The *given* can sometimes be left out because a "known" referent can be assumed in communications. So, we might say, *Now we've done that* (given), *let's party!* (new) or just *Let's party!* Another reason for leaving out the given element relates to *initiation* of discourse where there is no "given" in the conversation.

Given and *new*, also correspond to "theme" and "rheme". Given and new reflect the *listener's* perspective, while theme reflects the "speaker's point of departure" and the rheme reflects the speaker's way of developing or adding to the subject introduced in the theme (ibid.). In unmarked *written* language it may be hard to discern emphasis and meaning (information unit), since it relies more on grammatical structure. However, where the written word is personally known (e.g. by the author of the text, or where there is familiarity with the text), information units not strictly related to grammar may still be discerned.

The *information unit* thus described may be an appropriate unit for textual analysis in psychotherapy. The transmission of information in a conversation requires processes of reception, response and recognition to constitute an *exchange*. Such exchanges are continuous in human lives across an infinite number of information units, building into the long conversations and life stories that define each person.

Building narrative

From the patient's perspective a minimal unit of exchange, relevant to growth of self, would relate to a communication, a response (not always verbal, perhaps gestural or "mood sign") and recognition of that response by the patient (again not always verbal). As discussed, this would relate to a longer period of time than the "present moment" (spans of experience accessible to self) because it involves at least one other person. A clue to what such a meaningful span of time may be in human experience is provided by observations of infant-carer vocalizations.

In his classic description of the component of felt experience termed "vitality affects", Stern emphasized the rhythmic, surging, fading, pulsatile and melodic properties that accompany human interactions (Stern, 1985). In observations of a mother with her neonatal baby, pitch contours and melodic patterns were recorded (see Malloch & Trevarthen, 2009, p. 5 [Figure 1.2]). What is evident is that both mother and infant take turns, contributing to a "mini-narrative" that unfolds over about 30 seconds, with the mother responding to the infant's vocalizations, in a way that reflects coordination of vitality affects. While the mother vocalizes more than the infant, the shape and melody of the narrative episode display interdependence: it is a mutual creation.

In analysing this exchange, a classical four-part narrative structure is seen with "Introduction, Development, Climax, and Resolution" (Malloch & Trevarthen, 2009). This is an inherently musical structure also seen in other forms of interaction characteristic of play (e.g. physical movement has dance-like rhythmic properties), leading to the proposition that "it is our common musicality that makes it possible for us to share time meaningfully together" (ibid. p. 5). This example demonstrates *musical* vocal information transfer that precedes verbal-conceptual information transfer. Its central phenomenon is affective interplay and continuity, aspects of the interpersonal dimension of language. The timings of *phrases* within this narrative structure correspond roughly to the timings of the present moment discussed in the previous chapter. However, narrative-like episodes of vocal exchange last 12–30 seconds (ibid.) or, in more complex forms, minutes or longer (Osborne, 2009). These time frames relate to "the creative interpersonal coordination of expression in time generated by the brain and active body, constitut(ing) a crucial basis for subjective experience" (Gratier & Apter-Danon, 2009). These patterns emerge spontaneously, reflecting infants' innate participatory and imitative propensities: "Infants, like jazz musicians, may create their spontaneous music within any 'grammatical' structure of the musical culture that they have absorbed" (Bannan & Woodward, 2009).

Time frames relevant to meaningful conversational exchange and the emergence of narrative structure, will hence be referred to as **narrative units**. This is based on the conclusion that "information units" (in language) and "narrative units" (in language, music and embodied interactions) are related. The relevant time for examination of such units relates more to a sense of inter-subjective time than it does to the timings of a one-person system, consistent with "an essential dynamic **intersubjective consciousness** of human communication from its beginnings" (Trevarthen, 2015). Simple units of 12–30 seconds, and more complex units of varying length, might conform to the sense of a narrative which, in its simplest form, has a beginning, middle and an end. Such simple narrative units could be considered the minimal unit of exchange for co-creation of narrative, an activity at the heart of psychotherapy. Units of time reflectively accessible to a particular self will be taken to be in the range 2–12 seconds and the timings of simple *narrative units* will be taken to be 12–30 seconds in the next chapter, where some preliminary research findings are reported.

In the next section the challenge of finding ways to "measure" the inter-subjective field of "self and other" is considered. The intent is not to come up with a standard measure to gauge against a normative sample, but rather to engage patient and therapist in a reflective process that has the effect of "thickening" the available information in the synchronic (self) dimension of language. This involves enrichment of the sense of significance as well as measurement. This is consistent with a form of research that seeks not only to find new data but which may also contribute to the therapeutic process by actively engaging patient and therapist in reflection.

Measuring self-state

During a brief discussion I had with Gerald Edelman, following a lecture he gave on the subject of consciousness in 2006, he described his view of consciousness as a "resonating system with digital characteristics" (Edelman, 2006). This seemed to refer to the resonating characteristics of affective life and the circumscribed properties of conceptual life. Elsewhere, he compares consciousness to a sequence of discrete images (specific "digital" units) on a film that, when played, give the illusion of continuity of movement (aliveness; "resonating" interplay) (Edelman & Tononi, 2000). These discrete units of consciousness can be very short to the extent that much of the stream of consciousness does not get integrated into memory or become available to self-awareness. It has been argued that the present moment, related to the rhythm of breathing and the linguistic rhythms of phrases or clauses, is an appropriate unit of study. However, because higher consciousness requires interpersonal, intersubjective processes (involving language) for significance to be felt, it is also necessary to consider the larger *narrative unit* as necessary to understanding the interactive, conversational level of experience.

In considering the way in which self operates interactively, it should be remembered that initially the carer serves an important homeostatic function for the infant (Bowlby, 1969; Lichtenberg, 1989). Others continue to play a role in the regulation of self throughout life (Kohut, 1971), although the individual becomes less dependent upon a specific carer. Homeostatic dynamics maintain individuals in a zone of comfortable functioning, both physiologically and psychologically. In interpersonal terms, as described by Piaget, individuals will prefer to *assimilate* interpersonal and other environmental information into pre-existing internalized schemas where possible; while processes of *accommodation* normally come into play when stimuli cannot be so assimilated (Piaget, 1954). The bias towards assimilation will mean, in relation to conversation, that not every piece of what is new in spoken "information units" (Halliday & Matthiessen, 2004) will be responded to as if it is really "new". The self that sticks to a pre-existing (unconscious) schema will not "see" what is new, in the other's offering. This constitutes an aspect of difference in perspective, between one person and another, in relation to many messages shared in conversation. While the "representation" (semantic meaning) may be known to both, the precise message will often have different shades of meaning for each. These factors will affect the frequency with which changes in self-state are experienced.

Since self-states are private experiences, their measurement requires a subjective report by the protagonists. In the next chapter an instrument designed to capture personal reports of self-state from *both* patient and therapist is described as part of an intersubjective approach to research.

Communicative embodiment: "selved beings"

A whole is that which has a beginning, a middle and an end.
Aristotle, *Poetics*

The simplest form of spoken language, perhaps suggestive of the manner in which language began in humans (although this is unknown), involves three sorts of word:

1 words for physical things: notably body and body parts; animals; objects; kinship terms (father, mother, etc.),
2 words for simple actions (run, throw, eat, etc.) and,
3 a third small group of "pointing words" (this, that, etc.).

(Deutscher, 2005, p. 213)

These make the distinction between objects and actions, laying a foundation for the development of more complex communications and symbolic language (ibid.). Verbal "pointing" reflects the innate human capacity for shared attention and understanding (Tomasello, 2010). It is preceded developmentally by gestural pointing as a means of facilitating shared attention (ibid.). The beginning of separation between objects and actions through vocalization, becomes established before verbal language. The creation of mental space requires both safety and an enlivening field of play, allowing for participation in communication.

Humans are the only species to have developed a reflective function, as far as is known (Greenspan & Shankar, 2004). The process of language acquisition and symbol formation requires affective investment: "relevant emotional experiences must invest symbols as they form" (ibid.). These symbols arise in the actual people and objects provided for the infant by the environment. The second developmental condition for symbol formation is that "a symbol emerges when a perception is separated from its action" (ibid.). Relevant emotional experiences become incorporated into the emerging sense of self. Even before proto-conversation, there is a *proto-self*, consisting of body image, and the sense of movement in space (Damasio, 2000). Emergent relational experience and capacities gradually become integrated with the proto-self, as it gradually takes on affective properties, becoming a vehicle for symbolic communication as it develops, by stages, into a mature self.

The human world does not exist apart from its symbolic values or meanings. This is true even when a person is not conscious of her symbolic contributions to communicative exchanges with others, as in the case of infant with carer. Indeed, we are never fully conscious of all possible "meanings" that may be conveyed in a particular message. Even in death, significance is read into facial expression by the observer. The relationship between symbolic and actual is interpenetrated: the infant's need for care demands response but at the same time exerts influence through the significance of the infant's expressions. The symbolic level offers order, both consciously and unconsciously. At the same time the individual is affected by messages and symbols that have an impact emotionally and physiologically, sometimes beyond conceptual understanding.

Language can impinge upon us in unexpected ways, where we lose the sense of mental space that allows us to separate object and action. Barthes, in a discussion of the story *Sarrasine*, refers to the "asymbolic code", where an experience may shock one out of conventional interpretation of a scene. A woman is preoccupied with someone whose appearance she finds strange, being subsequently reassured by a companion:

> Is he alive? She reached out to the phenomenon with that boldness women can summon up out of the strength of their desires but she broke into a cold sweat, for no sooner had she touched the old man than she heard a cry like a rattle. This sharp voice, if voice it was, issued from a nearly dried up throat.... "Come" I replied, "you are being ridiculous, taking a little old man for a ghost." from, "Sarrasine" (Honore de Balzac)
> (Barthes, 1974; Project Gutenberg, 2010)

This brief passage corresponds more or less to a relatively simple narrative unit, describing a communicative gesture ("reaching out"), a response ("a cry like a rattle") and what seems to the woman like a disturbing kind of recognition with autonomic accompaniments ("cold sweat"). It illustrates the embodied nature of communicative interactions, and the time required to respond and then to recover.

Some additional prose examples of simple narrative units are given:

1   He opened the envelope. Saw the first word. Everything else was irrelevant. Went to black. People were with him, talking. He didn't respond. He wasn't there. They asked him if he was OK. He said, "I don't know, I'm numb".
(Anon)

2   That was my first time too. He frowned, looking straight ahead. His face was white as a plastic bag. Then a change came over it as though he was going to be sick. Then his face changed again and he smiled, but now the smile only affected his mouth.
(from, "Cartagena", in *The Boat*, Nam Le)

Both of these vignettes, similarly to the extract from *Sarrasine*, involve an action and a response, in an interpersonal context. In the first example bad news is received and the man is "hit" by a physiological response: he is "beside himself", having temporarily lost his sense of self, with sudden alteration in bodily feeling accompaniments (dissociation). In the second, the scene is of a man with an accomplice, who has engaged in a murder. The man appears to be overcome by the strength of the autonomic response. He weathers the storm, with the final "mouth-only smile", suggesting self has survived but is changed (the "mood sign" is transformed). In both cases there is a simple narrative form, with a protagonist whose experience has an internal dimension of relatedness as well as external relationships: they are "selved beings".

Embodying the symbolic

According to the polyvagal theory (PVT), evolution has contributed to primacy of the social engagement system in human interaction under conditions of safety. The PVT invokes the evolutionarily more recent myelinated division of the parasympathetic nervous system as an important physiological mediator in this process, allowing nuanced affective life to come into its fullest expression. Physiological systems have arisen supporting "closeness without fear". Everyday examples of this kind of behaviour include sexual intimacy, infant nurture and affiliative closeness (e.g. friends confiding or sharing close company when they feel safe). These states are associated with pleasure. Pleasure, from an intersubjective perspective, is more about doing things together with a sense of fellowship and collaboration, rather than consummation of desire or aggression. A feeling of safety is central to such experiences. Creation of a sense of personal safety is a central psychotherapeutic goal. It should be noted that "safety" in this context is an apperception, underpinned by unconscious *neuroception*, not a linguistic or verbal concept: we share this kind of evaluation of safety with other mammals. The difference is that other species do not react to communicative symbols in embodied ways, as do humans.

The emphasis in the PVT is on:

1 a release of the "vagal brake" when there is neuroception of threat, allowing the "orienting response" to occur,
2 move back to social engagement mode when neuroception engenders feelings of safety,
3 shift to "mobilization" of sympathetic defences when continuing threat is perceived,
4 shift to "shutdown" mode when "life threat" is perceived.

(Porges, 2011)

The PVT also points towards quiet, meditative or low stimulus states as assisting maintenance of a healthy vagal tone supporting social engagement. When a sense of safety is maintained consistently, oxytocin may play a role in pleasurable affiliative states (ibid.). States of social engagement and reverie are important to the development of self.

In contrast, the "drive-defence" model that dominated psychoanalytic thinking in the first half of the 20th century depended upon an understanding of emotions and drives in conflict with "external reality", leading to states of arousal and distress. The emphasis was on "arousal" and the sympathetic nervous system was seen as the primary mediator of emotion, with the associated perception of emotions as having a basis in defensive action (ibid; Redding, 1999). This gave "emotions" a "bad name", associated with defence, often contrasted to calmness and rational thought. For the PVT, emotional life is seen as serving normative social engagement and evaluative functions. Porges characterizes this distinction as follows, "drive-defence lives in a world of threat and polyvagal lives in an optimistic world in which love, trust, and connectedness serve as a biobehavioral platform for emergent properties including intimacy, creativity, etc." (Porges, 2019).

For the CM there are two systems of consciousness: the system of self and that of trauma. Nuanced feeling supports complexity, creativity and the growth of self. For self, feeling is firstly an intrinsic value system, with defensive manifestations having value in relation to survival. The orienting response involves evaluation, allowing the individual freedom to deploy attentional resources where there is a sense of safety. The "giving of attention" amounts to focussing or shedding light on the environment, in a manner that permits exploration and growth of consciousness (Edelman & Tononi, 2000) and hence self. More complex forms of feeling emerge. When defensive physiological systems *do* come into play there is a constricted focus of attention, with diversion of metabolic resources away from the central nervous system (Porges, 2011) and a shift to self-protection, often associated with traumatic experience: either mobilization of the "fight-flight" response (sympathetic nervous system) associated with high arousal, or the "shutdown" response (freezing, death-feigning, dissociating) associated with hypo-arousal or hypo-metabolism (ibid.).

The development of language is associated with more complex systems of social engagement and higher forms of consciousness, mediated through the verbal, symbolic system of language (Edelman & Tononi, 2000). Language constitutes an essential part of the human maturational environment. It is not an abstract "added" element. Language is engaged with developmentally before linguistic and conceptual competence is attained. Turn-taking, rhythmic responses, narrative form, tonal matching and amplification are all evident from very early in life (Malloch & Trevarthen, 2009). The physiological systems that support social engagement are already operational from birth. When "language cuts to the quick" (Butt et al., 2007), it must be recognized that symbolic systems impact upon physical states, causing not only radical and rapid shifts in feeling, but also in overall physiology. This is particularly true of spoken language. While this can occur in a fraction of second, it takes longer periods for such shifts to be reflectively available to self. Initial response can, at one extreme, be both a psychological and bodily "shock". With written language, it is easier to sustain the illusion that language is "abstract", or "distanced" from the body.

Conversely it is also plausible that the body's physiology influences the "symbolic orders" that get realized in language. "Symbolic orders", in a pragmatic sense, are organizations of ideas, behaviours and modes of relating that represent a "way of living", in a sense similar to *language games* (Wittgenstein, 1958). In the dynamic interplay of life, autonomic systems become engaged in patterns of behavioural interplay and affective expression that could reasonably be termed "embodied symbolic orders", relating to particularized bodily experience as well as language.

When the social engagement system ("face-brain-heart") is operational, there may be a sense of social harmony: language is likely to be relatively coherent with personal significance and associated with appropriate expressive affect that isn't disruptive to the individual. The resonating intonations of vocalization, in themselves, may be sufficient to trigger the neuroception of safety, as frequently evident in the calming effect for the infant, of the mother's voice. The sense of safety allows listening and expression *with other*. It also facilitates processes such as recognition and realization. The sense of safety can be maintained in the "spaces" between interpersonal contacts (i.e. in solitude), where much reflection and realization occur. This is evident in a child with a secure attachment who feels empowered to explore while alone. Symbolic representations related to the social engagement system might be expected to include themes of resonance and harmony. The primary kind of embodied order might be the coherent story, the narrative of self, with a texture and timbre that resonates with others.

When the sympathetic system is activated metabolism shifts away from the brain towards muscular systems. Hence, one would expect a more restricted range of language to be used in these circumstances, with themes relating to conflict, fear and aggression being dominant. The quality of the voice is also likely to be more constricted. Of course, *mobilization* is necessary and people may be trained in deployment of these forms of behaviour. For example, soldiers and sports people may be trained in "controlled aggression". Within the overall society such behaviour may be idealized. Within subcultures, or in deprived circumstances, opportunistic aggression may be rewarded. The associated stories, whether of heroism, corruption or escape, are likely to emerge when the protagonist is in a calmer more socially engaged state. In the midst of high-stress emotional intensity the capacity for story-telling is lost.

When the phylogenetically ancient "shutdown" system (unmyelinated parasympathetic) is in operation, there is a response to the sense of *actual* life threat. Death becomes a dominant symbolic motif. The person may have a sense of "something dying" internally. In many ways, the experience is sensed as outside the social order. Hence, one might refer to symbolic orders of alienation, horror or the "non-order" of chaos. These states, as experienced from within, are often beyond words, potentially perceived as *worse than death*. The disruptive effects on the internal sense of self lead to *dissociation*. The individual is in a fragmented, traumatic, "not-me" state of alienation. This internal state can be so distressing that the person will behave in ways that don't make sense to an outside observer (e.g. self-laceration) but may afford a way out of the dysphoria, at least temporarily. There may be a temporary restoration of a sense of cohesion although ultimately such efforts tend to be futile because there is no resolution of the dissociated state. Resolution requires social engagement, or "re-association".

Finding a way in consciousness

What is remarkable in humans is that these autonomic systems can be activated by language (including its spoken vocal, visual and gestural accompaniments). We respond to neuroception of threat in the absence of actual immediate external threat, in part because social connection and interdependence is of such importance to the individual's survival. The sense of self is not a given in development. Although feeling forms an important basis for self (Korner, 2002), it is often experienced as "background feeling" (Meares, 2005). We are caught up in the *world knot* (Edelman & Tononi, 2000), the intersection between each individual and the environment. Interactive experience and apperception tend towards an external focus. Awareness of the "inner" is often vague, particularly as it relates to the "I". We achieve "object consciousness" before "subject consciousness" (Jackson, 1931–2; Meares, 1999b).

Put another way, Hegel refers to the development of knowledge of the world of facts (object consciousness) as the "unhappy consciousness" because it is essentially an empty kind of knowledge. Further developments in thought derive from involvement, participation and the development of an empathic apprehension of self and world, a fulfilling kind of knowledge (Hegel, 1807). The distinction between *autobiographical memory*, necessary for development of knowledge integrated with self and significantly based in right hemispheric systems (Schore, 2012; Siegel, 2015) and the more conceptually based *semantic* memory, more based in left hemispheric processes (Schore, 2012; Meares, 2012), may be of relevance in the distinction of these forms of consciousness.

In most human societies, systems of belief have been relatively homogeneous and cohesive, organized within relatively small communities such as tribal groupings. This has radically altered in the modern era with development of mass societies, urbanization and globalization changing the face of human experience. We are no longer born into *orders* that have broad community acceptance. In many cases, people experience an inner sense of fragmentation in the face of the information overload of modern life. It is up to the individual to find her way. This leads some to psychotherapy, where patients struggle to find order and make personal sense of life. It is not sufficient to be aware of intellectual arguments in favour of particular ideologies. People need to be able to make sense in a way "that is felt in the blood and felt along the heart" (Hobson, 1985, p. 81). In psychotherapeutic conversations this could be termed "ascending to the concrete" (Butt et al., 2012), denoting when something that had been understood intellectually takes on a personal, emotionally integrated form. Psychologically, for something to be really believed and owned it has to be felt in an immediate way, i.e. *felt concretely*.

These perspectives contribute to an understanding of the process of psychotherapy as the development of a fuller, more empathically based knowledge of self. The process of expressing and revealing self, often including disclosure of traumatically based and emotionally distressing self-perceptions, demonstrates the challenge and work of psychotherapy. Often trauma dominates consciousness, making it hard to appreciate anything that may be "going right". The aspect of psychotherapy that brings what is "lively" or "right" for the person into conscious awareness is recognized by the CM as a creative process.

The struggle to *know oneself more fully* characterizes the psychotherapeutic journey. It is in a sense never-ending even though therapy sessions come to an end. Each session needs to be understood as its own journey with a narrative form and two contributors. Each psychotherapy session tends to reflect the whole therapy in microcosm. As with any conversation there tends to be a statement of the theme, followed by development, an emotional climax and a return to the theme, in modified form. This has been compared to a *Schenker analysis* of musical forms (Malloch, 2012), where music is seen to have three-part form, with beginning, middle, and end: "home starting point" (theme; "tonic" musically), movement away (exploration reaching a climactic point; shift to "dominant" musically) and return to home point (resolution; return to "tonic"). The apparently simple quote from *Poetics* "A whole is that which has a beginning, a middle and an end" (Aristotle) is profound. We all think we know what a "whole" is but when put in this way and as it might be applied to living human beings, it takes on a different perspective, one that is temporal and contextual as well as material. In relation to an individual, a whole (self) becomes a sensible, reflectively aware, body-psyche moving through time in a network of relatedness and significance.

Four story types

Four forms of "self-story" are outlined. *No story, script, chronicle* and *narrative* are described with reference to clinical material. *No story* is the situation of failure to thrive. *Script, chronicle* and *narrative* are described with illustrative clinical quotes. In contrast to the *no story* situation, these latter three forms are language-based. When considering traumatic forms of story, it should be born in mind that patients can't always speak coherently about trauma. Some illustrations of trauma occur later, once the person is able to find the words to talk about it, rather than when in the grip of trauma. Even allusions to such experience, however, may engender a level of anxiety or re-experiencing. Each of the three language-based forms is considered in terms of *fuzzy logic* (Zadeh, 1965), contributing to understanding how organizing principles, established early in life, manifest in conversation.

No story

The medieval anecdote of the Emperor Frederick is recalled: in a situation of extreme emotional privation, with no communicative interaction, "the children all died" (Fernandez-Armesto, 1997). Modern evidence is also found of the severe effects of such privation (Spitz, 1946). Put bluntly, such circumstances can and do lead to death, although this is rare in developed societies. Medical people are one group more likely to come into contact with this reality. The trauma is not so much of impingement as gross neglect. As a medical person, it was a source of some distress and helplessness for me to witness this kind of event. The experience has not been forgotten. My account may not fully convey the horror of this "psychological absence" but, suffice it to say, it was a truly *bad place* for a human. The outcome was fatal. In the course of my professional life I have seen many patients with severe pain, others near death, people devastated by violence or subject to degradation, loss or misfortune. Yet I can think of no sadder situation than this:

> *I was working as a young doctor, in a country with limited medical facilities, on a paediatric ward. A young girl was there perched on her bed, unmoving with wide eyes. She was nearly five, although only had the weight and size of an infant of 15 months. She had arrived without a name. The nurses gave her one. She sat upright with a vacant stare. There were nurses trying to engage her, to talk to her, to cajole her but there was no response. She wouldn't take food. It was too late they said. They had seen it before. There wasn't any specific illness that could be found. She was malnourished of course but nothing else. She sat hour after hour. Not sleeping much. Not really awake. Some sort of limbo. Staring, no word, no language, no response, no self at all, or so it seemed. After about 16 weeks she disappeared in the night. The next day it was said that she died at night, alone. It was a life that never happened. No family, no traces left. Her stare looks through me still. I don't remember her name.*

The girl was alive but forgotten as far as significant others were concerned. Psychologically she had never really lived. The situation of being left, or forgotten (French, "*oublier*"), was utilized in medieval times as a final torture following the many predations of torturers. The *oubliette* was "a secret dungeon with an opening only at the top" (Delbridge, 1981): a place where there was no possibility of escape and people were simply left until death. Whether at the beginning or end of life, neglect can be of such severity as to effectively obliterate mental life, leaving the individual in the situation of a psychological vacuum.

This deeply traumatic psychological space is perhaps what is meant by existential "voids". It is, arguably, the instinctual fear driving the *isolation call* (MacLean, 1985). It is the *no-thing*: no connection, no self at all. It contrasts with *script*, *chronicle* and *narrative* where trauma at least takes form. Isolation and emotional privation (the absence of communication) are universally feared. Given that language becomes a significant aspect of what constitutes *self*, this is a form of *darkness* central to human fear and vulnerability. Complete isolation is symbolic darkness characterized by *no story*: no recognition, no connection, no sense of existence. Such fears, deep within the psyche, mean that language has a function in relation to the prevention of, and healing from, trauma. Some form of self-organization through language is preferable to none.

The script

> *I was defenceless . . . they would shout at me and say I was stupid . . .*

Here a patient is recalling states of trauma dating from familial interactions that have occurred repetitively throughout life. For some people such states will be the main form of relatedness and adaptations are made to an *ongoing* traumatic state where an "impinging narrative" of "other(s)" dominates experience (Meares, 2000). In adapting to a situation of traumatic relatedness the most effective response is to restrict activity and consciousness to a very limited scope, a set of *invariant* organizing principles based upon acceptance of the impinging script (ibid.). In the example given, were that to dominate ongoing experience, such a script might be something like, "I'm weak and helpless, *I'm defenceless*". This is barely a story at all, but may, nevertheless, allow some relational organization. To use the *if . . . and . . . then* form of fuzzy logic, such a limited script might allow for an organization like: "*if* I am so weak *and* others keep shouting at me *then* I need to keep out of their way and do what they say". When such a form of organization is dominant, it is likely that change will feel threatening. It takes considerable time to establish new patterns. Transformations won't be possible on the basis of instruction as this involves repetition of the old pattern. The establishment of safety and development of analogical forms of relatedness are required. The presence of language and communication provide hope for self. A basic understanding that the need for adaptation has stemmed from the need to protect a self with value will assist the therapist to maintain a therapeutic position.

The chronicle

> *When she [mother] died the family fell apart . . . . it was a case of everyone for themselves . . .*

In this short passage the emphasis is on a stress to which both patient and family were subject, where the outcome was psychological isolation: "*everyone for themselves*". If this circumstance is sustained, the child is left feeling everything is up to them, that existence is only possible if effort and activity are maintained. If such a situation dominates before a sustaining sense of self has emerged, the person is likely to be in a state of stimulus entrapment (Meares, 1998, 2005), where the sense of existence is inextricably tied to externally orientated activity and continuing stimulus from the environment. This is a situation of constricted traumatic consciousness lacking the duality of self (Meares, 2005; Benjamin, 2013). Since experience is reliant upon stimuli, the patient's language is likely to be reflected in *chronicles* involving recitations of events and facts without the colour of personal experience.

Looked at in terms of fuzzy logic, there could be a principle in operation along the lines: "*if* I keep doing things *and* I keep working hard *then* I might survive".

A limited kind of story is possible here, although it is without expectation of success or growth and with little expectation of intimacy or connection. In terms of affect states such a strategy is sometimes associated with inhibition of affective expression (Tomkins, 1995), or in fuzzy terms: "*if* I notice a feeling or emotion *and* it gets stronger *then* I better hide it or escape, or even shutdown completely".

The narrative

> So many spatial metaphors today . . . . the big citadel and the city surrounding, the roads radiating every which way . . . . like a map inviting you to go off away from the pack, find your own path . . . it's like Ulysses, so many possibilities . . . (silence) . . . it's so vast yet somehow it holds us all.

In this passage, we see a sense of connection, use of analogy and metaphor, future orientation and a sense of inner life, where silence feels safe and the world "*holds us all*". Felt experience has a lively narrative form that can be shared with access to the common sense of language. There is a poetic quality to the language consistent with the possibility of change (Meares et al., 2005b). There is the sense of possibility rather than dread or dull repetition. This flexibility reflects a coordination of personality (Tomkins, 1995). From an emotional viewpoint, the "fuzzy" view might be: "*If* I notice a feeling or emotion *and* there is no threat that can be seen, *then* I am free to direct my attention as I please". There is room for exploration.

The concrete enrichment of personal texts

Signs that make up language are not abstractions but *concrete entities* that exist when linked to sound-images (Saussure, 1959). This is to say that for any given individual, language is part of material reality. Language is also a *network of differences in value*, existing independently of the individual (Saussure, 1959). While language is part of material reality, the arbitrary nature of signs and their independence from individual instantiations, means that the combination of sound and thought (signifier and signified) "produces a form, not a substance" (Saussure, 1959, p. 113). Here lies a paradox: language is part of concrete reality, yet produces form, not substance. How, one might ask, does this paradox play out in actual lives, and specifically in the situation of psychotherapy?

Recall the claim, "inner speech just **is** higher-order or symbolic thought" (Thibault, 2004, p. 273). Thought is dependent on language: "apart from its expression in words (thought) is only a shapeless and indistinct mass" (Saussure, 1959, p. 111). To a large extent thought uses language that has been appropriated by the individual, for her own use. In contrast, James considered that "feelings are the germ and starting point of cognition, thoughts the developed tree" (James, 1890, p. 222). To apply James' idea to Thibault's reasoning, we might see feeling as the germ of language, if language and thought can be considered equivalent, as suggested. However, this would be misleading. The independence of language from the individual means language has to be acquired before it can be used. The relation of language to developed thought is one where language has formed part of the initial environment. In relation to James' metaphorical "tree", language forms part of the *earth* from which the personal self is realized (Korner, 2003).

It has been argued that *self* corresponds to Saussure's synchronic dimension of language. The sense of significance and the capacity to discriminate aspects of the environment grow over time through communicative exchange, as the culminative dimension of the life text. As is the case for language, self can only express some particular aspect of this growth, at any given time, in the diachronic dimension. While the individual self has no control over the language into which he or she is born, each individual develops in a relationship of dependence to the mother tongue.

The representations of language (the semantic value that exists independently of individuals) can be considered formal, rather than having material substance, when it comes to their instantiation in particular lives. Yet speech has an impact and is often felt concretely. Selves start from the "ground zero" of proto-self, a reference point with no text (Damasio, 2000). The messages and "images given and received" are materially expressed within the body of an individual, accounting for specific differentiation over time. This is reflected in measurable biological realities, where the distinctiveness of each brain increases over a lifetime (Edelman & Tononi, 2000).

When personal realities are sustained through communicative interaction, there is a degree of *revocability* in the experience of life. That is to say that new experience may lead to reappraisal. This is in contrast to situations such as violent injury, where something *irrevocable* has occurred. The notion of revocability may have some relationship to Saussure's conceptualization, of language having form but no material substance. The world that people live in when they are focused on mutuality through communication, rather than domination through violence or coercion, can be "formed and transformed" without unbearable loss. The psychotherapist endeavours to work with the patient in such a zone.

The dimensions of language that relate most closely to *self* are the interpersonal *metafunction*, or *clause as exchange*; and textual *metafunction*, or *clause as message*. These relate to the affective, prosodic elements of language and the building up of messages, self-knowledge and the capacity to express *self* with a sense of integrity. A sense of connection is required for this culminative building of a text. Given that it is not possible to access the entire stream of consciousness over a lifetime, the personal *text* relating to individual selves can only ever be partially expressed. The textual elements of self are recognized within the synchronic dimension of language. The diachronic succession of external events does not speak to the whole inner life. The process of psychotherapy can be understood as the patient striving to give expression to states that disclose and enrich recognition of this synchronic dimension of language in the intersubjective field, with an associated growth in terms of self-knowledge and relatedness.

The vehicle for this process is the language of *clause as representation* (shared conventional language). However, without emotional expressiveness, and *images given and received*, this dimension of language remains experience-distant, failing to engage.

Feeling is the *germ* of self, as well as of developed thought. Affective experience is inseparable from self, a psychologically concrete aspect of personal reality. This property is shared with Saussure's language sign as *concrete entity*. Feeling can't be considered to have existence independent of individuals, although it is characteristic that much human feeling is generated during interpersonal interaction serving communicative functions that pre-exist and complement the exchanges of verbal language. Affect remains the key motivational influence on communication throughout life (Panksepp, 2008). While *feeling* shares some of the characteristics of language, it is tied to the indexical present. For *self* the acquisition of language provides the potential, through the mental spatiality inherent in grammar, for entry into a conceptual world not dependent upon specific others, thereby enabling personal transcendence of the indexical present. Self becomes an actor in the world of symbolic exchange.

In psychodynamic psychotherapies empathic responsiveness is central to the work. Empathy was considered by Freud to be "the comprehension of the mechanism by means of which we are enabled to take up any attitude at all towards another mental life" (Freud, 1921). This seems to imply the possibility that empathy may be important in transcending the indexical present in interpersonal situations. One is not simply bound to respond in kind. The progress of psychotherapy would be greatly impeded if therapists did not have the capacity to tolerate and transform difficult feelings. Similar processes are required of carers in the developmental context. Empathy and affective transformation are central to change in psychotherapy, and human development generally. The mature self generates time for others (McLean & Korner, 2013), potentiating the imagination through communicative interaction in a kind of therapeutic alchemy.

In considering psychotherapy process, the CM argues that intersubjective exchange precedes individual growth in a manner analogous to the developmental situation, where *proto-conversation* precedes development of the sense of interiority necessary for emergence of self as a relatively autonomous being. In linguistic terms this involves the patient making himself the psychological subject in a relationship, introducing themes that meet with therapeutic response. If the *new* in conversation is recognized and amplified, there is likely to be *new experience*. This may allow reflection and the reconstruction of logical relations. Experience in conversation within the affective dimension (*interpersonal metafunction*) and responses that create relevance to context (*textual metafunction*) need to occur before growth and reorganization can take place. The syntax of language is linear in nature (Saussure, 1959). Inner language, with its wandering and associational properties, is non-linear (Vygotsky, 1934; Meares, 2005). It may be that processes of exchange with others, via the continual introduction of *new* components for *self* contribute to renewal and growth of a personalized, enriched text.

Chapter 5

Two minds greater than one: an intersubjective approach to research

Overview

A rationale for an intersubjective research paradigm is offered, arguing that this must provide information relevant to understanding an effective psychotherapy process. An example is given of a project where both patient and therapist make ratings reflecting changes in their self-experience during a therapy session, with concurrent measures of breathing and heart rate. Heart Rate Variability (HRV) and breathing are considered with reference to their relevance as markers of autonomic state, with likely variability in relation to feeling states. The frequencies of the self-experience ratings are demonstrated to relate to the timings of the *present moment* and the *narrative unit*, suggesting that self-states accessible to reflection do not correspond to minimal conscious states. Psychotherapy process is considered in relation to a therapy where the patient begins from a relatively alienated position but undergoes transformations that relate to recognition and protection of the *vulnerable self*. Tentative connections are made between the experience of self, as reported in ratings, and physiological, autonomic state, with reference to the Polyvagal Theory.

In search of an intersubjective research paradigm

The work reported in this chapter was motivated by the wish to consider the psychotherapeutic setting as one with two embodied participants involved in a prolonged interactive exchange. Despite the relatively high public profile of psychotherapy and competing claims about outcome and efficacy, "research into the processes and effects of psychotherapy remains much less known" (Lambert, 2013). While the dominant approaches to research utilize quantitative measures, it is the qualitative approach to research that appeals to many clinicians because "it remains closer to the actual phenomena and lived experience of therapy" (McLeod, 2013). It provides a sense of "being able to hear the voice of the client" while "offer(ing) an understanding of the meaning that various aspects of therapy hold for (clients)" (ibid.). In a standard text on psychotherapy research (Lambert, 2013), a whole chapter is devoted to qualitative approaches for the first time, "evidence for the 'coming of age' of qualitative research" (McLeod, 2013). Subjectivity and intersubjectivity are terms that reflect the centrality of personal meaning in mental life and the sense of significance experienced in interpersonal interactions.

An intersubjective research paradigm would consider the whole person in relational context. In individual psychotherapy both patient and therapist would be given a voice in understanding the interaction and its correlates in personal experience. Traditionally, research has largely taken the position of looking at the experience of the patient from the perspective of the therapist. The patient's voice has been under-represented. This creates a situation where only half the story gets told. There are advantages to research that recognizes the singularity of each person and the distinct voice with which the person represents himself.

Applications may include elucidation of psychotherapy process and recognition of change over time. *Self* and *person* are not objective constructs. Rather they have intersubjectively based meaning. Linguistic analysis of spontaneous conversations, on the one hand and physiological markers of the internal value system (i.e. feeling) that vary in relation to stress and emotional state, such as HRV and Respiratory Rate, are good candidates for providing objective correlates to *self*. Another objective marker, not explored in detail here, is the intonation of the voice, the acoustic qualities that can be objectively represented and serve not only "to communicate . . . relevant features in the environment, but also reflect the physiological (autonomic) state" of the speaker (Porges & Lewis, 2010). In this chapter preliminary findings using an intersubjective research paradigm demonstrate links between the subjective and objective domains of measurement.

An intersubjective approach to research should be seen as one form of research with strengths rather than as a paradigm to replace existing approaches. Differing research paradigms all have their own merits. Quantitative research can have great instrumental power. Phenomenological research helps establish a mental vocabulary. Perhaps intersubjective research might be found to have evocative power in bringing the patient's voice into play.

An illustrative project

In a psychotherapy session there is an ongoing conversation involving a continual flux of meaning and significance for both patient and therapist. Much of this experience of significance is not captured by the words of the conversation. The communicative exchange is partly unconscious. The illustrations in this chapter are taken from a research project that explored changes in self-state for both patient and therapist utilizing audio-recordings of actual therapy sessions (Korner, 2015). Both subjects were simultaneously monitored using a non-invasive system that records heart and respiratory rate, providing a measure of some objective correlates of subjective experience. The project also recorded comparison dyads, involving an interviewer conversing with an interviewee regarding their life story.

The process of recording and rating was designed to fit within the timing of a normal psychotherapy session in order to minimize disruption to therapy.

Following the recording session, a transcript was typed with copies given to therapist and patient (or control "interviewer" and "interviewee"). The therapist rated the "Change in Self Experience Rating Scale" (CSERS), an instrument developed for the study, prior to the next session, noting where shifts in the experience of self-state occurred. In the subsequent therapy session, the patient (or interviewee) spent the first 30 minutes making his or her rating. The researcher then interviewed participants for feedback on the experience of the procedure.

Previous study of micro-processes in therapy has been divided into two types: "interpersonal process recall" (IPR), and "conversational analysis" (CA) (McLeod, 2013). The study under discussion has elements of both of these approaches: the actual transcripts of single sessions are studied (CA) and both patient and therapist are subsequently asked to reflect on the experience of the session (IPR). However, the precise methodology is original. A contrasting example of existing methodology is the "Core Conflictual Relationship Theme" approach, which identifies patterns of interaction between patient and therapist involving the "response of the other" (RO) and the "response of self" (RS) (Luborsky, 1977). This enables identification of repetitive patterns of rejection and the like. Analysis of the "RO to RS" sequence "goes a long way toward assisting joint understanding of the meaning of symptoms" (Grenyer, 2012). However, this method relies upon the researcher carefully reading and interpreting the transcript (Grenyer, 2012), without directly involving the patient in the process. The present study, in contrast, employs both patient and therapist as active participants, independently rating the transcript.

A measure of self-state: background

An instrument was developed based on the notion that all human experience can be considered to vary in its sense of "liveliness" from high degrees of liveliness to experiences that feel deadening, or even incompatible with sustaining life (i.e. overwhelming-intolerable). This variable has been chosen because it is likely that it corresponds in a meaningful way to affective experience from the beginning of life as a separate being (from birth). This reflects a reformulation of Freud's two principles of mental functioning, the pleasure and reality principles (Freud, 1911), utilizing the principle of liveliness (Korner, 2000).

The seven-point scale and associated instructions appear in Figure 5.1. The selection of "seven" as the number of points is common in psychological testing, possibly reflecting an aspect of human discrimination and judgment propensities (Miller, 1956). It is designed for independent use by *both participants* in dyadic conversations. It brings additional information derived from affective and contextual experience (*self-state*) to the written transcript, as well as information about correlations between the experiences of two individuals. Hence it is a measure with personal, *within subject*, as well as interpersonal, *between subject*, dimensions. Although there is an element of "forcing choices" for subjects in any instrument or questionnaire, providing the subjects with the option of choosing their own word descriptor for the shifts in self-state leaves room for independent specification of experience, while still asking for the subject to mark a point on a seven-point scale. The subject is also free to choose *where* in the transcript choices are made.

Given that it takes time to reproduce a transcript for rating, there is a necessary interval between the original experience and the rating. This brings into play differences between the experience as it occurred originally and the "re-experience" of reading the transcript, mimicking natural reflective processes and re-creation of memory in the context of present experience. Memory, itself, is a creative process influenced by present contexts, rather being strictly re-duplicative (Edelman & Tononi, 2000). At least in theory, it might be expected use of this type of scale actually contributes to self-knowledge through reflection, in contrast to scales that provide information without opportunity for reflective consideration.

Using this scale brings word descriptions to an element of conversation not normally seen, the realm of private self-experience (self-state). The nature of self-experience is such that this can only be done in an approximate way as there is simply no way of being precise. Commonly used quantitative methods that seek to bring precise definition in terms of "either–or" paradigms of set membership can be misleading when it comes to experience in the "intermediate zone" (Winnicott, 1971). The uncertainty and vagueness of much human experience is acknowledged when we place emphasis on the centrality of feeling to self-experience (James, 1890). The need for modes of measurement of control systems that have a "language base", rather than a strictly numerical paradigm, was discussed in Chapter 3, with reference to "fuzzy logic" (Zadeh, 1965). In fact, complex human levels of organization and culture can be attained without the development of complex numerical bases (Sapir, 1951). CSERS is a language-based measure. It combines elements of previous approaches taken to the study of micro-process in therapy: "interpersonal process recall" (IPR) and "conversational analysis" (CA) (McLeod, 2013, p. 57). In this pilot study, conducted with CSERS, three patient-therapist dyads and four control dyads utilized the instrument, generating data discussed in later sections.

Change in Self-Experience Rating Scale (CSERS)

Choose one word and one letter to describe changes in the experience of your-self on the scale below at the points where you notice these changes as you read the transcript. If you cannot find a word that fits with your experience, use a word of your choice that corresponds to one of the letters. Mark them at the side of the transcript.

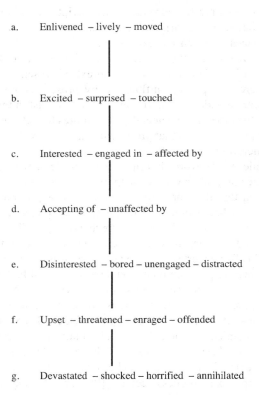

Figure 5.1 Change in Self-Experience Rating Scale: CSERS

Heart Rate Variability (HRV)

Respiratory Sinus Arrhythmia (RSA) is an index of vagal tone relating to activity of the myelinated division of the vagus, where higher RSA values reflect greater HRV (Porges, 2011). As mentioned in Chapter 3, this measure was conceived as useful in a variety of clinical situations: "I had the vision that monitoring physiological state would be a helpful guide to the therapist during the clinical interaction" (ibid.). The decision to record breathing and heart rate in this study related to Porges' use of these variables as a measure of autonomic state.

HRV is the measurement of the variation in inter-beat intervals, usually defined as the "R-R" interval, on successive QRS complexes of the ECG. With improved digital signal processing techniques, it has become possible over the last 40 years to analyse subtle beat-to-beat variations in various parameters (Billman, 2011). Interest in HRV has grown since the demonstration that foetal stress was preceded by reduction in HRV, before any change in average heart rate could be detected (Hon and Lee, 1965). More recent findings have found a relationship to other conditions, including cardiac problems, diabetes, depression, and obesity (Task Force, 1996). Interest has grown in HRV as a positive marker of health status. It is thought to be "a measure of the continuous interplay between sympathetic and parasympathetic influences on heart rate that yields information on autonomic flexibility . . . (representing) the capacity for regulated emotional responding" (Appelhans & Luecken, 2006). A similar interpretation is made by Porges who argues that the amplitude of RSA, a relatively easily measurable component of HRV, provides a proxy measure for vagal tone reflecting the fine-grained influence of the "*smart*" *vagus* on the cardiac pacemaker (Porges, 2011).

HRV is not a direct measure, so its interpretation remains a matter of debate. Current recommendations are for measuring heart rate averaged over 5-minute periods, although this method loses much fine-grained detail of HRV. Several approaches have been taken to measure HRV but there is currently no "gold standard" of measurement (Task Force, 1996). Other factors, including baroreceptors and the mechanical effects of respiration or cardiac muscle can exert non-autonomic influences on HRV.

Whilst this demonstrates that conclusions about HRV require caution, it is likely interest in this area will remain strong. Application to psychotherapy is novel. For psychotherapy it is argued there is particular relevance in studying timeframes corresponding to experience available to the process of self-reflection. This would require measures of HRV sensitive to the "present moment" of 2–10 seconds, relating to the timings of autonomic response, breathing and language. This does not represent the minimal time for neural or emotional response to stimuli but may reflect a minimum time for awareness of the significance of events to register. It would be a considerable advantage if a method of measurement could be developed that could yield meaningful data over relatively short periods of measurement, significantly less than the 5-minute periods currently recommended. With this in mind, we developed such a method, allowing measurement over short recording windows, with demonstrated accuracy and reversibility, unlike techniques that require averaging (Melkonian et al., 2012). However, its application in uncontrolled settings remains speculative. Porges, using his own method, reports a capacity to estimate RSA every 10 seconds, a considerable advance on the Task Force measure (Porges, 2019).

CSERS group data

Subjects were asked to rate typed transcripts from a session recorded approximately a week earlier. This, in effect, gives the subject an independent, personal voice in relation to the "public" data of the verbal transcript. For the rating using the CSERS scale, 30 minutes was allowed. The 30 minutes rating time was chosen so the rating could be completed along with recorded feedback on the procedure within the span of a normal psychotherapy session. This minimized disruption of the therapeutic framework and maximized the applicability of the method to a naturalistic psychotherapeutic setting, bearing in mind that sessions were conducted at regular times and were 50 minutes in length. Some people did not complete the rating in this time – where it as clear that the rating was incomplete this was indicated in data collection which reports on the number of shifts in self-experience reported by different subjects and the time range between shifts. The total number of shifts reported per session ranged from a low of 11 to a high of 75. The range of *shortest* time between changes in self-state for all subjects varied from a minimum, in this series, of 3 seconds up to a maximum of 85 seconds. The *longest* time between changes in self-state for all subjects ranges from 3 minutes to 12 minutes. These data described are set out in Table 5.1.

The shortest time intervals between alterations in self-state rating would be expected from earlier discussions to relate to the timings of the present moment. The findings here are consistent with this range, with the majority of subjects (10/16) recording shortest gaps between ratings within the range 3–12 seconds. Of course, even in these cases, the majority of self-observed shifts are longer, often in the range of minutes. Some of these shifts are likely to correspond to "narrative units" which, in their most simple form, are expected to take from 12–30 seconds. The universal bias towards assimilation of new stimuli and towards psychological homeostasis, makes it unsurprising that many intervals are substantially longer, up

	Number of shifts reported	Time range of shifts (approx.)
Pilot 1 – Patient rating	21 (rated 12 / 18 pages)	4 secs–4 mins
Pil 1 – Therapist rating	21	10 secs–6 mins
Pil 2 – Pt rating	27	7 secs–7 mins
Pil 2 – Th rating	37	7 secs–7 mins
Pil 3 – Pt rating	54 (29 indicating change)	9 secs–9 mins
Pil 3 – Th rating	34	11 secs–4 mins
Pil 4 – Pt rating	14 (rated 15/18 pages)	30 secs–8 mins
Pil 4 – Th rating	37	20 secs–3.5 mins
Control 1 – Subject rating	14 (short recording 23m)	20 secs–3 mins
Con 1 – Interviewer rating	14	10 secs–3.5 mins
Con 2 – Sub rating	66 (39 indic. change; 15/17p)	4 secs–4 mins
Con 2 – Int rating	23	15 secs–6 mins
Con 3 – Sub rating	13	25 secs–12 mins
Con 3 – Int rating	74 (59 indicating change)	4 secs–4 mins
Con 4 – Sub rating	11	85 secs–12 mins
Con 4 – Int rating	52	3 secs–4 mins

Table 5.1 Frequency of self-state report, and time ranges between self-reports, for study and control dyads

to 12 minutes in this series. It is likely that, within such long intervals there would be smaller narrative units that are formed into more complex units. The data support the idea that *changes in self-experience that can be accessed by individuals do not occur on the very brief time scales (20–150 milliseconds) that characterize brief conscious states (transient attentional "blinks")*. As such the data lend face validity to the notion that **"self-states" are experienced on a time scale distinct from minimal conscious states**. The data described are set out in Table 5.1.

The timings of self-awareness relate to the timings of breathing and language, making it reasonable to speculate that a sense of self is realized through the medium of language and that self can only be *understood* through this medium. Hence self, as far as it can be understood, is realized as a text, although one that can only ever be partially expressed. At the same time language, in its lived verbal and affective dimensions, involves an accompanying brain-body state at any given time.

Developing a psychologically relevant measure of HRV

The need for a measure of HRV sensitive to changes over short time periods has been highlighted. The current recommendation is to take measurements over periods of five minutes, assuming a regular process over this period, i.e. averaging heart beats over this period (Task Force, 1996). While this allows variability between successive standard time-frame periods to be measured, it involves altering data in such a way that information about the moment-to-moment variability of beats is lost. The mathematical technique of averaging effectively means loss of the original fine-grained variability. This is a paradox, given that fine flexibility in response is the process thought to have implications for self-regulation. It also limits recording information that reflects the responsiveness between people in psychotherapy.

The Similar Basis Function (SBF) algorithm is a mathematical approach for the estimation of Fourier integrals, allowing measurement over short periods by accepting both uniform and non-uniform intervals into the analysis (Melkonian, 2009). It involves transcription to digital form and is applicable to signals of arbitrary length. It has been applied to another physiological signal, the evoked response potential (ERP), providing data that differentiated a clinical psychiatric population from control subjects (Meares et al., 2011).

In order to further assess the application of the SBF to the measure of RSA-HRV we decided to do a study where breathing was controlled to verify the methodology could produce accurate measurements. The procedure was carried out in an office setting. In this experiment data was recorded from one subject only as the purpose was to look at the relation of breathing to HRV and RSA rather than correlations between subjects. Throughout breathing wave form and R-R intervals were recorded to allow measurement of HRV and derivation of RSA, following Porges' method (Porges, 1985). In Porges' method RSA is considered a proxy for vagal tone.

Respiratory rate was timed, using a metronome, with the following conditions: (1) resting/baseline (uncontrolled breathing); (2) 5 breaths per minute; (3) 10 breaths per minute; (4) 15 breaths per minute; (5) 30 breaths per minute; (6) a recovery period (uncontrolled). The duration of the recovery period was approximately two minutes.

Vagal tone was expected to be relatively high at rest. A reduction of vagal tone was anticipated at higher breathing frequencies in response to the controlled condition of metronomic breathing, reflected in reduced amplitude of HRV and decreased RSA. Following such a controlled period it was expected that, after a brief recovery period, an increase in vagal tone might again be observed. A subsequent review of the method cautioned that very low breathing rates (below 7–8 breaths per minute) may be "difficult to interpret because the slower variations in heart rate that have baroreceptor feedback influences become intertwined with RSA" (Porges, 2019). This is interesting from a clinical point of view because many of the currently available apps that support regulation of HRV through finding one's optimal breathing rate encourage breathing in this slow range.

The main findings of the study were of decreasing HRV with increased respiratory rate, suggesting decreased vagal tone consistent with other studies (e.g. Hirsch & Bishop, 1981). The data also demonstrated that HRV shows dominant frequencies corresponding to the respiratory rate, consistent with the phenomenon of Respiratory Sinus Arrhythmia. At lower breathing rates there is a strong relationship between

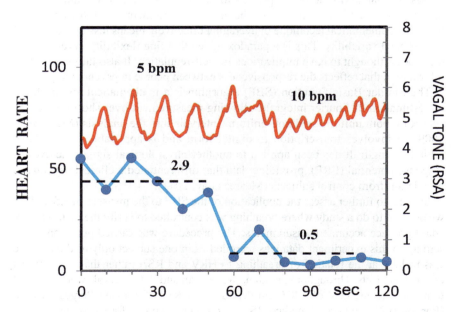

Figure 5.2 Illustration of transition in RSA, as subject alters rate of controlled breathing. Red: HRV; Blue: RSA. The amplitude of HRV is reduced as breathing rate increases; RSA is reduced in magnitude as breathing rate increases. RSA values are in natural logarithm units per millisecond squared.

RSA and breathing rates (5; 10 breaths per minute). This relationship is much weaker at 15 bpm and there is virtually no relationship evident at 30 bpm.

In Figure 5.2 there is a demonstration of the transition from a low frequency of breathing (5 breaths per minute) to a higher frequency (10 breaths per minute). This shows how the method is able to detect changes in vagal tone over time frames corresponding to the present moment that are likely to be relevant to the experience of significance within relational interactions involving communicative exchange.

The detection of variability in RSA over short timeframes suggests the "Non-Stationary time-frequency analysis of HRV" using the SBF algorithm may have utility in measuring moment-to-moment changes in RSA. Overall, the findings were consistent with reduced vagal influence at higher breathing rates with relatively rapid restoration of vagal influence upon cessation of controlled breathing.

Impact of speaking and listening on autonomic function

In order to be clearer about the relationship of breathing patterns, speech and RSA, a session was designed with two participants. It was carried out in office conditions as described previously. In this session there was a silent resting condition; followed by one person speaking for about 3 minutes; then, the other person speaking for a similar period. The instruction in this case was simply to speak about whatever came to mind, with the interest being on the effect of speaking rather than on the content (i.e. this was not an attempt to simulate psychotherapy). Although specific turns for speaking were *prescribed* in this session, the person was speaking to the other subject about matters of mutual interest. Hence, the condition was one of a conversation, where one person could be designated as "speaking" at a particular time, and the other person could be designated as "listening".

During the silent phase, both A and B were breathing at a rate of 14 breaths per minute. Significant synchronies were evident in breathing, as illustrated in Figure 5.3. In this session it was evident that speaking had the effect of slowing breathing, bringing it close to resting levels. Conversely, respiratory rates were more rapid when the subject was listening.

The effect of speaking was not associated with reduction of RSA, which remained similar to the resting condition. This is consistent with a previous study showing speech doesn't decrease RSA (Kotani, 2007). In the case of the "listening" condition in relation to RSA, there was also not much change in absolute value. Listening conditions in this sample were associated with breathing rates below 20 bpm, perhaps suggesting that breathing rates under conversational conditions remain consistent with predominant vagal regulation in both speaking and listening conditions. This is consistent with the PVT around social engagement, where communication within an acoustic frequency range of perceptual advantage (as in normal level conversations) may have evolved under vagal regulation, to "promote social interactions and social bonds in safe environments" (Porges & Lewis, 2010).

Overall, the data in this study were consistent with the hypothesis that conversation may serve a metabolic function, in slowing breathing. Slowing of the breath

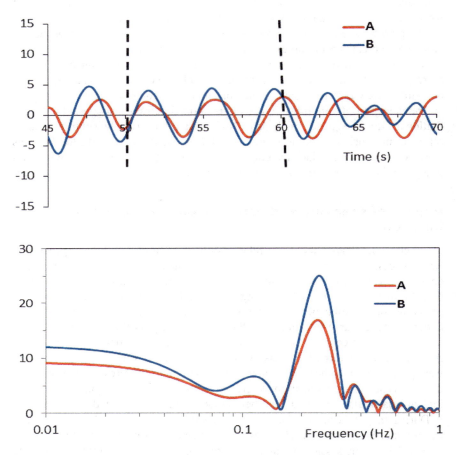

Figure 5.3 Dyadic breathing during silence; subjects A and B; silent phase. Top graph shows time domain; lower graph shows frequency domain.

is a condition with an established association with higher vagal tone. Resonances were demonstrated between people in breathing (Figure 5.3). This may be more likely to occur during periods of silence.

The findings overall are consistent with the idea of Porges that social engagement mediated through a high level of vagal activity is associated with rapid autonomic modulation of the cardio-respiratory apparatus. Levels of vagal activity are likely to vary, according to the polyvagal theory, depending on the sense of significance at the time. A hostile argument, for example, would have different implications for autonomic recruitment, compared to a socially harmonious interaction. Meaning and context make a difference. Measuring significance requires integration of the autonomic data with report from the private space of personal experience.

Application of CSERS: a case illustration

Psychotherapy is concerned with the inner world of the patient. The therapist attempts to maintain attention and facilitate understanding of self with the patient. Shifts in self-state may occur with greater frequency in such a setting. CSERS provides a tool for tracking such changes in experience.

The psychotherapeutic conversation is an example of a spontaneously occurring asymmetric dialogue, with a focus primarily on the *self* of the patient. From a linguistic point of view, the study of this interaction may be best approached using actual transcripts. The CSERS methodology involves use of transcripts. A short extract from one of the therapeutic dyads (see also Chapter 1) is presented, with discussion of CSERS findings for the session. To demonstrate longitudinal changes in therapy, I have drawn on other clinical experiences to illustrate later stages of therapy.

Vignette I

Recalling the exchange in Chapter 1,

Pt: ..... *I just .... I ..... it's like I wanted (my ex) there 'cause I'm used to it .... (becomes emotional) I don't like to be reminded that he's gone. There you go, there's feelings.*
(*few turns later*)
I'm glad he's gone in a sense. I'm glad that the limbo is kind of over. I know where we stand. .... I'm glad of the separation but there's elements that I miss.

Th: *Of course, 'cause you're telling me that he has a number of really positive features about him that he has been a good man in your life.*

Pt: *I miss him when I'm feeling bad he'll just give you a hug and sometimes you feel so much better you know it doesn't take away what I'm feeling or anything but I just don't feel alone with that feeling.*

Th: *Sure it's kind of soothing to have somebody there who just holds us and comforts us.*

This extract is an edited segment occurring over roughly 2 minutes and occurring in the last 15 minutes of the session. It includes material that is salient to the patient's current experience. The patient's only rating is "d.accepting of", made when she says, "*I'm glad he's gone in a sense*". This, although neutral, occurs in a session where the patient's predominant ratings are in negative hedonic range. The therapist makes two ratings in this segment: "b.excited" at the beginning, where the patient says, "*there you go, there's feelings*" and at the end when he makes a rating of "a.lively", as he responds verbally to the patient's comment "*I just don't feel alone with that feeling*". In this case the semantic content, on its own, gives clues to what is of concern to the patient: the need for intimacy and connection, while at the same time feeling some relief at there being some resolution of her position in a relationship. The therapist's responses suggest that when she gives emotional cues of vulnerability ('mood signs'), he responds warmly, with two consecutive positive ratings suggesting engagement, and perhaps a felt response to her sense of isolation. In this case the data could be seen to be providing a window onto the relationship. There is a sense of lively emotional expression, although confusing and unresolved to the patient, with a lack of cohesion at this point. The capacity to express feeling seems hopeful, to the therapist.

The session, with patient ratings

In this session, once the therapist frames the session as beginning (*"What's been happening?"*), the patient quickly moves into a definition of the main theme (*". . . . I'm still functioning OK. . . . I'm very tired but I think that's got to do with the kids"*), which relates to "parenting". At times emotion is expressed around efforts *"for the kid's sake"*, and recognition that this is also, *"for my sake"*. The patient describes interaction with the child's father, from whom she has separated. While she values his help and company at times, she also places value on having separated, and becoming more her own person. She says, *"I'm glad he's gone in a sense. I'm glad that the limbo is kind of over. . . . I know where we stand"*.

At one point she refers to past self-harming behaviours, saying she has a sense of, *"taking a responsibility for those behaviours . . . . God it's so nice to say 'used to'"* (i.e. no longer self-harming), conveying a sense of movement or progression, as her reflection takes on some coherence. The theme of parenting is recapitulated, with a statement of goals and aspirations: *". . . I'm testing myself . . . see if I can manage. To see if I can manage to my standards as well as to other people's – To keep myself together and to give my kids what they need. And I don't feel like I'm doing that good right now"*. The theme of "tiredness" as a parent has been elaborated into a sense of flagging or failing, despite efforts at being a good parent. Her sense of responsibility to her children keeps her going but is hampered by her lack of self-worth.

The patient makes 14 ratings, completing ratings for 15 out of 18 pages of transcript. This is a relatively low number compared to other patients and controls. Of these, one rating is in the positive hedonic range ("b.excited"); 3 are in the "neutral range" ("d"); while the remaining 10 are in the negative hedonic range (9 "f"; 1 "e"). This is consistent with someone who has been, and remains, depressed, a condition recognized explicitly in the transcript.

Of interest is that episodes of becoming emotional are typically rated as "f.upset", suggesting negative personal evaluation of emotion. On three of the four "f.upset" ratings there is a subsequent "f.angry" rating. Taken together, this sequence might suggest that there is an experience of *threat to self* when emotionally vulnerable, leading to a "mobilizing" kind of (internal) response. The positive rating comes when she recounts an episode where her son shows a new behaviour, of actually asking for help. The therapist subsequently recognizes this as an achievement for the son, and a development in her relationship with him. The therapist's recognition seems to provide a significant amplification that allows this realization to occur.

During the session the patient also defines her problem: "*I remember ten years ago telling myself I've got to stop telling myself this same thing hating myself just as much saying you know it'll run its course . . .*" The problem, defined as "*hating myself*", speaks to a disturbance of internal relationship. The emotional contours of the session are reflected in language that displays increased negative self-evaluation at times when she becomes emotionally expressive, suggesting an implicit devaluation of vulnerability.

Patient report on rating process

The patient's responses as reported the week after the session, when the transcript was rated, were indicative of greater emotional complexity than was evident from her self-state ratings. A selection of her responses follows:

> In response to how it was for her, ". . . *it was fine*"; " . . . . *in the beginning I felt a little nervous*"; " . . . . . *after about five or ten minutes it just all kind of happened . . . I stopped taking notice, it just didn't matter, I didn't think about it*". (referring to the recording process)

> In response to how it was, "going through the transcript": "*Umm OK, it gave me a bit of laugh*" . . . "*like inside I can't believe I said that (laughs) it is interesting looking at what I said*".

> In response to, "is it different to what you recall of the session, actually seeing it there in writing?", she says:

> *Different from where it was more amusing umm I didn't, like I was aware that I had said it and that but umm boy leader ummm that is just kind of funny . . . . . Umm as I was reading it the emotions and that became quite clear I could remember umm and when I read it the same emotions sort of comes up . . . . Yeah umm for me it wasn't so much recollection it was when I am reading that I can umm how do I put it when I am reading a novel, I get really into it and I can feel the emotions of the novel and it was similar . . .*

> In response to "what was easier, rating it with the letters or is it rating with the words?", she said,

> *The words was hardest, yeah . . . . it didn't really cover the emotions I was feeling . . . Yeah there were moments of anger there was moments of upset but there was moments of just you when I thought, excited is the wrong word, but uplifted by what I was saying and then I could tell that there was a drop in the way I was speaking and you know that I felt kind of flat but I wasn't upset I was just kind of dropped.*

Overall these comments, made at the time of rating, suggest the original ratings made by the patient don't fully capture the complexity of her responses. Although the predominant ratings were in the negative hedonic range, she indicates that often there were positive feelings of interest and "*uplift*". The fact that she found it "*a bit of a laugh*" and that it was "*amusing*" suggests that the process of reviewing the transcript carried elements of surprise for her. The fact that she found it engaging in the manner of "*reading a novel*" and that she could "*feel the emotions*" suggests that the rating process was found to reproduce, or realize, actual emotional responses.

There was a period of silence, where she referred to being "*off with the fairies*", consistent with a possible dissociative period, with an effect on expressive function (she comments, "*nothing is coming out of my mouth*"). There are strong indications that she found the process acceptable, despite her basically negative self-evaluation.

Therapist ratings

The therapist makes 38 ratings, covering 17 out of 18 pages of transcript. The spread of ratings is greater, and more evenly distributed, relative to the patient: 2 "a" ratings; 5 "b" ratings; 10 "c" ratings; 6 "d"; 9 "e"; 6 "f". The "c" and "e" ratings reflected whether the therapist felt "interested" or "engaged with" vs "disinterested", "distracted" or "disappointed", suggesting times when there was a relative loss of attention, while other periods were associated with an adequate sense of connection.

The period of about 32–46 minutes into the session, including material in the vignette, is the period of greatest positive CSERS ratings by the therapist. The peak rating of "a.lively", for the therapist, related to a passage where the patient reflected on a need for soothing ("*Sure it's kind of soothing to have somebody there who just holds us and comforts us*"); and another passage, where "a.moved" is rated, as the patient seemed reflective about past self-harm behaviours ("*Yeah I mean it was never . . . . when I did it, it was never a suicide attempt, it was never a . . . and I want attention, because it was like I don't want anyone to see. . . . It was just like I needed to release something . . . . like the balloon about to burst*"). On several occasions "b" ratings relate to the sense that the patient has realized something, such as, "*God, it's so nice to say 'used to'*" – referring to cessation of self-harm.

It is notable that, at times when the therapist is making ratings of mildly positive or neutral hedonic tone (e.g. "c" or "d"), the patient tends to be rating "f.upset". This suggests that the therapist feels interested in the patient when the patient is expressing emotional vulnerability, but that the patient is more focused on her own state. The period of most positive ratings by the therapist relates (for the patient), to: (1) a transition from "f.upset", to "f.angry"; (2) a further shift for the patient from "f.angry", to "f.flat but not upset" (possibly suggesting a more manageable, although still distressing position); followed by a shift to a neutral "d.accepting of". However, this is followed by an interesting shift by the patient back to "f.upset" then "f.angry", followed by the therapist peak rating of "a.moved" near the end of the session. This contrasting rating suggests that the therapist is moved by both the patient's predicament and emotional state *and* her apparent efforts at mobilization as she grapples with her problems.

Session as a whole

The content of the session is revealing of the patient's inner world, or self. As might be expected, given that the focus of the session is on the patient, it says less about the self of the therapist. The central themes of the session relate to parenting and relationship with significant others, leading to consideration of aloneness and disconnection from, or loss of, significant others. While the session is never in a state of emotional decompensation, it points towards states of feeling alone and outside social connection that may be transiently experienced in the session, and more intensely in external experience. Hence, there is the suggestion that the patient experiences states involving "shutdown", or dissociation, which might suggest preoccupations with death and alienation, reflected in sensitivity to cues in language that related to loss, separation and devaluation.

The two sequences of "f.upset" to "f.angry" suggest that one of her responses to these states is to "mobilize", perhaps employing relative activation of the sympathetic nervous system. The therapist's positive response to one of these episodes, when the patient says, "*God, it's so nice to say 'used to'*", suggests that this strategy may indeed lead to an enlivened response on the part of the patient, as does her comment the following week where she refers to an "*uplifting*" experience, not evident in the rating itself. At these times the sense of "fighting the good fight" may be relevant for the patient. However, the greatest value, on self-rating, is allocated to remarks involving recognition and the sense of a step forward in the relationship with her son. This is consistent with a symbolic order of "togetherness", or social harmony with a significant other, and the sense of success in her role as mother.

There is a sense of someone who has suffered in the context of her own early relationships, and who has taken the difficult step of breaking an unsatisfactory relationship, while trying to carry on as a mother to her children. In the process there is confrontation with her *self* and tension between expectations of herself and her emotional experience of the vicissitudes of parenting. In the session she shows some capacity for self-reflection, and is able to give value to relationships with her ex-partner, her mother and her children. She has greater difficulty giving herself credit, but does so to an extent in relation to recognition of a step forward with her son and the realization of progress in relation to self-regulating behaviour (a shift from self-harm to greater other-relatedness). In all of this there is disruption by emotional states and the sense of "shutdown", followed by the effort of "mobilization". These disruptive states make it difficult to sustain a consistent sense of self, conveying the sense of a temporally "broken up" (i.e. dissociated) life. Nevertheless, there is also the sense of gradual forward progress, and a continuing struggle towards self-realization.

Vignette 2: a later session*

*The first session is taken from study data. The second and third sessions are drawn from other clinical experiences with more longitudinal contact. They create a personal situation congruent with the psychophysiological findings in Figure 5.4 (also drawn from study data). The reader is invited to imagine the sessions as involving one person.

Pt: *Inside feels so hateful to me, I don't want to be here . . . (becomes tearful)*
Th: *(pause) . . . . I sense the pain inside, deep down . . . that you're suffering . . . (therapist emotional) (pause)*
Pt: *(tearful) . . . . you know I kind of believe you. Nobody's said that to me before . . .*

This session, from a later stage of therapy, shows a brief exchange from an emotionally charged session, occurring about 30 minutes into the session. The patient had been expressing despair and frustration at the slowness of her progress. Until this point such feelings had been couched in terms of self-criticism or self-hatred (as in Vignette 1). Finally, the patient becomes tearful and sobs for some minutes. Although she has cried before in therapy, there is a different, less attenuated quality to this emotional display. The emotional intensity is such that the therapist feels a need to wait to respond. Ultimately, a comment is made which, although at one level banal, was deeply felt. There was a very strong sense of connection and this moment was one that was remembered and referred to by the patient a number of times over the following year. It seems likely that the therapist's intonation, the sound of his voice, may have been more important than the content of the comment. She said it was like the first time she had been heard. Perhaps it was also the first time she had felt safe enough with another adult to really express her vulnerability.

In an analogous session from study data, both patient and therapist rated a similar moment very highly in terms of positive experience and also in terms of frequency of ratings. It related to the expression by the patient of the vulnerable self and a responsive acceptance by the therapist of the vulnerable state. Although at one level the semantic content appears negative *('hateful')*, the sense of connection in therapy will sometimes be sufficient to make the experience a positive one. It is possible to see that in the earlier phase (Vignette 1) it is the therapist responding positively to the patient's expressions of vulnerability, while the patient remains somewhat alienated from herself. Now, in this session, the positive response to the expression of the patient's vulnerability is shared by both and made all the more moving to both parties because of this togetherness. There is a measure of growth of self.

Vignette 3 — later still

Pt: Someone said to me, it was such a great thing to say, "you can't avoid the storms . . . you have to learn to dance in the rain".
Th: Makes me think of "Singing in the Rain".
Pt: Makes me see what I have to do . . . . (silence) . . . . I don't know, I think I'm more tolerant . . . . there's a sense of space . . . . (silence) . . . . it's like there's room for everyone . . .

This session is from a late stage of therapy. This segment comes at the narrative highpoint of a session where the patient has conveyed a strong sense of agency. Her language has changed gradually over preceding months – away from the language of self-doubt and indecision. While recognizing that "storms" will still occur, there is the sense that they can now be managed. The patient is able to bring in associations found to be personally meaningful. She conveys a sense of resolve and direction. The therapist joins in by making an association, referring to a song that had come up months earlier in the therapeutic conversation. Quiet moments can be sustained in the conversation without anxiety, as indicated by a silence of about 90 seconds. The therapy ended within a few months. Occasional further contact supported the sense that the patient continued to function well, with a robust sense of self and progress in her career and relational world.

In an analogous session from study data, the therapist rated a similar moment very positively while the patient's rating, perhaps surprisingly, was neutral ("d. relaxed"). To the therapist it seemed like a moment of realization, born out by the subsequent clinical course. Possibly such a finding is consistent with a strong vagal influence associated with a relatively calm self-state. This was born out in study data by a slowing of the breath, indicating vagal up-regulation (Figure 5.4).

In terms of self, it now appears there is a greater autonomy and comfort both with togetherness and being alone. A far cry from Vignette 1. Perhaps an achievement of the state of *alone togetherness*.

Transformation of the vulnerable self

In Vignette 1, the patient says, "*I'm glad that the limbo is kind of over*". While this is a specific reference to the experience of separation, *limbo* could also be taken as a metaphor for states of disconnection. Seen in this way the comment might resonate with a journey begun but not completed. In fact, she still is quite often in states of dissociation, a kind of *limbo*. This changes over time. "*Dancing in the rain*" is a contrasting metaphor for a self that can move even in adversity. The *limbo* is not forgotten but the self is now coherent and expressive. The intermediate state of a strong sense of connection with someone who recognizes and accepts the *vulnerable self* might be seen as an important intervening episode in this progression from *limbo* to *dancing*. While both could be said to involve "dance", the

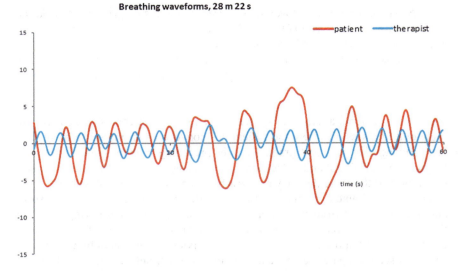

Figure 5.4 Breathing forms around period of narrative climax showing slowing and increasing amplitude of patient waveforms, possibly reflecting vagal upregulation. Therapist waveforms are on average smaller in amplitude with faster respiratory rate, relative to patient.

sense is of a contrast between a dance requiring one to deform oneself and a dance of freedom and exhilaration.

This re-application or development of an original metaphor has been described as a "moving metaphor" (Hobson, 1985). The moment of connection described in Vignette 2 speaks to a process of re-association which has followed a long period where the patient dissociated in response to expressions of vulnerability *perceived as weakness*. In Vignette 3 there is a shared referent, reflecting the development of common ground in the associative world of the therapeutic relationship. "Smooth communication" between people requires the development of such "mutually known common ground" (Tomasello, 2010).

The application of CSERS suggests repetitive links in the first session between emotional states and physiological states, reflecting various forms of autonomic regulation or dysregulation. Dissociative moments reflect a likely defensive parasympathetic response, sometimes followed by mobilizing, angry responses in relation to the "upset" of the emotional state, with a likely correspondence to sympathetic up-regulation. By Vignette 3 the patient has arrived at a state that is connected, yet calm, arguably reflecting a non-defensive, vagally up-regulated condition. These changes speak to a progression from disconnection to relative autonomy via experiences of communicative connection and exchange where both patient and therapist are affected. Even in the first session, the therapist's engagement with the emotional content of the patient's contributions to the conversation may lay the groundwork for later changes. In all of these cases the CSERS rating adds information about the relation of the internal state to the therapeutic conversation and potentially to physiological correlates.

The exchange illustrated physiologically in Vignette 3 is associated with a distinct slowing of breathing, suggesting vagal upregulation (Figure 5.4). Perhaps, following the therapist's sense of the exchange, it illustrates the human process of *realization* (Korner, 2018). Arguably, the process of recognition and acceptance of vulnerability in the earlier session and the realization that occurs later are examples of the kind of social engagement underpinned by vagal regulation described in the polyvagal theory (Porges, 2011). It may also provide demonstration of a link between the sense of significance and its objective correlate in breathing patterns.

The emergence of self

All of these sessions had a reasonably clear narrative form with development of themes, narrative climax and recapitulation of themes. The language, with shared referents, is part of a larger conversation. The earlier session refers to a self who is struggling with self-alienation while retaining motivation to *fight for* significant others. While she sees value in others, she sees herself as an object without much value. While "object consciousness" figures prominently, there is also an evident struggle to connect, even in the first session. This implies an actively striving subject ("I"), an aspect of the "becoming" of self that has been described philosophically (Hegel, 1807) and in relation to the psychoanalysis of normal development, as the so-called "forward edge" transference (Tolpin, 2002). The sense of ongoing disconnection from others in the first session impacts the patient's sense of agency. By the third session the patient is using a different sort of language with self-assertion and metaphor. There is emergence of a more coherent and confident self. In this session a more self-aware "subject consciousness" is evident (Meares, 1999; Jackson, 1931–2).

Both subject and object consciousness could be considered, in a dynamic sense, "moments" of self, remembering that self is a whole. These moments are initially outside conscious awareness. They are not things of which one can ever be completely aware. They are always present in self, reflecting self's dependence on grammatical structure: self can be an object of attention, but is also always present as subject in relation to experience. This grammatical structure is not completely language-dependent since the infant is also both object and subject in interpersonal, communicative exchange.

However, *development* of self does depend upon language and its elaboration. The grammar of subject, object and verbs describing process allows differentiation. In this sense language is different from mathematics. A "verbal equation" is not equivalent to a mathematical equation, because there is differentiation implied by occupying the position of subject or object. If one considers this in relation to the two pronouns "I" and "it", one could state two verbal equations, "it is it", and "I am I". In both cases the general sense of the clause would be that one side of the verb (subject) would refer to the "general case", while the other side (object) would refer to the particular case. Understood in this way, we can see that the declaration of "I-ness" with respect to oneself would refer to something beyond the bare "I" or "me" of subject and object. This is "myself", the area of personal growth capable, under therapeutic conditions, of continued development throughout life (Meares, 2000). Self is manifest in conversation and the expansion of that conversation through the medium of symbolic exchange constitutes therapy.

A passive experience of object consciousness occurs when we experience life happening *to* us, one is "object" of others' actions. This is often associated with the sense of external forces controlling experience. While becoming a "doer" helps the individual's sense of agency, providing a more "owned" form of object consciousness, subject consciousness is an aspect of a larger process of self, beyond specific states of consciousness: "Consciousness in its intentional, or object, mode is not self itself, but a revealing of self" (Meares, 2012: citing Jackson, 1931-32). The revealing of self may be more important therapeutically than the identification of specific states. The revealing of the *vulnerable self*, the human condition of greatest universality, may be of particular significance.

Hence the therapist empathizes with the struggle of the vulnerable self to be recognized. Later, growth in self is evident, having occurred whilst maintaining recognition of vulnerability rather than denying it. Core vulnerability, represented paradigmatically by the infant's cry and affective expression, is seen as indicative of personal value, within an embodied value system that persists throughout life. Considered in relation to the sequence of *cry* and *response* in a network of *self* and *other*, the case illustration could be described as an initial *cry* from the patient with a warm *response* to the mood signs from the therapist that goes somewhat unnoticed by the patient because of her tendency to dissociate. This is followed, in the second session, by an undissociated *cry* with a *response* from the therapist that is finally heard and felt concretely by the patient, providing an important shared emotional experience for the therapeutic dyad. One might say that the *cry of self* has found a *home* in the therapeutic relationship. Finally, in the third session the patient shows agency and there is a sense of mutuality in the exchange. One might say that *self* now feels *at home* within herself and is confident in her exchanges with others.

CSERS

Feeling operates as a continuous mode of organization within the individual and between people through the interpersonal dimension of language. It is akin to an analogue scale with continual variation and movement determined by felt experience, allowing only relatively approximate "takes", *sensed* by self, rather than being subject to precise measurement.

The scale introduced in this chapter, CSERS, allows the participant to score at any time they choose as they read a transcript, allowing freedom in the choice of descriptor. It is intended to access moments felt as significant on the continuous analogue scale of affective experience. The measures obtained are not strictly objective. They rely upon language (choosing words) for changes in feeling state. Words for feeling are not precise measures. In a linguistic sense words for feeling are "dead metaphors", which is to say we have come to accept a word such as "sadness" as an "entity", which "originally meant heaviness", a metaphor for a state of the body (Meares, 2005). CSERS is a method of externalizing the participant's own understanding of his or her experience. It is a collaborative tool, requiring the application of reflective function, rather than a means of revealing a fixed inner state. As such it has face validity in relation to study of self but does not have objective properties allowing for tests of reliability, in a scientific sense. However, CSERS does provide additional information regarding interpersonal exchanges and self-evaluations in therapeutic conversation that go beyond the information discerned from the semantic content of the transcript. It sheds light on interpersonal and intrapersonal dynamics. In linguistic terms it provides a window onto the *interpersonal metafunction* of the conversation.

CSERS does generate some measurements that *can* be considered objectively. For example, the number and timings of ratings made, can be considered an objective measure (although one which is likely to vary were ratings repeated). While this does not give direct information about self, it illustrates that people do not rate every distinct conscious state that originally occurred, as they go through the rating process. Given that states of consciousness are often very brief, it would be impossible for all of these states to be captured in a reflective process. The shortest time between ratings in this series was 3 seconds, corresponding roughly to the timing of the "present moment". The longest interval between ratings was 12 minutes, a period that extends well beyond the "present moment". The data support the idea that *shifts in self-experience that can be accessed by individuals do not occur on the very brief time scales (20–150 ms) that characterize brief conscious states*. As mentioned, such data lend face validity to the notion that self-states occur on a distinct time scale. Self-states perhaps reflect a chunk of experience relevant to the development of the personal *text* that is *self*.

The commonality between feeling and language is that both are understood to be networks of value. While language has been considered, following Saussure, to be independent of any given individual, it is clearly not independent of human beings as a collective. In an evolutionary sense, it has been suggested that the earliest forms of language relate to bodily experience and the immediate environment. The re-evaluation of emotional life as primarily an internal value system and only secondarily as relating to defence, makes it necessary to see language and affect as complementary functions when instantiated in actual lives. Forerunners of symbolic language are seen in capacities for play and the dynamism of affective experience, mediated through the ANS.

There were various examples of paradoxical ratings in this series. Some found the need to make more than one rating or use more than one descriptor for a self-state, as well as the need to use phrases rather than single words, with use of arrows or other markers of emphasis. These aspects of rating reflect the complexity of self-state and the fact that experience can't always be reduced to a particular emotion or clearly defined state. They are consistent with selves that are internally complex. At times repeated affect sequences were evident (as in the session discussed in relation to Vignette 1), reflecting the particular affect signature of an individual.

The fact that the process can still be enjoyed, as in Vignette 2, even where semantic content appears to be in a negative emotional range, might be seen as analogous to the type of pleasure that an audience experiences watching drama or tragedy, as described by Aristotle in *Poetics* (Aristotle, 1996). More important to self than the positivity or negativity of specific states, may be that the states can be expressed in a "containable" way, contributing to the development of a coherent narrative. In the second session the patient experiences the narrative climax positively despite disclosure of a vulnerable state. Self, in linguistic and psychotherapeutic terms, has been defined as a text, although one imbued with personal meaning and embodied affective qualities.

CSERS is an intersubjective methodology that is collaborative, with both parties contributing to an understanding of the interaction. While correlations with bodily state remain uncertain, it provides a means of punctuating conversational interaction, in terms of perceived significance, reflecting a particularization of the language that goes beyond its standard representational function. This may mean that it is more likely to correlate to bodily (and brain) states.

Chapter 6

Becoming who we are: personal realization

Overview

Self is not a given, yet it grows from the experience of relatedness and the seeking of attachments, organically, entwined with the rhythms of bodily existence. Living in a symbolic milieu confers great flexibility on human relatedness and the development of this *self*. The power of association and the wandering nature of individual human thought takes us to unexpected places, warranting reconsideration of the value of "primary" and "secondary" process. Thoughtful well-being is realized in communicative exchange through shared experience in situations of trust, creative play and friendship, as also found in effective therapeutic relationships. Processes of personal instantiation and recognition characterize emergent realizations. Realizations also occur in quiet spaces where a self-process has been established, as in experiences related to dreams. The forward orientation of self in time brings to mind a person who grows as a *prospective self* in a community where openness and shared experience create many personal possibilities.

Self as second nature

Language is at the heart of the human world. Whether one grows in an environment sensed to be hostile or supportive makes a big difference as far as the emergence of self is concerned. It also influences how feeling gets invested in relationships and activities. Self is a private experience although equally it grows in the public domain. Exchanges of meaning occur whether or not they are articulated at a verbal level. Given that the speech fellowship involves a symbolic network of relatedness held at the level of communities (language), the exchange of meaning must occur through primary exchanges in spoken language, vocalization and gesture involving more than one person, a matrix of "self and others". Even with the written word one recognizes a process involving more than one person.

In terms of psychotherapy process, *self* is understood as the emergence of an effective narrative voice providing the necessary analogical fit in relation to the world in order to sustain personal coherence and resonance. The private experience of self can then be represented in the public domain of interpersonal life.

As we journey through life, we are always at the forward edge of a past that is embodied within us, a past that literally "*beats within*". Through processes of memory, language and acculturation, this becomes our *second nature* (Edelman, 2006). When we consider that much attention is directed towards the future, it would also make sense to say our *expectations*, conditioned by personal worldviews and organizing principles, are carried within us and provide another *beat* in daily living. The importance of language to this bodily beat of experience is that it is a chief way of organizing self, given "we are the only species with a syntax-based language" (Edelman, 2006). Syntactic language supports "metaphor and analogical reasoning" so that "we're always planning ahead, imagining scenarios for the future, and then choosing ... in ways that take remote contingencies into account" (Calvin, 1996).

Sensorimotor sequences (relatively automatized co-ordinations involving the basal ganglia, in concert with motor, sensory and prefrontal cortices) also give us "a kind of basal syntax" related to skill acquisition and emotional intelligence (Edelman, 2006). Memory does not provide replicas of experience. Rather, "memory, which is recategorization influenced by value systems, trades off ultimate precision for **associative** power" (Edelman, 2006, p. 33, my emphasis). This evolutionary selection for **associative power** demonstrates the importance of non-linear, non-logical wanderings of the stream of consciousness to individual development. Logic and linear thought are secondary developments. *Selectional* brain processes "lay the grounds for the emergence of a self" and are involved in differentiation (Edelman, 2006). Understanding the personal value of individual selves requires elaboration of feeling, not through naming of individual affects, but rather through expression of stories that fit with personal, familial and cultural contexts.

Self prioritizes association in relational life following the principles of affective experience: maximizing positive experience, minimizing negative experience and allowing affective expression (minimizing affect inhibition). Forward orientation contributes to the sense that the growing self applies these principles prospectively.

Earlier, we considered the philosophy of Hegel, describing the journey of the individual from desire through a process of exchange with significant others, where knowledge of the environment is gained and applied, leading to a more empathic engagement realized through participation in the world, constituting the *becoming* of self. The self grows and seeks, making use of the most universal affect system, the *seeking system*. There is a link between communicative exchange in humans and the basic orientation of all living creatures to seek what allows them to thrive from the environment.

Language always operates at three levels with respect to the lived experience of significance. The most *immediate* is the level of felt experience of the exchange (what is felt at the time), the *enduring* personal aspect is that of message received (what is personally understood and taken in, becoming part of the text of *self*), and last is the level of representation as communally defined (formal semantic representation, required for the expression of personal stories). Listening and expressing are as much a part of our bodily existence as breathing in and out and are analogous to such fundamental physiological processes. They are necessary for homeostasis and growth. The elaboration of personal reality requires a flow of images, thoughts and feelings and the capacity to reflect and share that experience. Telling one's story opens up the possibility of transformation.

The power of association and its significance in social terms justifies a revision of its place in mental life. Non-linear associative processes are at least as important as logical conceptual-verbal processes. It is the coordination of these functions that reflects higher levels of adaptation.

In therapy the emergence of a coherent flow of association gives rise to the distinctiveness of each individual, allowing recognition of each person as a singularity. For some, a sense of safety in the therapeutic relationship needs to be established involving a flow of conversation between therapist and patient before it becomes possible to sustain a nourishing inner conversation. Eventually this leads to the patient sustaining a distinct personal flow of experience with a non-linear form and a diversity of life outcomes. Free association and social plurality go hand in hand.

The emergence of self reflects those aspects of being that are felt to have value. The interpersonal process that supports growth of self involves giving value to the person's experience. It involves shaping and growth. Given that many people enter therapy with lives dominated by trauma and associated vehement feelings there is a lot of work to do before this kind of flourishing can occur. Rather than being supplanted by verbal language, as had been foreshadowed by Freud, the forms of feeling at the heart of the therapeutic relationship require coordination and eventual integration enabling effective representation in a social network.

Heart to heart: the associative pathway to therapeutic growth

The relationship of language to the development of self, primarily informed in the first place by feeling, is critical to human growth in general and to psychotherapy in particular. Self-growth requires coordination of language and feeling within a social network. Such integration facilitates "the true voice of feeling" (Hobson, 1985), implying a capacity for genuine engagement in a community.

Language is constitutive of who we are as people. Play between infant and carer has a strong influence on how language is acquired and the way it becomes generative of self. It is the communicative exchanges of life that create one's sense of self and significance. When individuals enter into therapy, they embark upon an associative pathway where distinct associations form the basis of an emergent self, significantly mediated by right-hemispherically determined communication.

The role of right hemisphere and right hemispheric thinking in communication is now better understood. Where the left hemisphere deals sequentially with events and representations, looking at problems analytically and taking things apart, the right hemisphere is involved in the processing of simultaneous perception. It is essential to solving previously unencountered problems and "putting the synthetic picture of the multimedia world around us back together" (Goldberg, 2005; Meares, 2012). "Neuroscientific studies . . . now clearly indicate that right (and not left) lateralized prefrontal systems are responsible for the highest level regulation of affect and stress in the brain. They also document that in adulthood the right hemisphere continues to be dominant for affiliation, while the left supports power motivation" (Schore, 2012, p. 389). A range of research leads to the conclusion that when it comes to managing moment-to-moment engagement with life, it is the right hemisphere that should be considered "master" and left the "emissary" (McGilchrist, 2009). Functionally the left hemisphere is dominant in analytic logical atomistic thinking while the right hemisphere is dominant in associative synthetic thinking, crucial to social engagement. The importance of right-hemispheric regulation in the psychotherapeutic setting calls for re-consideration of the significance of *primary* and *secondary* process. The affective basis of associational life needs to be seen in a normative, integrative way rather than as an unruly process to be overcome by a rational ego.

The role of language in healing is crucial to talking treatments. In psychoanalytic theory, the question of whether understanding relates to agencies within the mind (as in tripartite structural theory: *id*, *ego* and *superego*) or to the whole person concept of *self* is of central importance. The role of gender has also been a concern in psychoanalytic theory, evident in the writings of Freud, Lacan, and Klein, amongst many others. However, if the primary emphasis is on self and relationship, in themselves non-gendered terms, gender may come to be seen as somewhat less critical to the development of mental life. This is not to deny the importance of gender in development. The embodied nature of self speaks to the importance of gender. However, what is considered *primary* to self in this book is personal feeling and the flow of consciousness, shaped by the environment.

In elaborating his ideas about primary and secondary process in *The Interpretation of Dreams*, Freud recognizes a difficulty:

> I have set myself a hard task, and one to which my powers of exposition are scarcely equal. Elements in this complicated whole which are in fact simultaneous can only be represented successively in my description of them, while, in putting forward each point, I must avoid appearing to anticipate the grounds on which it is based: difficulties such as these it is beyond my strength to master.
>
> (Freud, 1900, p. 745)

Although he may not have been aware of it, he could be making the distinction between synchronic language and diachronic language or between the whole and its parts. While his elaborations are in terms of interacting parts, it can be seen that there was awareness of a whole, greater than the parts. He goes on to say that "primary process" is dominated by "activity . . . . . directed towards securing the

free discharge of the quantities of excitation", while secondary process "succeeds in **inhibiting** this discharge" (ibid., p. 759, his emphasis). Inhibition is crucial to the development of secondary process and is central to the Freudian theory of repression: "it is key to the whole theory of repression: the second system can only cathect an idea if it is in a position to inhibit any development of unpleasure that may proceed from it" (ibid., p. 761).

Thus, classical psychoanalytic theory sees secondary process (logical, goal-directed, rational thought, in touch with "external reality") as an achievement that results from inhibition of the unruly, illogical, emotionally based primary process. As such, it is a form of rationalism, seeing development as the triumph of reason over passion. *Ideas* have an inherently linguistic form while the term *cathect* means to *affectively invest*. It could be argued that the process of affective investment ("cathecting") is primary in development rather than ideas, given the pre-verbal infant has limited access to the world of words, clauses and concepts that constitute ideas.

Freud's rationalist position is developed further, when he puts forward his structural theory of mind in *The Ego and the Id* (Freud, 1923). The German version refers to "*Das Ich*" and "*Das Es*", considered here in relation to the terms *I* and *it*, which seem closer to his intent. By using the Latin nouns *ego* and *id*, Strachey may have contributed to reification of these terms, making them more thing-like, relative to the original use of pronouns emphasizing the *personal* or *impersonal* nature of the process in question.

Freud states, "all perceptions . . . received from without . . . and from within – what we call sensations and feelings – are conscious from the start" (ibid., p. 18), thereby recognizing the centrality of **feeling** to conscious states. Although this is not a notion he develops, he later states, "We approach the id with analogies" (Freud, 1933), suggesting an understanding of the need to approach the representation of feeling through analogy. While he recognizes the primacy of thinking in images, he sees it as a "very incomplete form of becoming conscious . . . . unquestionably older than the latter (words) both ontogenetically and phylogenetically" (Freud, 1923). He refers to a passive experience in life where "we are 'lived' by unknown and uncontrollable forces", seeing this as the perceptual system present from the start and referring to this system as the *it*, consistent with "*whatever in our nature is impersonal*" (ibid.).

The impersonal *it* is seen as something "upon whose surface rests the 'I'" (ibid.), leading to the Freudian metaphor of the *I* being "like a man on horseback" (ibid., p. 24), with *it* being the horse. The *I* has ever "to hold in check the superior strength of the horse" (ibid.). Specifically, he states that "the ego ['I'] represents what might be called reason, and endeavours to substitute the reality principle for the pleasure principle which reigns unrestrictedly in the id" (ibid., p. 24). Reason is identified with language, known by Freud to be located in the left brain, reflecting the state of neurological knowledge at the time: "as we know . . . its speech [centre] . . . [is] on the left-hand side" (ibid.). In contrast the "scene of the activities of the lower passions is in the unconscious", the "location" of which is not known (ibid.). In the current state of understanding, feeling is seen to have a basis in deeply subcortical networks, while "The 'id' knows more than the 'ego' admits" (Solms, 2015).

In his discussion of superego and ego ideal, Freud asserts the significance of early relationships, while indicating a primary paternal influence in relation to this development: "in the origin of the ego ideal . . . . . there lies hidden an individual's first and most important identification, his identification with his father in his own personal prehistory" (ibid., p. 30). He sees social feelings as arising out of the frustration of hostile impulses and feelings, "social feelings arise in the individual . . . . built upon impulses of jealous rivalry against brothers and sisters. Since the hostility cannot be satisfied, an identification with the former rival develops" (ibid., p. 36). Social engagement is not seen as primary need, or primary instinct, in this description, but rather as a compromise formation. He does not consider that hostility may arise out of traumatic circumstances. He contends "Psycho-analysis is an instrument to enable ego ['I'] to achieve a positive conquest of the id ['it']" (ibid., p. 55), re-framed later as, "Where id was, there ego shall be" (Freud, 1933).

An alternative view is of the primary importance of social connection supported by right-hemisphere-mediated communication and subcortical networks, involving resonance and affiliation that is to be found in the earliest interactions between carer and infant (Trevarthen, 2015). The evolutionary need for care over the prolonged period of human dependency may have brought about the situation where interactions between child and carers are associated with a sense of reward not available to child or parent in isolation (Meares, 2016).

In a discussion of the relationship between language, healing and silence, the views of Hegel, Kierkegaard, Freud and Lacan are considered (Berthold, 2009). Hegel saw language as essential to development of self, referring to the "divine nature" of language (Hegel, 1807). Freud, in keeping with Hegel, argued that "the talking cure . . . puts the obscure, fermenting 'something' of insanity into words, and in this way gives a sort of clarity which, as Freud saw it, was the best that could be hoped for" (Berthold, 2009). Kierkegaard is more suspicious of words, suggesting that professors, full of fine talk should be "stripped", to see what they are really made of: "Yes to strip them of their clothing, the changes of clothing, and the disguises of language, to frisk them by ordering them to be silent, saying: 'Shut up, and let us see what your life expresses, for once let this [your life] be the speaker who says who you are" (Kierkegaard, 1967, cited in Berthold, 2009, p. 300).

Lacan, while critical of Freud in relation to his emphasis on rationality, is identified as neo-Freudian for his emphasis on the *nom du père* or " 'the symbolic', the domain of language, the key vantage point from which all other 'registers' of psychic life must be approached" (Lacan, 1966). He sees therapy as essentially a task of evoking speech, "it might be said [therapy] . . . amounts to overcoming the barrier of silence" or "to get her [the patient] to speak" (Lacan, 1964). Kierkegaard, while suspicious of language, recognizes his dependence upon it, saying he gets ill when he doesn't write (Berthold, 2009). He has a version of "talking cure", involving "indirect communication . . . designed to lead the reader to take responsibility for self-authorship – . . . a cure whose talking will be elusive, strange, and mysterious" (ibid.).

For Hegel, Freud and Lacan the development of self is seen as the development of symbolic order related to the ascendancy of language and repression of instinctual life (ibid.). Kierkegaard's version of the place of language in healing could be taken to refer to recognition of its value as a form of expression, related to Freud's *primary process* or, in the CM, related to the primary flow of conscious experience reflected in non-linear, associational thought. His reference to letting one's life "*be the speaker*" would be consistent with humans as *living symbols* occupying embodied places in communicative space that go beyond verbal language. He also contrasts the view of faith in objective knowledge expressed in Freud's work, arguing that "truth is subjectivity" (Kierkegaard, 1967). For the CM this would relate to recognition of the personal reality of the patient taking precedence in the therapeutic setting.

Rather than seeing language as the instrument for attainment of an order that is imposed upon life, it may be more relevant to understand *language as lived* being *constitutive* of human lives (Taylor, 2016). One might speak of a level of symbolic order that refers to an integration of internal, affective value systems with language, reflecting a less abstract concept than the symbolic order implied in the work of Freud and Lacan, where language is seen to be involved in conquest of emotional forces.

The recognition of the value of silence is also crucial to the notion of a space where self can grow. One might recall the patient discussed in the previous chapter where it was noted that there was a sense of the creation of personal space in the later session. There was a significant amount of silence and reflective space with a moment of personal realization. In such moments, arguably, *I* differentiates and self becomes. There was emergence of a more poetic, universal tone and a peaceful silence: "*you can't avoid the storms . . . you have to learn to dance in the rain . . . there's a sense of space . . . . (silence) . . . . it's like there's room for everyone*". In becoming who one truly is, quiet "alone" space is as necessary as shared space.

Mothers and fathers have always figured prominently in psycho-analytic theorizing, with good reason given that they are primary players in the developmental process for any given individual. Benjamin, writing from an intersubjective perspective, highlights the significance of the relationship with mother in shaping development (Benjamin, 2004) as have countless psychodynamic writers. Her interest is in elaborating development of the self beyond the experience of "doer and done to", focussing on the importance of mother-infant engagement through what she calls the *moral third*: a relationship based upon recognition of the vulnerability of the other that motivates care. She contrasts her position with Lacan's: "Unfortunately Lacan's oedipal view equated the third with the father, contending that the father's 'no', his prohibition or 'castration', constitutes the symbolic third" (ibid.). Her description of the development of the *third* relates more to processes of resonance and empathy, whilst still incorporating limit-setting arising out of care. This is a version of personal development not relying upon prohibition and inhibition but rather seeing growth as an outcome of resonance and playful interaction.

Inevitably, when either "mother" or "father" are emphasized, theories become polarized or characterized as having a maternal or paternal bias. There is an advantage to seeing that what is being described is personal process, taking place in relationship. The "passions" represented by the horse in Freud's metaphor of "rider and horse", for related parts of the mind (ego/id; I/it), devalue feeling as being of a lower order than the reasoning faculty of the mind, the "ego/I". The metaphor is about learning to tame or at least exert influence over the dangerous, beast-like passions, naturally inclined towards aggression, competition and hostility. Language, as the tool of reason, is seen by Freud to be embedded in the left cerebral hemisphere, suggesting that the processing of the logical left hemisphere needs to inhibit and control the emotional right hemisphere. In this view, dominated by drives and the theory of repression, it is little wonder that expressions of disagreement and failures to respond to the analyst's expressed understandings are classed as "negative therapeutic reactions" or "resistance". After all this would simply reflect natural hostility to superior reason. Indeed, Freud says, "We tell him that he is dominated by a resistance" (Freud, 1923).

Other theorists have come to see the situation differently. In working with patients that displayed negative therapeutic reactions, Brandchaft comments that,

> I believe that observation is being obscured in psychoanalysis by continuing to regard primary factors as defensive or secondary, while secondary factors are installed as primary. The primary factors in these patients proved to be the particular self disorder emerging from the transference in the forms of archaic, intensified, distorted longings, now out of phase, which originally should have formed the basis of sound psychological structure. . . . . The factors that proved to be secondary in these cases were drives; conflicts . . . castrations; separation; and superego anxieties.
> (Brandchaft, 1983, p. 348)

The emphasis is on the need to see the legitimacy of the patient's position and the value of self. The therapist is required to help understand the patient's position, not to provide correction.

We currently recognize that early development is informed by patterns of feeling, with affect regulation achieved through dyadic care and play. Such activity is modulated through right hemispheric influence, involving inhibition by the right orbito-frontal cortex of right-sided limbic and mid-brain structures (Schore, 2012; Panksepp & Biven, 2012) associated with effective regulation of affective experience, in relationship to significant others. The left hemisphere can also exert an influence on affect but is less effective in doing so. When the left-brain attempts to exert control through "'verbal', 'logical' and 'analytical'" functions, with deficient right hemispheric modulation, the left brain may tend to "overpower" the right brain (Doidge, 2007). This gives rise to a dissociated, traumatic form of consciousness, rather than to an integrated experience of self.

Social engagement and the need for relationship are *primary* motivators, utilizing feeling as an internal value system in relationship to self and other. Language can be affectively invested through playful and imaginative engagement. Indeed, without affective investment language is empty and lacking in conviction. Many features of language arise from contributions of the right hemisphere, particularly in relation to motivation, affective expression and prosody.

The id or *it* takes on a different value, when seen to include the *affective heart* of experience. Far from being "impersonal", it is felt to be highly personal, while at the same time being an aspect of experience *shareable* with others, where similarity ("fellow feeling") is sensed. A functional understanding of brain and mind needs to include the *sharing* of experience in relationship (Siegel, 2015). Feeling is a critical bridge to communicative understanding, although there is also always an element to feeling that is beyond description and can't be fully communicated (Williams, 2019). The process of therapy involves the effort towards sharing whilst respecting the limits of the process.

Patients are likely to experience a challenge in finding "The words to say it" (Cardinal, 1984). Cardinal refers to finding the courage to express what is heartfelt. The neutral form of pronouns ("it"; "one") may have the interpersonal value, in psychotherapy, of allowing difficult matters to be talked about, without the sense of *pointing* often inherent in the use of personal pronouns. Rather than representing something impersonal or "beast-like" that needs to be tamed or mastered, the affective heart of a person is a central motivator that can be harnessed creatively and is, indeed, the basis of creativity for any individual. Imagery is also to be understood as central to personal process and thought. It is not an inferior or primitive aspect of thought. Experienced therapists will be familiar with the evocative power of shared images.

When we speak of *self*, we speak of the whole, alluded to in pronominal language. It is a process which includes but is greater than "I" and "me". It is a singularity defined through the personal inscription of feeling, not the generic inscription of conceptual language. Linguistic analysis of healthy people expressing their experience tends to show alternation between *I* and *other* perspectives, reflected in the use of pronouns (Pennebaker, 2011). This suggests that the capacity for conversation, initially reliant upon the *actual* other, is carried on within the inner stream of thought. Where trauma has significantly constricted this capacity, there is a need for facilitation of an effective voice of self through the therapeutic conversation.

The communicative response of self, both external and internal, is understood as a coordination of language and feeling, not a subjugation of feeling. In traumatic circumstances the nuanced responsiveness of social connection is lost. The individual is subject to domination or neglect giving rise to constrictions and dissociations in consciousness that limit development of self, understood as an unfolding process with inherent value. Trauma leads to failures in maturation and delays in the realization of self. "A **mature self**, when it emerges, is a generator of bodily space and time, in the first place for the person's own self and then, with further development, becoming a generator of the kind of **space for others** that **engenders players** in the human world" (McLean & Korner, 2013, p. 7). The personal nature of feeling and imagery, involvement in conversations (in words **and** images) with others and within ourselves, constitutes what is significant in human lives. While based in personal experience, it can be seen as transcending the personal, part of a chain of continuity with past and future generations.

'Ascending to the concrete': knowing from the inside

The growth of self might be thought of in relation to a growth in *worldview*. There is a sense of growth in the breadth and depth of vision. A strictly objective view misses what goes on internally within the mind, often involving experiences such as dreams or moments of picturing and imagining in waking life. In these experiences there is a relationship to external reality that is felt concretely and sometimes associated with a sense of self-enhancement that isn't accessible to objective measurement. Philosophically, there is an argument that the data of experience goes beyond that simply derived directly from the senses (*empiricism*), rather including the sense of meaning and relationship that is integrated within individual minds (*radical empiricism*) (James, 1890). While all experience can be said to hold meaning, much of it passes by in the stream of consciousness as unconscious or at least un-noticed content. Moments that capture the attention and are felt distinctly take on a particular significance for the individual. They may become an important element in personal narrative, motivating in terms of larger life goals and purposes. They reflect the highly individual and somewhat mysterious process of affective investment within the stream of associative thought.

Such moments may take on major significance in a person's life or they may be smaller chunks of experience that enrich *self*. It is the ascension to the level of distinct feeling of the experience as *mine* that gives it the sense of concreteness. In the last chapter the patient who has the sense of "*see*(ing) *what I have to do*" could be seen in this way. The dreams described in this section are seen to have been important influences on the worldviews of the dreamers that can be plausibly related to the course of their life and work.

In the first example, Judy Atkinson, who has mixed Indigenous Australian (Jiman/Bandjalung) descent as well as German-Celtic forbears, writes of a dream where she was visited by her "great-grannie". They sat in a circle with other relatives.

> *We began to talk. I was so happy to see them but I could feel a great sadness around them and in them. I went into their sadness and suddenly – suddenly,*

we were in another time and another place, and we were running, running in terror through the bush, running in terror from the thundering horses and the guns of the white men.

The dream was of a massacre including the killing of children. The women began their grieving for their children. Rain came in cloudbursts, eventually

cleansing us and cleansing the trampled and defiled earth. After the rain came the stillness, the silence . . . listening to the silence in the stillness brought seeds of awareness and then a Deep Knowing – Spirit to Spirit. We are women. With that knowledge came new life and movement. . . . We danced a women's dance of birth and re-birth, of life healing, of re-generation, of re-creation. My great-grannie gave me a gift – she taught me. We are women, We have creation powers, We are the Creators of the Future.

(Atkinson, 2002, pp. 2–3)

Although the content of the dream is disturbing it is also associated with "Deep Knowing" and informs Atkinson's life work of healing for those in Indigenous and other communities within Australia who have suffered trauma. Her way of working has resonances with the Indigenous tradition of *dadirri* ("deep listening") and with evocative processes, as illustrated in a group she ran (which I attended). A Cambodian woman told the traumatic story of her escape from oppression and abuse and her journey to a new land. Everyone was moved by the pain and courage of this young woman, even though the woman herself felt unhappy and unlovely. Judy responded with a song that she encouraged everyone to sing:

How could anyone ever say you are anything less than beautiful,
How could anyone ever say you are less than whole,
Don't you know that your love is a miracle,
That connects you deeply to my soul.

In this way of working there is an emphasis on fostering a strong feeling of connection, amplified by the participation of the group. It works with feeling as ally of the healing process.

The second example is a dream described by Martin Buber, a dream that kept recurring throughout his life in various forms. He is in a "primitive world, meagrely equipped". The dream begins with some frantic terrible event like having an arm torn off by an animal. Then the pace abates and "I stand there and cry out". It can be a cry of joy or pain or both although there is a certain rhythm, a rise and fall that is always present. It swells to a fullness that couldn't be endured when awake and the cry becomes a song (Buber, 1947).

When it ends my heart stops beating. But then, somewhere, far away, another cry moves towards me, another which is the same, the same cry uttered or sung by another voice. Yet it is not the same cry, certainly no "echo" of my cry but rather its true rejoinder, tone for tone not repeating mine, not even in a weakened form, but corresponding to mine, answering its tones . . . [He then has the sense that] *Now it has happened.*

(ibid., pp. 1–3)

This call of the other to which we find a response that is not a repetition but a *true rejoinder* is what underlies the *I-thou* philosophy of Buber and what defines the truly human response. This kind of dreaming is a source of knowledge that goes beyond the facts of the world. It is a key element in Buber's life work.

Lives are composed of many more modest experiences than these two dreams. Yet day-to-day experiences that are felt concretely also serve to thicken the texture of lives. Two illustrations from waking life make the point. Both are first person accounts, the first by someone recalling a joyful childhood moment.

I'm not really one for casting my line into the past, but I do have one small memory that often springs to mind. As fleeting and seemingly insignificant as it may seem I remember it vividly. I was around ten years old and was in the company of my best friend. We had just come out of his house and we were both lazing effortlessly down the side of a long sweeping stairway handrail. Orange sunlight filled the air through some large windows (unusually for Scotland), it was warm, it was calm, we were both in unison, both at peace, all was good in the world. We had no worries, no fears, just joy and fulfilment. We looked at each other and grinned. We were boisterous boys and this was an unusually quiet moment for us, locked in time and in memory forever. Poignantly, for me anyway, was the fact that at that very moment I knew I would retain the memory for ever, I clearly remember thinking this out loud. It sometimes puzzles me how such an ordinary occurrence could register significance with me at such an early age.

As the author states, it's an "ordinary occurrence". Yet it has a concreteness in his experience that involved an experience of knowing, even as a child, that this would stay *in memory for ever*.

In the second illustration a moment occurs for an adult experiencing an image that stands out in the mind:

I was sitting outside on the deck. There had been a family gathering at which one of my sons had been absent. I sat looking at some succulent plants and cacti that had been a gift from him. After a few seconds I had the experience of seeing the central plant, a small but tall spiky cactus, as representing my son. The sense I had was of knowing something more about him. There were many associations that no doubt contributed to the moment. This plant that was hardy and able to grow in all sorts of difficult conditions. That wanted to grow. That was quite different to me but that could stand alone. That had a

> *certain radiance in that moment. I had an appreciation of him that filled his absence at the table.*

These waking moments might be thought of as *perchings* in the associative stream of consciousness (James, 1890). These moments, characterized as experiences of *ascending to the concrete*, can also be seen in the course of psychotherapeutic conversation.

"Given" and "new" as process in psychotherapy: instantiation, recognition and realization

Finding our way in a world where lives are full of an uncertainty that isn't alleviated by known facts presents everyone with a challenge. Finding oneself involves communicative exchange with many others. For some the security of a therapeutic relationship provides a space where a conversation can be developed over time in exchanges with the therapist that, in good enough circumstances, constitutes a spiral of growth.

The structure of a conversation was described in Chapter 4 in terms of *given* and *new*, when viewed from the listener's perspective; or as *theme* and *rheme*, from the speaker's perspective. This is to say that a conversation proceeds on the basis of exchange: there is something *given* and then responded to with an additional *new* piece of information. From the speaker's point of view there is a topic or "theme" introduced and then development of the topic, the "rheme".

In this section, a selection of clauses from a session of therapy is presented as an illustration of this spiral growth in meaning. The selection is made on the basis of perceived significance, without it being possible to analyse or explain in detail, why the particular selection was made. This process has been termed *motivated selection* (Butt et al., 2012) and is partly conscious and partly unconscious. It is also typical of conversational responses more generally. The style of analysis here is not objective clausal analysis. Rather the *motivated selections* used are discussed through reflective consideration of the transcript, an *impressionistic analysis* likely to be closer to what psychotherapists actually do during a session, where the therapist is always in the position of *participant* as well as observer.

This is in keeping with the notion of *information units* where the boundaries of the units are marked by emphasis and the affective qualities of the communication (Halliday & Matthiessen, 2004). In therapy, responses are made with a degree of self-awareness, without time and space for detailed objective analysis of every word or clause. However, it should be noted that the selections are actual utterances from the session, rather than a remembered account. The selection is discussed with regard to the process of change in psychotherapy, in terms of the minute particulars of conversational exchange (Hobson, 1985; Meares, 2005).

The detailed selection is from the first half of a therapy session. Exchanges are numbered into 14 groupings corresponding to narrative units, as described earlier. Some of the longer units have been abbreviated and some of the units are brief (3,

4 and 8), largely represented in the selected quotes. The emphasis here is on the process of *given* and *new*, as a model for exchange and personal growth in psychotherapy. Growth relates to the culminative nature of the development of self as living text. Self becomes increasingly defined and specified over time.

Clause selection in narrative unit groupings with commentary

1 Pt: Can't the institute provide you with any more?
  Th: Well, there's . . . . . .
  . . . .
  Pt: But you just haven't figured it out yet . . . . . .

Comment: This is a selection from a longer unit, constituting about 5 minutes. The patient's opening comment relates to her sense that the therapist should be better equipped by the parent organization. The exchange is notable for the therapist not showing mastery as they discuss technical matters relating to recording the session, with the sense that the patient knows rather more than the therapist. In response to what is given, the therapist is happy to reveal his lack of knowledge.

2 Pt: I take it all back. Tell you what, it's like dressing, dressing – like you actually have to present, it's hard work.
  Th: You have never, sort of – I always get the sense, but I'm not sure if I'm right, but I always get the sense that you never really enjoy the girlie things?
  Pt: No, that's not true.
  Th: OK. Well I'm glad I raised it.
  Pt: Sorry?
  Th: I said boy am I glad that I raised it.
  Pt: (Laugh) Um.
  Th: So, I can get that sorted out.
  Pt: Well. It's not true and it's true. It's – I . . . once about 10 years ago, asked my friend G, why she thought I was incapable of actually living in a reasonably tidy, clean, organized flat. Because she came over one day and it looked something in Kabul and um, and there are other things too.
  Th: Hmm-mm
  Pt: And, after so much prompting, 'cause she really didn't want to saying anything hurtful or could be interpreted the wrong way. She, she said that she felt that it was as if I'd missed out on the feminine input.
  Th: Right, so she was approaching it from a –

Comment: As is usually the case, spoken language tends to be somewhat agrammatical as evident in this and other narrative units throughout this session. The patient establishes the theme for this session by referring to "*dressing*" as "*hard work*". This *given* reflects a common referent, in that the therapist knows what is being referred to relates to matters discussed before, the effort of getting prepared to "look the part". The therapist's response is to introduce an association that goes beyond what is expected, wondering out loud whether the patient "*never really enjoyed the girlie things*" (a *new* to the patient's *given*). This meets with denial by the patient ("*No, that's not true*"). Rather than confront the denial, the therapist uses humour, again surprising the patient who double checks what has been said ("*Sorry?*"). Surprise suggests that the response is experienced again as something *new*, in an affective sense, for the patient. Eventually the patient comes around to conceding that there is some truth to what the therapist is saying . . . "*it's not true and it's true*". Others have noted that, "*I'd missed out on the feminine input*". She is giving an **instantiation** from her life of the validity of the therapist's speculation. The theme has been transformed from a relatively offhand comment into a matter of significance in the life of the patient.

3 Pt: Which is interesting because it was, it was my mother, as you know, was totally neurotic.
  Th: But I'm not sure I understand what that means in the . . .
  Pt: The feminine input?
  Th: Well, yeah, in terms of the context we're talking about!
  Pt: Well I think, well, oh sorry you mean girlie?
  Th: Girlie, feminine.
  Pt: I think she was still talking about a sort of softness –
  Th: Do you feel any twinge of sadness as you're saying, as you're saying that?
  Pt: Yeah, it's very sad.

Comment: The patient redefines the theme (one could say there's a development or rheme), making it more personal and specific – about her relationship with her mother. The therapist, rather than interpreting or attempting to show specific understanding of the situation, undercuts the patient's comment (perhaps again surprising her a little) by saying . . . "*I'm not sure I understand what that means*". Now the patient confirms that the therapist's earlier comment had been apposite ("*oh sorry you mean girlie*"). There is an implicit indication that the therapist has **recognized** something important to the patient. She uses an evocative phrase to capture that what has been lacking has a certain quality, "*a sort of softness*" that suggests tenderness and intimacy. Her "lack" has emotional weight, recognized by the therapist, "*Do you feel a twinge of sadness . . .*" and confirmed by the patient, "*Yes, it's very sad*". There is a deepening of the affective engagement.

4 Pt: I didn't quite know what she meant, but it wasn't, it wasn't like completely foreign concept –
  Th: Hmm
  Pt: I mean, I knew there's something, When um, when I'm with the, the little girls, it's taken me quite a few – I – I, find that, it's taken me quite a while to sort of get into the girlie thing then.
  Th: Hmm. Hmm.

Comment: There is a further development of the theme by the patient, demonstrating how, in the affective realm, things are often "partially true" or "relatively lacking" when she says, "*it wasn't like completely foreign concept*". She refers to a gradual process of **realization**, "*it's taken me quite a while to sort of get into the girlie thing then.*" The therapist's responses are minimal but enough to show solidarity with the patient. The narrative is growing in complexity.

5 Pt: But I do now. And more importantly.
  Th: Hmm.
  Pt: The other day when I brought my new bra, I brought a very girlie one.
  Th: Um, is there some suggestion then that sort of like, joining them in that sort of playful dimension.
  Pt: The children.
  Th: The children.
  Pt: Mm
  Th: Is also kind of helping you in some way?
      . . . .
  Pt: Yeah, but it's any play with children has always helped me.
  Th: Mm. It's kind of fan- . . . lovely, isn't it?
      . . . .

Comment: The patient takes ownership of the situation, "*I do now*". She confidently asserts her femininity in a playful way, "*when I brought my new bra, I brought a very girlie one*". The therapist makes a link with the children and play and both agree upon the importance of play, and the helpfulness to the adult of engaging with children in this way, "*any play with children has always helped me*". There is *mutual* **recognition** here and also the recognition that asymmetric relationships (adult-child) can be rewarding to both parties (perhaps paralleled in the therapeutic relationship). The specificity of the purchase of the bra is another example of **instantiation** in the patient's life relating to emotional investment in a recent experience.

6 Pt: . . . I said before, you know R and, and the afternoon tea parties.
      There follows an exchange which provides examples of relationships with children that been important for the patient – a source of joy and also of learning about people through participation in relationships.

Comment: While not represented in detail, there is further instantiation in relation to more relationships and specific experiences that have the effect of enriching the complexity of the narrative even though, taken in isolation, some of the events may seem trivial ("*the afternoon tea parties*").

7 Pt: She's quite – because she used to be absolutely adore me. Now I (pause) she gets irritating things . . . I think she's incredibly sensitive and she'll

take her father . . . suffering from depression . . . And they also recently split the property so it's been extremely fraught . . .
There follows an exchange which shows empathy for the life difficulties faced by some of the people she's been involved with.

Comment: This narrative unit begins with a strong statement about feeling loved in a relationship with one of the children she has cared for, "*she used to be absolutely adore me*". This seems to indicate self-recognition as someone who can be loved and feel close to another – a **realization** helped through the asymmetry of the adult-child relationship. She goes on to elaborate her feelings of empathy for others – perhaps reflecting a capacity that has grown, given the sense of emotional deficit that characterized the patient's early life.

8 Pt: *Hm. And the other child I'm very girlie with is V's youngest . . . she's got four children, three girls . . . . . the youngest is 5 and she's very girlie . . . everything's like fairies or princesses – I mean I . . . doll or nothing but I don't really, hmm (long pause 30 secs)*

(directly followed by (9) below)

Comment: The patient gives a more specific iteration of the theme, defining "*girlieness*" in relation to her engagement with children. This passage has been counted as a narrative unit even though the therapist says nothing. The long pause is affectively significant and marks a transition for the patient. Sometimes the restraint of the therapist in not responding verbally (while being present emotionally) constitutes an important form of "staying with the moment" with elements of non-verbal exchange.

9 Pt: *Why do you say that I'm not girlie?*
Th: *Did I say you weren't girlie?*
Pt: *What did you say?*
Th: *Kind of lost track as well.*
Pt: *You said I get the sense that you weren't very girlie.*
Th: *Yeah, something like that. It's more like a sense like um because last week we were talking about your girlie attributes and you were comfortable and proud of them.*
Pt: *Yeah.*
Th: *So, it's not as if kind of like there was a tomboyishness or you know some kind of discomfort.*
Pt: *Well I certainly was a tomboy when I was younger when I was little.*
Th: *Yeah. Yeah. But I just got the sense that sort of like, you know maybe girlishness wasn't quite the right sort of . . .*
Pt: *Yeah, I don't think it was encouraged because the thing is that my role model for it was such a disconnected sort of role model.*

156 Becoming who we are

Comment: The theme is recapitulated, now in the form of a direct challenge, "*Why did you say that I am not girlie?*". It reflects a patient feeling emotionally safe-enough to address the therapist in this way. The therapist's response is playful, "*Did I say you weren't girlie?*". For both parties this exchange is best understood as approaching something serious through play. Rather than try to reconstruct a correct version of the conversation, the therapist aligns with the patient, saying "*Yeah something like that*". There's a playful paradoxical exchange around tomboyishness and the therapist shows the uncertainty and the approximate nature of the understanding, "*I just got the sense that sort of like, you know maybe girlishness wasn't quite the right sort of . . .*". This leaves the patient the prerogative of making a more definitive statement, " '*I don't think it was encouraged because the thing is that my role model for it was such a disconnected sort of role model*". The conversation remains on the agenda of the patient. We see a playful negotiation of meaning in response to a challenge.

10 Th: *Yeah, I was going to say I think it's more than girlishness . . . or girliness I should say, it's almost like you missed out on a whole lot of stuff.*
    Pt: *That's what my friend G said when that I missed out on the feminine input.*
    Th: *Yeah, yeah. Now you've really had to kind of like work your own way through the morass of relationships, all the complex relationships with other females, with other men and some the – almost like I don't know if this is a fair way of putting it but I'm just wondering whether we could say something like not having had a lot of input from mother made negotiating the subjects of some relationships with older – other women as an adult quite fraught at times.*
    Pt: *Maybe, mm*
    Th: *It's almost like there wasn't a lot of education whatever the hell that means.*
    Pt: *No.*
    Th: *The knowledge, you know, imparted from mum.*

Comment: This narrative starts with something *given* by the therapist rather than the patient, although it represents a development of the patient's theme, rather than introduction of a new theme. It involves a feeling-based empathic representation. The comment, "*I was going to say I think it's **more** than girlishness . . .*" respects the fact that the person and her narrative is always *more* than we can glimpse at any given moment. When the therapist comments, "*it's almost like you missed out on a whole lot of stuff*", emotional **recognition** is represented, going on to enrich this recognition with reference to how the patient has "*really had to kind of like work your own way through the morass of relationships*". There is a move from the more abstract "*not having a lot of input from mother made negotiating the subjects of some relationships with older – other women*" to the more concise, "*almost like there wasn't a lot of education*" (with the self-deprecating qualifier, "*whatever the hell that means*") and finally to something more concrete, one might say *ascending to the concrete* with the comment, "*The knowledge, you know, imparted from mum*".

11 Pt: *I mean she was constantly imparting knowledge that you know – asinine crap basically. She's bloody cheap. I mean she's not like she listens to talkback radio or anything like that. But she – she's not big on thinking herself with it. Like she'd be completely swayed by one argument and – not that I'm saying I wouldn't – have . . . . but she'll go in like . . .*
Th: *Can we imagine what that was about? I mean I get a sense that mum may have been taking care of some of her feelings or anxieties or something.*
Pt: *When?*
Th: *When she was kind of like with you shutting down.*
Pt: *She's shut – she's all the time.*
Th: *It's all the time?*
Pt: *Yeah.*
Th: *I'm just trying to imagine that's got to be a terrible experience.*
Pt: *For her?*
Th: *No, for you! To be you know, in a relationship with a mother who is chronically shut down.*
Pt: *Yeah it was awful.*

Comment: The patient gives voice to strong feelings illustrating the extent of the problem with which the therapist had resonated in the preceding passage. This suggest that the therapist's intervention was effective – there is an expansion of the theme, with voice being given to difficult emotions in a safe way. Rather than joining in with criticism of the mother, the therapist appeals to the imagination and the possibility of a mother struggling to "(take) *care of her feelings or anxieties or something*". The subsequent question suggests the patient is a little surprised. The severity of the situation is now clearly characterized in terms of the metaphor to shut down, "*She's shut – she's all the time*". The therapist recognizes the dire nature of this for the daughter, giving voice to the reality of her experience.

12 Th: *You know when you say that it's almost like you become slightly detached from yourself.*
Pt: *Well I have (Th: yeah, yeah) Because I don't sit still. Don't want. Don't know how to deal with it. (Th: Yeah) And I think for many, many years I was still angry and – so what's that did for me for . . . completely paranoid around it. You know anything I did made . . . her jumpy and I was . . . . and she just fights back in kind. And occasionally loses her temper and says awful things you know, you're a bitch.*
Th: *I guess as you were saying that, I was acutely aware of the absence of any warmth or caring or compassion. Any softness.*

Pt: Mm
Th: I mean I don't know whether the word "brutal" is too strong a word . . .
Pt: I think she was. I don't think she is now. (Th: Hmm) Only because she's older and not as . . . But I mean I can remember – I think a long time ago that I ran into that friend of hers you know of 10 years ago . . . . . . she said how's your mother and I said well you know. I only had a certain sort of relationship with my mother and she sort of realized that . . . she clicked and she said, "oh, it's impossible to have an intimate relationship with your mother".
Th: Yeah yeah yeah. Tell me how that would have felt hearing that for the first time?

Comment: The therapist makes a significant transition, bringing the conversation, that had been somewhat focused on the past, very much into the present, "*You know when you say that it's almost like you become slightly detached from yourself*". This meets with a confirming response by the patient, highlighting this detachment as present reality, "*Well, I have*". Past conflicts are talked about with present feeling. The therapist's response draws upon the patient's language from earlier in the session (a non-linear association) with the reference to the lack of *softness*. The therapist's use of a strong affective word, *brutal*, elicits a warmer response by the patient towards the mother, leading her to recall an earlier referent in the conversation (the friend who said, "*oh, it's impossible to have an intimate relationship with your mother*"). One can sense, even in this single session, the building of common referents, the creation of a language singular to the therapeutic relationship. The therapist frequently responds with "*yeah*", seemingly a recurrent affirmation and encouragement of the patient. The difficult experience of dissociation has been approached without it being seen as unusual or defensive.

13 Pt: Well when I heard it from her, the truth is I don't think I understood what an intimate relationship was . . . . Now . . . as I said, it was about in fact it would have been before my father died. So, we're talking 12, 13 years ago?
Th: Yeah. Yeah.
Pt: Yeah. So I don't think I – I . . . or something I don't know I suppose maybe I do now.
Th: Well that's interesting to speculate. Because my sense is you know in terms of when . . .
Pt: Open a door . . . go on.
Th: My sense is that you do get it now and that saddens you.
Pt: It's the lack of –
Th: The intimate relationship.
Pt: Well –
Th: And it's almost like you're learning how to cope with the lack of that intimate relationship.

Pt: Yes.
Th: *Instead of – and what I noticed is that –*

Comment: The patient begins with a very direct recapitulation of the main theme of the session, saying, "*the truth is I don't think I understood what an intimate relationship was*". She also acknowledges, in response to the therapist's encouragement that "*I suppose maybe I do now*". The therapist makes an indeterminate comment (*'interesting to speculate'*) which arouses interest in the patient. Her comment, "*Open a door . . . go on*", speaks to a relationship with the therapist in stark contrast to the *shut* quality of the relationship with her mother. In therapy feelings and the tender emotions can be recognized. This affirmation (*Open a door*) by the patient has a playful quality where she looks forward to what will happen next. There is a sense of movement towards a future, "*you're learning how to cope with the lack of that intimate relationship*".

14 Pt: *And not only learning but also – but learning but managing it.*

Comment: To round out the discussion of the narrative units that have been represented, the patient makes another statement alluding to an awareness of herself as *more* than just her deficit or her capacity to learn, she's "*not only learning but also – but learning but managing it*". This seems like a realistic kind of self-assertion.

There isn't space to detail the remainder of the session but it certainly didn't stop here. There is an expansion of the representation of her experience with mother. Additional referents come into the lexicon of this particular therapeutic relationship (the word *imperious* becomes notable, as something played with by both therapist and patient, referring to an aspect of character that is not only a flaw and a compensation but also a strength and a form of coping. *Discombobulates* is another referent adopted as a descriptor of emotional complexity). We hear of the realization of intimacy in current relationships. The patient conveys a sense of growth in tolerance and recalls her old "intolerant" self. She now sees herself as someone who could "*put myself on the line*", although the question is left open, *will she*? The therapist recognizes the progress that has been made and the patient recognizes the compassion that has been felt from the beginning of the therapeutic relationship.

Overall there is a sense of *communicative exchange* with a growth of feeling and value as the session progresses. This value is built upon a language which constitutes a common ground for *this* therapeutic dyad and which has been built over some substantial period of time. We can see the addition of new referents to this relationship, even within this session – phrases and metaphors that become part of the synchronic dimension of therapeutic language from which personal messages are acquired and a growing, spiralling sense of self is realized. The personal instantiation of self, the recognition of the other and the *new* elements of self, coming from the response of the therapist ('other') to the patient's *given* might be seen as central to the process of psychotherapy.

The prospective self

Personal stories develop in relationship and in communities. For self, a story is better than no story. Even a rudimentary, bare *script* is at least something. While in such a life there is little sense of continuity, there is at least a form of organization, a faint ember of life. A limited, convention-bound story (*chronicle*) can sustain life, albeit of a limited kind with a constricted sense of self. A developed self has the sense of her place in the world, being a protagonist in the action of life. There is a capacity to dream of many possible adventures and to bring what is imagined to a degree of realization, negotiating external constraints in the process. Not only that, there is also a capacity to share experience. This is the sense of a narrative self. Even so, life is still coloured by stories of trauma and loss.

The situation referred to as *no story* in Chapter 4 is the place of horror and alienation, instinctively feared. We shy away from this level of experience, *not wanting to know*. It is outside the social realm. One's response is akin to the message, inscribed on the gate to hell in *Inferno*: "Surrender as you enter every hope you have" (Alighieri, c. 1310). In Sartre's existential version, hell is the place of "*no exit*" (Sartre, 1958). The "city" of Hell in *Inferno*, is "*Dis*" where inhabitants are tortured by the "confusion of tongues .... denying all possibility of clear communication or thought" (Kirkpatrick, 2006). Horror or "hell" in the western literary canon relates to being denied the possibility of connection through language.

Trauma throws the person off balance into helpless or reactive states, limiting the development of personal narrative. Emotional balance is attained, in the first place, in early dyadic interaction. Balance occurs through affective and gestural exchange, in the proto-conversation. The loss of communicative connection, as referred to in the vision of "*Dis*", also occurs in this pre-verbal domain. Balanced *mental* life depends on communicative exchange throughout life. It has been suggested that the capacity for myth-making and story-telling, that is, for leading shared lives that are both actual and symbolic, has been revolutionary for humankind in terms of evolutionary significance (Harari, 2011).

Individual maintenance of balance through openness is highly valued in some communities. *Nungurrayi*, a *Kukatja* elder, comments on a young man in her tribe: "He is good dreamer; he is open" (Poirier, 2003, p. 111). For the *Kukatja* people, the spirit or *kurrunnpa* reflects balance between the seat of emotions or *tjurni* sensed in the abdominal area. *Kulila*, the organ of thought, is sensed as inside the head (ibid.). Perhaps *tjurni* reflects, to some extent, what is referred to, in English, as "gut feeling". For aboriginal people thought doesn't occur in isolation: "the mind .... stands in relation to whatever is acquired through listening to other people or stories; and second, through the tjurni, the seat of emotion, from which the kurrunnpa departs for dream experiences" (ibid., pp. 111–112). Balance is attained through the sharing of personal worlds, a collaborative belonging to the *mob*. This is an important aspect of what Australian Indigenous people mean by *The Dreaming*: "dreams as human action in the world, and as social process – is more valued than actual dream contents, or dreams simply as objects" (ibid.). Expressing personal experience, that which comes from within, may be more important to the economy of self than language that conforms to stereotypic public expectations.

Given that lives unfold into the future, the ongoing *balance* the individual strives for, is between the personally felt patterns, or *"feeling-toned complexes"*, of immediate individual experience and the received patterns of meaning from the community of fellows, the "archetypes" of the "collective unconscious" (Jung, 1934). Realization of stories requires engagement with others. There are more possibilities for realization where there is openness and collaboration, as opposed to isolation. Collective influences will draw the individual in a multiplicity of directions. Paths of opportunity, transgression and adventure may be more alive, for many than paths of convention and repetition. Life is carried on while the person is uncertain of her destination, or the ultimate form that her story will take. Each self is **prospective**, an emerging, embodied text with narrative form.

Openness is what characterizes the sense of flow in relational settings. This requires a balance between conceptual and affective expression. A dry recitation of events or facts, where intellectual or conceptual expression dominate, tends to be boring, lacking vitality. On the other hand, communication dominated by emotion may be incoherent, also failing to engage. Extreme domination by intense emotion may be moving to others in one way but lacks cohesion and coherence. The sharing of emotional life requires the revelation of selves as players in interaction. We don't understand emotion by naming it, although this is often the emphasis in academic writing, as has long been the case:

> ... unfortunately there is little psychological writing about the emotions that is not merely descriptive. As emotions are described in novels, they interest us, for we are made to share them ... the trouble with the emotions is that they are regarded too much as individual things.
>
> (James, 1890, pp. 448–449)

A simple story may still have considerable personal value. In its essence, a story is conveyed by the clause that expresses action with subject, transitive verb and object: "each sentence is a little story" (Calvin, 1996). Minimalistic stories are not synonymous with trauma. They can be lively, having the virtue of accessibility. Consider the following quote:

> I am not saying they love each other. Oh, no. Football is not a matter of life and death ... it's much more important than that. And it's more important to them than that ...
>
> (Shankly, c.1961)

Bill Shankly, the person being quoted, was manager of the Liverpool football club in the 1960s. His comment is often cited by fans of football, and sports fans more generally. While the reference is humorous, it arose from genuine respect for the many individuals and families who were fans of the club, involved in their "eternal" rivalry with neighbouring Everton fans. For many people, such engagement in the life of a team is understood as a simple story, about belonging and support: "I/We support Liverpool". This has both efficacy and accessibility. It is associated with action in people's lives in a form that can be shared. It provides grounds for *prospective* action, in contrast to the traumatic script where constricted self-definition limits possibilities for prospective action, effectively enslaving the person in a traumatic past. For those invested in Liverpool FC the *I* is no longer isolated. It is a case of the "*I that is We and the We that is I*".

Modern sporting stadiums bring people together in ways that can be compelling and emotionally engaging. The Liverpool crowd, singing their team song, *You'll Never Walk Alone*, at Anfield Stadium represents, for many, a real experience of community (Korner, 2002). The song conveys sentiment that resonates with Shankly's words, speaking of the courage it takes to keep going, despite adversity, "though your dreams be tossed and blown". The ultimate reward is that *You'll Never Walk Alone* (Rogers & Hammerstein, 1945). It is about the relationship of the individual to his community.

The realization of a text has to begin somewhere. The realization of the embodied text that is *self* begins with the sharing of what is experienced. The secret of value, that which is inner, is brought into the public space of shared experience. It can be as simple as a single sentence that constitutes the beginning of a journey, of someone becoming who she is meant to be.

Chapter 7

The long conversation

Overview

In a scientific age, spirituality tends to be de-emphasized. However, we all develop whole person responses to the world into which we are born, which are a natural basis for spiritual life. Creation stories underpin *worldviews* and provide a symbolic *cradle* for members of a culture. The achievement of a sense of belonging may be nurtured by creation stories, although in the modern era we are confronted with a confusing array of such stories, sometimes limited by rationales that lack vitality and spontaneity, serving privileged individuals rather than communities. There are also further reflections on the long conversation for the individual over his lifetime, in psychotherapy and elsewhere. Trauma in early life, its dissociative impact and its transformation are considered, with reference to the literary example of *Jekyll and Hyde*. Main themes of human conversation over the whole of its existence have included trauma, healing and love. Current responses to mental suffering and thoughts on the possibility of human *civilization* in the sense of a less violent and conflicted world, with an emphasis on the role of joyful dreaming, will bring the book to a speculative and hopeful close.

Worldview

Humans have been in conversation from time immemorial. We can't conceive of humanity without conversation. We are born into a world of communicative exchange from the beginning of life through to the last breath. In this sense each person is involved in a transformative lifelong conversation from cradle to grave. Therapists enter into such conversations sometimes in a single meeting, sometimes over many years, becoming part of the process that shapes lives.

For millennia the human conversation was largely an oral tradition. With the advent of written language, conversations achieved more enduring forms that also provided a storehouse for memory and inter-generational knowledge. One might reasonably speak of the *long conversation* as the means by which humanity as a whole has transformed itself. The term has applicability to the individual life as *self-organizing system* and, in the global era, to humanity as a whole. The *Long*

Conversation is the human tendency to communicate with each other, between generations, within oneself and with the inanimate environment.

Oral traditions persist despite the rise of written and digital forms of communication. Psychotherapy is one of them. The immense written literature on the subject reflects effort to reach common understanding. Language is often taken for granted and not always taken seriously as an aspect of healing. Yet language is constitutive of who we are, remembering, "Man is not merely the symbol-using animal. He is constituted of symbols, because that is his nature, not because he is driven" (Levenson, 2017). The argument that transformation occurs through communicative exchange is made in the following passage from Levenson (added commentary in brackets):

> in the psychoanalytic process . . . change . . . [depends] on a dialectical interaction . . . . Like Oedipus confronting the Sphinx, we are asked, What is inside us yet between us?' "What is intrinsically mine yet intrinsically yours?" [while language doesn't belong to one or the other, this could be taken to mean language as acquired by one and as acquired by the other] What is there given, yet made between us?' . . . . The answer is, of course, language. [Language is "given", our common sense, what is "made between us" is the shared language of the healing relationship] And my claim is that the psychoanalytic process, the healing process is a language process which allows for, indeed requires, the synthesis of these two paradoxically oppositional aspects of therapy: the aspect of meaning [specific meaning] and the aspect of experience [with its non-specific sense of significance]. Rather than calling it a language process, I think it might be more precise to refer to it as a semiotic process, in the sense that it encompasses more than spoken language. It includes also sign systems, nonverbal cueings, distances, dispersions; the whole repertoire of interpersonal language.
>
> (Levenson, 2017, pp. 39–40)

Conversation can be dulled by convention and inhibited by trauma or strong emotion. Or it can be enlivened by association and reciprocity. It is a substantial element of the environment into which we are born. Ideas and beliefs are given birth in communicative exchange. Hearts and minds are won over, or not. Such is the crucible of a person's outlook on the world.

The notion of *worldview* is dynamic and perhaps elusive, not often referred to in English scientific literature. This may be in part because it is not possible to conceive of worldview in terms of measurement in a numerical sense. Jaspers referred to *"weltanschaung"* ("world outlook") as "The total mental achievement" (Jaspers, 1963). He says, "under favourable circumstances an individual can *become aware of his personal world in a systematic way* . . . The methods for knowledge in this field are only acquired through training in the humanities". This suggests that concepts such as person, personal worlds and self are relevant to the concept of *worldview*.

Man's efforts at "making sense" of the suffering and joy of living have developed as the variety of reflective and expressive practices in which humans engage. Of these the most ancient are spiritual beliefs that subsequently became systematized as religions. As a partial definition of religion, James said, "Religion, whatever it is, is a man's total reaction upon life . . . to get at them (total attitudes) . . . you must reach down to that curious sense of the whole residual cosmos as an everlasting presence . . . that everyone possesses" (James, 1902). This formulation sounds like an assertion that each individual has a "total reaction upon life" involving a relationship between self and the "whole residual cosmos". Something like *worldview* may always be present whether consciously recognized or not. In the modern era, this involves a complex interplay between personality and heterogeneous cultural influences.

"Total reaction upon life" and "total mental achievement" are similar statements and in a sense give credit for the effort towards adaptation that has formed each person. A person's whole mental achievement should be a matter for respect. When it comes to meaning and significance the relationship of the individual to her fellows is a meronymic one: she is a part of the whole. Growth and maturation involve a broadening of vision within that whole rather than a self-repudiation involving rejection of personal feeling.

Creation stories

Australia, like many countries in the 21st century, is a place where the influence of religion is on the wane. Old creation stories are often derided as unscientific metaphors. Perhaps this involves a denial of the metaphor inherent in scientific explanations. The dominant scientific "creation story" in the 21st century is the Big Bang Theory. Its name is a metaphor. It refers to the moment at the beginning of the universe which is the beginning of time and the beginning of energy expansion and transformation of matter. In reverse, one could use another metaphor and refer to it as the "vanishing point" where time and matter disappear. In any case it is a term derived from work in physics and related sciences to describe and explain recorded data. It doesn't have a strong connection to any explanation for the human world with which the average person could identify. As such it doesn't make a satisfying creation story at a human level. In human terms the metaphor sounds destructive rather than supportive of life.

Perhaps we need to turn to the biological sciences for such a story. Here the dominant "creation story" at the present time is the Darwinian theory of evolution. In popular imagination this is often translated into the phrase *survival of the fittest*. This is not a nurturing story but rather one which emphasizes individual competition. Many non-scientific religious or traditional creation stories may make a stronger case for providing social cohesion for their adherents. Terms like *eternity* and the *sacred* that have meaning in the human world may provide a sense of solidarity and connection, even though they may be considered illusions through an objective lens.

However, a version of evolution which sees survival of the group as the key element might account for the irreducibly interpersonal and social phenomena of language and symbolic communication. It also might account for the development of the relationships that underpin long-term learning and provide rewards that can't be found in isolation. This is a very much broader but no less scientific interpretation of the data. Communicative exchange in a symbolic dimension provides the basis for cultural evolution that has so transformed the planet, as well as individual human lives. Perhaps a creation story could emerge that is consistent with science although it would need to extend beyond facts to engender feeling.

Old creation stories, as in *The Dreaming*, emphasize the living connection to the land. When science sees objectification as its end, it loses this sense of connection. When applied to human relationships we miss the essence of what sustains us: the felt connection with our fellows. This is why objective knowledge was termed the *unhappy consciousness* (Hegel, 1807). Being open to ongoing communication and seeking what we need provide hope for the emergence of a better world.

It would be desirable for communities to have creation stories that enhance the individual's sense of belonging, promoting integration into the community. However, we are constantly faced with tendencies towards dis-integration and dis-connection.

Difficult places, dissociative spaces: the zone of trauma

People are often moved by witnessed trauma. Major episodes of loss often bring people together in solidarity. Yet frequently we switch off or dissociate from pain and suffering. The global era of communication means an enormous range of suffering, with explicit content, is continually on show. We prefer to be blind to it sometimes, finding it too much. This is done consciously and unconsciously. Much as one may bear witness to the suffering of others, one is also inevitably caught up in a personal experience of trauma. Transformation of suffering through literature or music may allow it to be heard by providing a form of expression that allows recognition of pain without the alienation of horror.

Experiences of loss and trauma are inevitable in relational life. Even on the battlefields dying soldiers call for their mothers. In extremity, it is still natural to seek comfort. Soldiers traumatized in war often suffer as much from trauma they have inflicted, as from trauma to which they have fallen victim. So it is with trauma based in the early relational environment: "borderline patients are not so much afraid of staying in an empty house as they are terrified of being trapped in a haunted house – a house haunted by the memories of what others have done to them and what they, in turn, have done to themselves and others" (Zanarini & Frankenburg, 1994). The role of the clinician is to remain supportive and non-judgmental, even when the patient may have perpetrated trauma. If concepts like trauma and violence, aggression and sexuality are to be approached with understanding, a developmental framework recognizing the bases of trauma is required.

The most basic form of aggression "is almost synonymous with activity" (Winnicott, 1950–5). Activity is essential to establishment of the self-world relationship. Movement may be towards (progression; contact) or back into oneself (withdrawal). Early on, the action of a young infant who kicks out her leg striking a carer will be almost universally "glossed" as *she didn't mean it*. It isn't seen as intentional or violent. The infant, in the first six months or so, is in a stage before the development of concern for, and awareness of, the separateness of others (ibid.). Excessive inhibition of the need to move and express instinctual capacities for aggression is thought to result in a form of dissociation, referred to as "splitting" (after Klein), where "good and bad" develop along separate lines (ibid.). In this situation "love loses some of its valuable (lively) aggressive component" (ibid.).

Movement can be taken back earlier as a function of the *proto-self*. The foetus is moving limbs and body in the womb. This could be understood as a form of "monadic" relatedness, because at this stage of life the foetus cannot relate to whole others. Rather, the totally dependent but whole (psychologically undifferentiated) foetus, only has access to the rhythms and sensations of others and the external world filtered through the body of the mother, truly "through a glass darkly" (Corinthians, 1:12, KJV). Meares describes two basic forms of relatedness: dyadic and triadic (Meares, 1998, pp. 876–879). Dyadic relatedness begins with the proto-conversation (ibid.). Triadic relatedness involves the development of symbolic play, an activity initially carried on by a child in the sphere of the carer, involving play with the objects of the world (toys and the like), which become invested with personal meaning (ibid.). This is the beginning of personification of the self-world relationship which carries on through adult life, in the manner described earlier in discussion of the Hegelian process of "becoming". *Monadic* relatedness, *in utero*, could be seen as a third form of relatedness.

Paradoxically, in the biblical quote it is the *adult* who sees the world *through a glass darkly* in contrast to *face to face* (Corinthians, 1:12), intended to convey the immediacy of the child's view in dyadic relatedness. When applied to the relationship of the foetus to a world that can at most be perceived dimly, it refers to a stage of life preceding explicit communicative relatedness as a distinct being. Even here a kind of learning through communication is possible, relating to the rhythms of the mother's body, with the maternal body as conduit for the "music" of the world at large. The transition from the state of intra-uterine *monadic* relatedness through birth to the shock of a now physically separate relationship to the world and other, is itself a situation with risk of trauma, if supportive care is not sufficiently available. Where severe neglect results in failure to thrive the infant's experience can't be conceived adequately in linguistic terms. As discussed, it may represent a form, *no story*, defined by absence, rather than presence, of relationship.

While movement can be seen as beginning the self-world relationship, the cry is the beginning of explicit communicative relatedness and hence a foundation of great value to the infant, despite its initial reflex-like nature. The infant now participates in communicative exchanges, contributing to the sense of *significance* with carer. Self-world relatedness, starting rudimentarily with movement in the world, needs to be integrated with communicative gestures, to establish grounds for coordinated relatedness. Unintegrated aggressive impulses may later give rise to violence where the perpetrator, while conscious of the act, is not fully aware of the effect on others.

Sexuality involves the self-other relationship, requiring bodily and intersubjective coordination for it to be satisfying to both parties. Commonly this doesn't happen. The risk and sense of exploration of sexuality is part of what is exciting and pleasurable. It is often driven to the extent that individuals are blind to the experience of the other, so mismatches and traumatic experience are a frequent outcome. The coordination and integration required for sexuality, generally considered a private domain (with very strong cultural influences), for which children are often ill-prepared, may be such as to make it particularly susceptible to traumatic forms of experience.

It is difficult to discuss trauma publicly without making attributions of blame. When this occurs, it tends to be unhelpful, often leading to compounding of trauma and cycles of retributive pre-occupation. Yet trauma affects most, if not all, lives at some point. The experience of being haunted by such experience and in some cases dominated to the point of personal paralysis is common. When trauma is discussed people often think of violence, both sexual and physical. Other impingements like expressed anger, denigration and humiliation can also have major impacts. There is substantial evidence for links between emotional trauma and various forms of mental disorder (e.g. Kendler et al., 2003).

Relational trauma can be defined as involving ongoing impingement, violation or neglect. When physical abuse is involved the emotional effect includes the sense of helplessness and humiliation. When sexual abuse is involved the effects of helplessness and humiliation are compounded by an assault on the tender emotions (Meares, 2019). When this occurs the fine-grained feelings that support social engagement and relationship are threatened.

An understanding stance in relation to trauma needs to take into account that higher levels of mental function involve an ongoing synthesis of relational complexity essential to the integrated self, as outlined in the work of Janet and Meares (Meares, 1999; Barral & Meares, 2019). It is inevitable that there are failures in this level of functioning and trauma is a primary reason for this loss of function.

Literature often informs psychological understanding. Trauma is considered with reference to literature on dissociation and from the horror genre.

Dis-integration; the double life

> One great splitting of the whole universe into two halves is made by each of us; and for each of us almost all of the interest attaches to one of the halves; but we all draw the line of division between them in a different place. When I say that

we all call the two halves by the same names, and that those names are "me" and "not-me" respectively, it will at once be seen what I mean.

(James, 1890, p. 289)

The natural tendency is to divide one's experience of the world into that which is *me* or *mine* and that which is *not-me*, that to which I am indifferent. This kind of division, or dis-association, like that described earlier, occurs early in life, forming an implicit form of relational organization. Depending on the extent of such dissociation, the individual is likely to have difficulty tolerating difference. To some extent this kind of difficulty is evident in all people.

Under traumatic circumstances people lead restricted lives, based upon the *need* to adhere to *some* form of organization. Traumatic forms of organization have their basis in dissociation. Under good conditions the self has both multiplicity and continuity, maintaining a sense of unity. In traumatic dissociation, the sense of continuity and unity is lost. Different selves may be evident that seem incompatible, with little connection or internal capacity to communicate within self. Some areas of experience are hidden, sometimes even to the person himself (*not-me*, to myself).

These circumstances are not unusual in clinical practice. As an example:

A middle-aged man presents with recurrent depressive symptoms. He has a successful career as a teacher. He is also a devout Christian and works as a lay pastor in a protestant denomination. He has been married for 10 years and has two young children. His marriage is under threat after he was discovered by his wife looking at pornographic sites on the internet. Although he expresses very strongly how much he wishes to stop and reconcile with his wife, he finds it very difficult to do so. He finds it extremely painful to talk about and is very ambivalent about seeking help. After some tentative efforts to do so, he fails to attend an appointment and can't be contacted. A month later he commits suicide.

This kind of subject is much-favoured in media exposés as the revelation of the dark side of public figures who have led secret lives involving sexual indiscretion or criminal behaviour. Normally, secrets are kept as a matter of choice. When the secret takes up a substantial part of someone's life, the situation becomes one of divided affective investment with loss of integration. A separation between the public persona and private self is present in all people to some extent. It is most likely to lead to dysfunction when affect inhibition has been a dominant interpersonal strategy in the public domain. Shame is often a major affective influence, driving the person to hide what he is doing. One response to the frustration of chronic affect inhibition may be emergence of the "double life", a theme developed by Robert Louis Stevenson in the character(s) *Jekyll and Hyde* (Stevenson, 1886). The extent of this kind of phenomenon may be much more widespread than we like to believe, as evidenced within institutional cultures such as the Catholic Church (Martel, 2019).

The realm of the dis-social: trauma and horror

In the pre-verbal period there are a huge number of interactions between infant and carers. The communicative mode of exchange is feeling-based, carried in facial expression, the rhythms of movement and gesture. In developmental studies such as the "still-face" situation it has been shown how sensitive infants are to changes in this indexical "bodily syntax" (Tronick, 1978). When variations in parental mood or styles of communication fail to provide recognition and valuing, the infant is left in the position of having to adapt and does so at a cost in terms of optimal function. Infant feeling and expression that meets with hostility, indifference or rejection from carers becomes separated from the relational sphere. Re-organization occurs with division into what can be identified socially with self and what has to be held outside this space. This involves a loss to self.

Affectively toned complexes, held in implicit memory, may be felt as *not-me*. Traumatic events may be experienced as simply *happening to* a relatively helpless self ("me"), while processes of dissociation hold the affective complex out of consciousness ("not-me"). States associated with shame are especially prone to being hidden. This leaves the person in a state divided, where development is sub-optimal. The individual will suffer here, from dark states that cannot be shared socially and tend to go unnoticed. Even in good circumstances there is an element in developing experience that is beyond communication, *incommunicado* (Winnicott, 1963). These states remain "without speech" in implicit memory.

From the infant's viewpoint, the effect is to keep certain ("unacceptable to other") feeling states *separate* from dyadic, communicative space (the intersubjective field). The mechanism by which this occurs is most typically automatic (hence unconscious) and dissociative. The sense of significance is already being generated by proto-conversation. The movement under conditions of mismatch is towards some states becoming hidden.

This leaves the infant frustrated in relation to the third *General Image* of affect, relating to *minimizing affect inhibition* (Tomkins, 1995) (see also Chapter 3 for explanation of the four *General Images of Affect*). From a first-person perspective it is likely to be the lack of expressive space for feeling that is most significant. Current knowledge of early affect regulation suggests that mismatches and trauma lead to *failures* of right-sided inhibition of affect (Schore, 2012; Meares et al., 2011). This probably relates to inadequacies in and impingements on the early field of play, necessary to development of unconscious affect regulatory mechanisms.

Right hemispheric inhibition in early life is likely to contribute to effective regulation of feeling, whereas left-sided suppression of affect, later in development, is effortful and ego-dystonic. Chronic early impairment of affect regulation is likely to contribute to a dissociative predisposition and possibly left hemispheric dominance. These early experiences may be significant contributors to later episodes of mood disturbance (Winnicott, 1950–5; Meares, 2006). In some people processes of dissociation may lead to phenomena such as the "double life". The therapist is faced with the challenge of finding ways of recognizing, responding to and developing the story of self, even in the face of dark emotions.

The genre of horror, at its best, may serve a function of providing sufficient syntax, or story, for situations that would, in life, provoke "mental shutdown" (*no story*), allowing humanization and transformation of traumatic realms of human experience. This type of fiction emerged in the 19th century, perhaps influenced by conditions of industrialization with social dislocation, where many infants were abandoned, giving rise to the orphanages and workhouses of Dickensian times.

In both *Frankenstein* and *The Strange Case of Dr Jekyll and Mr Hyde*, new technologies of "medical science" play a role, although one cloaked in secrecy, danger and shame. In both stories there is a character that evokes horror in those around them (the *creature*; *Mr Hyde*) (Shelley, 1818; Stevenson, 1886). People are terrified, shying away in horror. The story of *Frankenstein* allows us to overcome this alienation, feeling empathy for the *creature*, abandoned by his creator and shunned or hunted by others, even though he is shown to be capable of responding to care. Shelley evokes the human qualities of the *creature* that allow us to feel a similarity with him, a *fellow feeling*.

The situation with *Jekyll and Hyde* is more complex: it is made clear to the reader that the character is divided against himself. The situation is analogous to that described previously for the infant, who learns to separate some affects from the dyadic space. Jekyll has, as long as he can remember, concealed that which he senses to be unacceptable to others. He contemplates the question of how this part of him might be *dissociated*, from the acceptable part, so that the "good" part would no longer be undermined (*dissociated* is a term used in the last section of the story, "Henry Jekyll's Full Statement of the Case").

When this "dissociation" occurs through the device of a chemical potion, the hitherto hidden side is given a life, although one cloaked in secrecy and deception. The hoped for strengthening of the "acceptable" side of the personality does not occur: Jekyll remains the same flawed character, although now fatally flawed. The ascendancy of elements of hostility, envy, aggression and hatred that make up Hyde's character can only lead to the destruction of his life. The story illustrates that the lifting of inhibition, as evident in the character of Hyde, does not lead to a good outcome.

What is required from a therapeutic viewpoint is the development of character through expression and understanding. This involves *re-association* (bringing experience into the social space of dyadic and triadic relatedness), in response to the "dis-association" (taking out of the social space) that has been the basis of suffering. This requires empathic imagination and the search for similarities that will allow the development of a recognizably human narrative. While *Frankenstein* presents us with a character who is essentially child-like and would respond to appropriate care, Dr Jekyll is an adult whose dark states are hidden and enigmatic. Treatment is likely to be difficult and language hard to find, although the fact that the story ends with a "full statement of the case" suggests that another outcome may have been possible if a communicative process had been followed rather than "blind" chemical disinhibition.

In mental health settings patients naturally present wanting distressing symptoms relieved. In the case of distress that has a long history, as in trauma with a developmental basis, this will sometimes equate to the wish to have "unacceptable parts" somehow removed. It is hard for people to see that what they wish discarded may have value to them. Yet all affects are part of the human range of adaptation to the relational environment. When they have been experienced in traumatic situations, they represent the best effort possible at adaptation made by the person at that time. The problem originally lies in the mismatches and impinging or neglectful relational environments that failed in recognizing value in the infant's affective, communicative and exploratory endeavours.

Mismatches may occur as a result of incompatible temperaments and don't necessarily imply abuse. The process of re-associating and allowing emergence of stories that not only integrate trauma but build upon the basic value of the person is the strategy in the direction of life. When people *write* about trauma, it has been demonstrated that the stories so created will be most therapeutic when there is a balance of words for positive and negative emotions (Pennebaker, 2011). Some negative words seem to be required, presumably relating to the need for recognition of trauma. However, positive language is also required if the effort of writing is to be associated with a sense of resolution (ibid.). These findings suggest simply "**having** a coherent story to explain a painful experience was not necessarily as useful as **constructing** a coherent story" (ibid.).

The prospective relationship of therapy needs to be towards development of the *good*, not elimination of the *bad*. Growth in the social realm has potential to contain the dis-social elements. This was evident to Dante in the 14th century. In *The Divine Comedy*, "he would not have written the *Inferno* and *Purgatorio* if he had not known from the first the extent to which intelligence is fulfilled in the perception and propagation of the good" (Kirkpatrick, 2006). Here *good* is to be understood as the *common good*, and *bad* not so much as that which is "selfish" but rather that which is *socially* destructive, leading, in the *Inferno*, to the isolated, tortured souls of *Dis*. Therapeutically, development of *self* is associated with differentiation and flourishing. This occurs in a system of *self* and *other*, not as an isolate. Stories of "the Fall", on the other hand, like *Dr Jekyll and Mr Hyde*, are stories with tragic trajectories where, if survival occurs at all, it is of a limited or distorted kind.

Therapy exclusively based upon analysis and interpretation is likely to lack a necessary element of prospective relatedness and narrative development. Analysis, by its nature, takes what already is, or has been, and is, therefore, intrinsically backward-looking. Ricoeur writes, "Freud can encounter morality only as a wounding of desire, as interdiction and not as aspiration" (Ricoeur, 1970,

p. 186). Moreover, the acceptance by the patient of the analyst's position inevitably involves a degree of wounding: "insight, must involve a 'humiliation', since it has encountered a hitherto masked enemy, which Freud calls the 'resistance of narcissism'" (ibid.).

For the individual with poor affect regulation, the "subsymbolic processing system, involving bodily and sensory experience, is dominant", reflected in arousal and lack of coherent verbal representation (Mariani et al., 2013). The process of referential reorganization can be seen in three phases, that of "arousal", where feeling predominates, then "narrative/symbolizing" activity, where there are "low levels of reflective language and fluent speech" (ibid.) and finally, "reorganizing", characterized by reflection and stepping back to "stand outside the experience" (ibid.). The role of imagination in the realization of this process requires interactive play with others.

People vary in their capacity to use imagination. Occupations don't always foster such abilities. Individual language use in many fields and often in the public domain, can often be characterized as *formal* or *analytic*. Some people have strengths in these areas, without having developed a *narrative* style of language use. Formal thinking may relate to concerns with status and power, while the analytic style is associated with cognitive complexity, distanced from emotion (Pennebaker, 2011). Analytic thinkers "work to understand their world" (ibid.). On the other hand, people with a narrative style of thinking are good storytellers, able to relate to others in ways conveying immediacy, evocative of emotion (ibid.). The development of narrative is necessary to growth of self, although there is a need to engage, at the level of the individual's linguistic style, for this to occur. Therapy which succeeds in fostering the growth of self, enhances the sense of aspiration towards a future. What hasn't been part of past experience can't be subject to analysis. Rather *new* stories need to evolve, and be elaborated in relational space in order to contain the tension between what was, what is and what will be. The "resistance of narcissism" may reflect the need to resist domination by the other and be one's *self*.

It is in the heart of affective experience that we find the core sense of self, waiting for development through language that facilitates exchange and growth, allowing the person to know and be known. The form of communication effective in this regard is *analogical relatedness*, based upon the kind of healthy interaction that constitutes *normal* relational conditions for psychological growth (Meares, 2009; Meares & Jones, 2009; Tolpin, 2002). This is to say relatedness focused on forms of feeling, encouraging expression through lively interplay and the language of metaphor and analogy. This needs to occur in the present, with an orientation to the future, to the becoming of *self*.

The long individual conversation

In most psychodynamic literature, development has been understood as *individual* development. However, development also has the form of roles and reciprocal interactions. The developmental and neurological grounds for such growth in mutuality have been characterized in terms of the pattern of *cry and response* and the traditional role progression from infant to child to adult to parent to elder. This was contrasted with the emphasis in many modern societies where the *adult* role is often equated with maturity.

Life paths have narrative form with a beginning, middle and an end. In human terms, this narrative is generally in the sequence, life at home, journey away, establishment of new home, engendering of new life and return, in the sense of the transmission of knowledge and estate to the new generation. The five role stages (infant, child, adult, parent, elder), expressed in terms of *call and response* can be considered in broad interactive terms of self-other and self-world relatedness.

Initially the infant *cries* and the parent/mother/other *responds*. In early infancy the infant can be seen to make calls relating to need, whereas it falls to carers to make calls to the infant, towards engagement in mutual play. The parental *call*, over the period of infancy, is important in bringing *self* into being. In childhood, the child broadens the scope of their calls whilst still relying on parents, who remain first responders to the child's calls of need. The child engages in calls to play in relation to an increasing range of others. As the self's knowledge of the world broadens, there is increasing responsiveness to the *call* of the *world*. The world includes the community of others. This call effectively becomes louder, drawing the person into activities that sustain her life until she *leaves home*, marking emergence into adulthood. To establish a place in the world, the adult has to respond by making an independent living and emotionally investing in intimate relatedness, the bases for foundation of a *new home*.

With the achievement of the *new home*, the self prepares the necessary resources to become a *generator* of time and space for developing others. This signifies readiness for the *parent* role. It should be noted that *parent* role does not necessarily imply actually having children. Rather it suggests having time for others and for generative activity. As *parents*, with the birth of children, a new family emerges, along with a new generation of developing selves. Having made the transition from child to carer, the parent gains an empathic appreciation of the human life cycle and takes the roles of *responder* to need and *caller* to less experienced others. When the new generation grows up and leaves home, the *self*, now an *elder*, is in a position to share experience with others. Ideally, the elder becomes a *representative* of the *world*, for others. Finally, as the body tires, its work done, there is the process of *letting go of life*.

Over a lifetime, the communicative exchanges that shape an individual life are between the self and *many* others. While there may be a progression from the "monadic" position of the foetus, to the dyad with a primary carer and then to participation in triadic relations, the reality is that a multiplicity of influences will have been present from the beginning, even though not necessarily discerned as such.

The painting by Redon captures something important about perception and the intersubjective field. It is "a picture from the reverse side of the eye" where the

The long conversation 175

Figure 7.1 Silence, Odilon Redon, (1840–1916), Silence, c. 1911. Oil on prepared paper, 21 $^1/_2$ × 21 $^1/_4$' (54.6 × 54 cm). Lillie P. Bliss Collection. Acc. n.: 113.1934. Museum of Modern Art (MoMA), New York

Source: The Museum of Modern Art, New York/Scala, Florence

rim of the orbit provides a frame and the subjects nose can be seen as well as the external image of a woman, possibly the mother or lover. There are two subjects, *self* and *other*. In reality, figures will move in and out of the field of exchanges with a passing parade of brief and prolonged relationships and situations that will form individual experience, shaping self. If one imagines an animated version of this image, one perhaps sees a mental model for intersubjective growth.

Personal realization doesn't only happen in the presence of others, although the presence of others and of the symbolic environment of language are *necessary* to individual thought. Much thought occurs alone, when the pressure for social interaction is relieved, allowing space for reflection and inner play. The possibility of sharing these experiences in the social space then arises, as it did with this dream:

> *Last night I awoke from a dream feeling somewhat unsettled. In the dream there was an image of myself, not in my usual form, but rather as a point held in a matrix or field that was itself moving or vibrating. I had the sense of "being here again" although I don't recall experiencing such an image before. The phrase came into my mind that "I was a rent in the fabric of time". This seemed to show some kind of engagement with the theme ("Time, space and the body") of a conference in which I was to speak.*
>
> *I think of this "self" (the "rent in the fabric of time") as something like an unfinished text. The image seemed to have the quality of a story that included repetition and finding oneself in the same place. It also had movement and the sense of going somewhere, although somewhere unknown. This is true for all of us: we have a story already that it is not complete and we move towards a destiny that is not known. When we engage with another in therapy, we are engaging in this journey with all its uncertainties, as we become aware of another person, another subjectivity, another self. We become part of another story, and we navigate our way through a world of unfinished stories. To so engage is to become involved in play and to sustain the conditions that allow for personal knowledge and development.*

The choice was made and the dream was shared at the conference. Even though it may be a phrase with which many wouldn't resonate, for me the sense of self as a *rent in the fabric of time* speaks to the relationship of a part to the whole which nevertheless retains its own distinctiveness.

There are turning points in every life. Some of them may be readily understood as part of a natural order. For instance, any parent is likely to recognize the birth of their first child as life-changing. However, many twists in the trajectory of life are much more unpredictable. Even those troubled by mental suffering and the dark spaces alluded to in the preceding sections may experience redemption. In Sydney, a child of alcoholics who became a petty criminal and alcoholic himself, experienced a change which has become part of the city's identity (Wikipedia, 2019):

> *There was a well-known Sydney character [Arthur Stace] referred to as "The Eternity Man". Many years ago, he embarked upon an epic task of writing, in a beautiful copperplate, the word "Eternity" on the pavement of every street in Sydney. He continued with this task for some decades, until his death. Older people may remember encountering such an inscription on various footpaths, written in chalk. Such a particular vision and mission perhaps reflects a kind of "play" for this man that involved the commitment of his entire being, leaving the public with a lasting story, a legacy that has become part of the mythology of modern Sydney.*

> *Nor did this story cease with his death. Indeed, at the beginning of the 21st century, the word "Eternity" lit up the Harbour Bridge at the Sydney New Year Celebrations. It was written in the copperplate style of The Eternity Man, now broadcast across the world.*

One might say Arthur Stace succeeded in achieving immortality in the context of *his* long conversation. In less obvious ways, the effects of our interpersonal relationships carry on in the lives of others even after the death of any given individual.

In human terms *eternity* implies the sense of timelessness characteristic, in the Australian Indigenous tradition, of *The Dreaming*. In the broadest human sense, it is characteristic of meaningful interplay with the environment, a whole world with which individuals engage in communicative exchange.

Intercultural conversation

In the colonial period there was an arrogance in western culture that extended to belief in its superiority. This belief and the rise of nation-states with a mission to extend their dominion led to coercive relationships with the first peoples of "new" colonies. Perverse forms of this belief were applied in both scientific and political arenas. The rise of ideologies that incorporated belief about superiority in relation to others may have been a consequence, contributing to the world wars of the 20th century. It is still evident in fundamentalist religious beliefs and other ideologies. Whether at an individual or a group level, the belief in superiority involves negation of the other, a negation of our mutual interdependence.

In countries like Australia this remains a current issue requiring resolution. Consider the following extract:

> *A nation chants,* **but we know your story already**. *The bells peal everywhere. Church bells calling the faithful to the tabernacle where the gates of heaven will open, but not for the wicked. Calling innocent little black girls from a distant community where the white dove bearing an olive branch never lands. Little girls who come back home after church on Sunday, who look around themselves at the human fallout and announce matter-of-factly,* **Armageddon begins here**.
>
> (Alexis Wright, *Carpentaria*, her emphasis)

The extract from *Carpentaria* (Wright, 2006) is an expression of the plight of dispossessed and traumatized Indigenous Australians. The book is also, in my view, a modern expression of *The Dreaming*. It is directed at all people. It is a story of survival in extraordinary circumstances and an illustration of the importance of *living* a *worldview*. The starting point, as illustrated, is one of traumatic helplessness. The rest of the nation is blind to Indigenous reality. The experience is of broken promises and children confronted with the end of their world. This is a bleak and overwhelming set of circumstances.

As Wright's book develops, intercultural and literal storms are ridden out and survived through a living, though uncertain, connection with land, sea and community. The vulnerability of individuals at all points on this journey and the lack of any complete or even satisfactory resolution of the situation is clear as the book unfolds. That is to say it is in many ways a realistic depiction. It is expressed in a way that has a basis in a worldview foreign to the nation of colonizers who are dismissive, saying "but we know your story already". It is all too clear that the nation *does not know* the Indigenous worldview and is blind to the extent that having to listen *again* is seen as an imposition that requires effort that is unwelcome.

When confronted with an external reality blind to their world, "innocent little black girls" confronted with "human fallout" see "Armageddon" as all that is left. *Human fallout* refers to the loss of spirit synonymous with the worldview that was central to the life of indigenous communities and individuals. A *worldview* has been devalued, people degraded. On many occasions they not only suffer indignity but are also blamed by the dominating culture that maintains its denial.

At the same time, *Carpentaria* represents an emerging form. A literature that is distinct and informed by the worldview of *The Dreaming* re-shaped through introduced forms of language and written expression. It provides a window onto the forms of feeling of *The Dreaming* for those who haven't grown up in the embrace of Indigenous culture. It creates an intercultural dimension to the long conversation.

The need for shared understanding and a measure of unity has never been greater than in the modern world. These needs are a matter for *persons* and *subjectivities* rather than *objects* or *organisms*. This involves *hearts and minds*. In the age of globalization, the need for unity takes on a broader dimension than it has in the past. The question, in our time, is whether "the innocent little black girls" will be heard and whether *their world* will be sufficiently validated to be worth living in. When we look at history, man's inhumanity to man is only too apparent. We see a litany of violence, conflict, domination and cultural blindness. Dominating cultures assert a version of "truth" that "trumps" the world of the subjugated. Public rhetoric is often merely a screen for a brutal reality. All cultures have rules that allow for inclusion and exclusion. The inclusion of different worldviews involves psychological work and psychological work involves attentive listening and responding as well as mutual respect. It also involves a willingness to be changed in the process.

The long conversation about suffering and alienation

Looked at over the last two hundred years, there have been two broad currents in the clinical approach to human suffering. The dominant trend has been based in the medical model of identifying pathology and finding treatments that aim to correct that pathology or at least relieve symptoms. The other has been primarily psycho-therapeutic involving careful listening and responsiveness in the service of understanding. The former model employs the strategy of objectifying disorders with the benefit, in some ways, of lessening stigma and the sense of responsibility for one's condition.

However, this may obscure the inter-subjective basis for the development of some conditions. While "we can . . . identify the metaphorical strategies the clinics use to understand and relate to these (unassimilable) experiences (medicalize, technologize or scientize them)", this doesn't necessarily constitute psychological understanding (Cammell, 2016). In the 20th century limitations in the psychotherapeutic model were exposed, with frustration at the length of analytic treatments and their lack of efficacy in the context of acute mental disorders. In the 21st century the challenge lies in developing therapies based on a normative understanding of development and integrating a variety of approaches humanely.

Psychiatry and related disciplines develop through extended conversations and debates with reference to what can be observed and understood. Scientific conversation tends to prioritize the objective over the personal. Current trends in classification have involved both changes in the boundaries between normality and pathology and the reification of many patterns of human distress into categories of mental disorder. Part of this conversation has involved questioning the very utility of the term *mental* and by extension, the validity of the concept of *mind* (DSM IV™).

For clinical practice this undermines respect for the patient's agency and may encourage an attitude of passivity. Any deviation from a course of prescription may come as a surprise. For one patient, "(he) had initially expected me to tell him how to 'get better', just like his previous therapists . . . . when this did not happen . . . . he realised that he could 'take part' in his own therapy" (Benjamin, 2013). In practice, some patients do choose to take a relatively passive role in their own care. This is not likely to yield optimal results when it comes to disorders with a developmental basis. There is a certain comfort, however, in submitting to expert advice and simply accepting what is prescribed. This may work for some. Others prefer to play an active role in their own recovery. This is the path required for the effective development of self. The becoming of self and realization of personality happens in fits and starts, with the odd quantum leap occurring on occasions, through the medium of interpersonal play.

The psychotherapeutic role is of *participant observer*, incorporating immersion in the world of the patient, emotional responsiveness involving the therapist's *self* and the capacity to reflect on and observe the flow of the relationship, as expressed in the conversation. This also involves the need for the therapist to observe her own flow of experience. The position is not one of detached observer or indifferent objective scientist. While self-disorder requires participation from the patient for change to occur, participation by the therapist is also necessary if processes of *exchange* are to be transformative. The medium of exchange is communication, taking place in the intermediate zone of experience (Winnicott, 1971), neither completely objective nor completely subjective. Rather it occurs in the personal intersubjective space required for communicational play and intimacy.

The dominant research paradigm in clinical science, including psychiatry and psychotherapy, is that of "Evidence-Based Medicine" (EBM), which seeks to establish the efficacy of specific interventions. While there has been some success in this regard, many treatments show only relatively small advantages over placebo, to the extent that the efficacy of some specific treatments is questioned (Thomas et al., 2013). For psychotherapy, reviews of evidence-based interventions have demonstrated that, for depression, most studies fail to demonstrate specific differences in particular therapeutic approaches, although the majority do demonstrate therapeutic benefit, compared to placebo (ibid.). When it comes to factors identifiable as associated with good psychotherapeutic outcome, those that account for the majority of variance are *non-specific* factors and therapeutic alliance (Norcross, 2011; Norcross & Lambert, 2013). One interpretation is that, in the case of depression, and probably other psychiatric disorders, non-specific, non-technical factors may be of primary importance in treatment (Thomas et al., 2013).

From the clinician's point of view things often look different to the data of EBM which is generally population-based. The therapist is inclined to view things in terms of the experience with the patient and moments which coincide with directly observable change (practice-based evidence):

A woman in her early fifties was troubled by somatic symptoms, fatigue and depression. Many antidepressants and psychological interventions had been tried. She had become chronically suicidal and was admitted to a private hospital. Her husband had become frustrated and angry with her and threatened to leave. In hospital, the therapist is struck by this woman's low self-esteem. A conversation focused on this aspect of her condition becomes a central pre-occupation for the therapist. She comes up with a formulation that seems generally true which she senses may challenge the patient's self-view. It is along the lines, "I exist therefore I have a right to exist; I occupy space therefore I have a place in this world; I am a person like other people". There was a session where the therapist shared these ideas with the patient. Perhaps they helped or perhaps it may have been the evidence for the patient that the therapist really had been thinking about her. In any case the patient's condition improved from that point. Three years later the therapist notices the woman with her husband on a train. They seem happy. The former patient sees the therapist, smiles and waves. They exchange a greeting.

The evidence for the role of specific precipitants in the onset of depression suggests a prominent role for interactive events involving trauma and loss. Background events involving loss *and* humiliation, combined, have been shown to be the most pathogenic in terms of predicting Major Depression and Mixed Anxiety/Depression (Kendler et al., 2003). Self-initiated separation or loss is associated with Major Depression but not with anxiety. Other-initiated separation, associated with a sense of humiliation, adds to the depressogenic effect, and is additionally associated with anxiety. This is accounted for by the experience of "humiliating events that directly devalue an individual in a core role" (ibid.). It is evident that interactive experiences of *significance* involving painful affect have a role in the development of common psychiatric disorders.

While current classification systems have hundreds of categories, they

> aggregate into three overarching domains, namely the externalizing, internalizing and psychotic experience domains, which finally aggregate into one dimension of psychopathology ... "p" ... the higher a person scores on "p", the worse that person fares on measures of psychiatric illness, brain function, childhood developmental history, and adult life impairment.
> (Caspi & Moffit, 2018, p. 831)

The likely candidate in explaining this "single factor" solution to understanding mental disorders is trauma exposure (ibid.). This speaks to the need for treatments that address traumatic injury to self as the common basis for a great deal of mental suffering.

There are potential dangers in the current paradigm of EBM, based upon objective evidence and justified as the "conscientious, explicit and judicious use of the current best evidence in making clinical decisions about the care of individual patients" (Sackett et al., 1996). In the same paper, a pitfall is recognized in that clinicians could be "tyrannized" if EBM was approached without the balance of significant clinical experience (ibid.). Indeed, for people without substantial clinical experience, like new trainees, the sense of having to slavishly follow the dictates of external sources of knowledge risks de-humanizing treatment. As previously noted, the rationale for EBM is the *optimal care of individual patients*. All clinicians need to regard the patient as the *primary* source of information, relevant to his or her care. This needs to be understood as a human source that expresses concerns in *communicative* forms irreducible to purely objective data. Care requires a human response. If this does not occur, the danger is people become reified as medical "diseases" or "disorders" rather than, first and foremost, being people. This may be particularly the case for psychiatry, where the proliferation of diagnoses and conditions, over the last few decades, has led one of the architects of the DSM IV classification system to question its clinical utility (Frances, 2013).

The DSM series, seen by many as an objective tool essential to EBM, is often revered, inappropriately, as a kind of *bible* in the profession (Benjamin, 2013). A model recognizing traumatic and developmental influences represents a move away from the DSM-influenced medical paradigm, dominant since the 1970s, an era sometimes referred to as the "second biological psychiatry" (ibid.). Indeed, this may be occurring, since the latest DSM 5 actually does place greater emphasis on the role of trauma.

The Conversational Model, in focussing on the naturally occurring form of communicative exchange (the conversation), seeks to understand and build upon non-specific communicative factors (Meares et al., 2012). This practice is not unique to the CM although is made explicit through use of the term *conversation*. While the model can be systematized and taught, it is based upon communicative responses analogous to the developmental processes of proto-conversation, translated into adult conversational situations. It is not the application of a technical procedure. It may be that the capacity to provide a human connection, encouraging the innate curiosity and creativity of self, is crucial to forms of suffering that have a basis in the psyche.

One of the dangers of reduction of suffering to *medical disorder* is loss of personal meaning. Stories and what we consider to be personal truths matter:

> a man is always a teller of tales, he lives surrounded by his stories and the stories of others . . . you have to choose . . . live or tell . . . . Nothing happens while you live. The scenery changes, people come in and go out, that's all. There are no beginnings . . . everything changes when you tell about your life; it's a change no one notices: the proof is people talk about true stories.
> (Sartre, 1964, p. 39)

The difference here between *living* and *telling* is between living blindly and living knowingly.

People live in the world *as* sociates in a social, collaborative world or as *dissociates*, living an isolated, alienated existence. Early trauma pushes people towards dissociated experience, without having experience of any choice in the matter, since implicit memory systems, inaccessible to declarative consciousness, are involved. Nevertheless, the movement towards expressing personal truth in conversation is the path towards re-association, shedding light on the dark spaces and creating new stories, reversing the constriction of trauma. When we choose to tell our stories, we discover the vulnerable self within us, we see it in our fellows and in those who relate their stories to us. We discover our common humanity.

The growth of self towards mature personhood has been emphasized, along with the crucial role of relatedness and language in this process. Therapy is a *temporary* relationship (Bowden, 2001). Indeed, all human relationships end at some point. For the self to be able to thrive, it needs to be able to bear loss and to grieve. For the patient to assume a position as full autonomous participant in the community, therapy needs to come to an end. As one conversation comes to a close, it is hoped that others will blossom. A successful therapy brings about a sufficient integration of affect, language and culture to bring to life the patient's *second nature*, her *self*.

Dreaming of better worlds

The sharing of personal realities with our fellows is the basis of community, reflected in a comment from the Kukatja elder, Napangarti, who expresses pride in her community's capacity to dream together: "This is good country, we are good dreamers" (Poirier, 2003, p. 113). A certain solidarity and willingness to share is implied.

How might we apply this in today's world? What do we have in common in this modern, mixed-up era? What would be a possible source of unity? We have human bodies that have a lot in common yet historically the perception of our physicality often heightens the sense of difference and division rather than bringing cohesion and unity. We share languages with many others but languages easily become a source of misunderstanding. Behavioural variability and diversity in patterns of emotional expression are considerable, often reflecting disparity in cultural tradition and belief. We might be left with the conclusion that there is no area of commonality and yet we all have the sense that this, also, is not true: we *do* all get sick and die, our bodies bleed when they are cut, there is enough commonality in human patterns of interaction that communication is always possible, languages can be translated and common understanding can be reached. We all feel. The *personal knowing* of feeling is embodied and connects us to the environment from the outset in a living relationship which for humans is both symbolic and actual. Feeling, experienced in the *knowing body* (Malloch & Trevarthen, 2018; Merleau-Ponty, 1945), represents, in humanity, "*a* turning point in natural history when physiological activity no longer results only in **public behaviour** but additionally in the **personal experience of feeling**" (Browning, 2017).

As the end of the Second World War approached, Franklin D. Roosevelt declared, "If civilization is to survive, we must cultivate the science of human relationships – the ability of all peoples, of all kinds, to live together, in the same world at peace" (Deacon, 1945). The basis for such a science must lie in an ecological appreciation of how balance is achieved in human relationships, a balance between self and other rather than domination of one by the other.

Neuroscience has an important role in elucidating the facilitation of relationships. The dominant model for neuroscience to-date has been a mechanistic one. This is more a model of central control rather than facilitation: "There are only two possible models: seeing it [brain] as part of a machine or part of a person. So we had a 50 per cent chance of getting it right. But we managed to make the wrong choice", quips McGilchrist (2012). A **better** model may be emerging in the increasing recognition of feeling as the basis of animacy and sentience (Browning, 2017). It may be the sustainability of human relationships that holds the key to efforts at re-shaping the world towards ecological balance. One might say, a principle of *conservation of relationship*.

Psychological growth is based upon sharing of personal experience. Such sharing needs encouragement and places where inner experience can be shared in an emotionally safe way. The 21st century scientific worldview now holds that all human groups are strongly linked by a common biological heritage without evidence for superiority of one group over another. Old claims for superiority often sought to characterize other groups as primitive or "savage". It has become clear that this is wrong: "Savagery is not a property of the past – just a defect of some minds that forswear the priorities of the group or the needs or sensibilities of others" (Fernandez-Armesto, 2019).

There is a truly common humanity, with myriad cultural variations elaborated in the various symbolically based traditions that have grown over millennia. Modern societies are often extremely heterogeneous and rapidly changing. Paradoxically, we also yearn for stability, for that which is "as it was in the beginning, is now and ever shall be, world without end" (Church of England, 1662). Individual growth depends on scaffolding of the infant's life by adults who facilitate the infant's developmental readiness in a joint performance (Browning, 2017).

Many pray for a civilized world without violence. The evidence for an historical trajectory towards any such realization isn't always obvious, although big data showing reduction in rates of violent death in the last 50 years gives cause for hope (Harari, 2011). There is more to be learned through reciprocal conversations that modify violent emotional states than by irrevocable action. Trauma is a frequent basis for such states and any move to a more civilized state would require measures to prevent trauma, whilst also recognizing trauma and loss as inevitable accompaniments of living, requiring a human response. Prevention of trauma relates closely to reduction of violence in communities. While we can't point towards an environment that *actually* exists in peace and ecological balance, without violence, it is natural to imagine one.

The renaissance painting *Madonna and Child with Book* (Raphael, 1503) is an idealized one. Looked at through the lens of human relatedness, it portrays elements necessary to growth of self: a loving, responsive relationship that is held within a world of knowledge, represented by the book, and a community that has provided a built environment within the larger context of the natural environment. The community of others is represented although not seen. A form of idealization is natural to the human infant who needs to look to adults to scaffold her growth in interaction (Kohut, 1971).

This tendency to idealization, rather than revealing God as an illusion, may contribute to understanding the psychological need for religion, as communities developed ways of life that could be communicated. It might also be a reason why human communities, as far as the archaeological record can reveal, have sacred sites and rituals around burial of the dead, marking respect for preceding generations. In many tribal cultures, including that of *The Dreaming*, rituals also involved communication with the environment or earth-mother. Conversations with one's elders and with the environment also form an ongoing part of the experience of self. In my own life, despite the death of my parents, I often find myself conversing with one or other internally. Similarly, I "speak" with my deceased grandparents, often with a strong sense of the place where these relationships happened:

> *My grandfather and I didn't speak all that much. At least not about anything serious. I remember him tickling and playing, sometimes growling while engaging in rough and tumble stuff that was mostly fun, occasionally a bit exhausting. He would watch things with me on TV that my parents*

The long conversation 185

Figure 7.2 Madonna and Child with Book, Raphael (Raffaello Sanzlo), Italian, 1483–1520, c. 1502–03, Oil on panel, 21 $^3/_4$ × 15 $^3/_4$ in. (55.2 × 40cm)

Source: Norton Simon Art Foundation

> *disapproved of, like the wrestling. I would roam around grandpa's house. I discovered things in my grandfather's office. He had an extensive library. Amongst them was a book entitled* Wonders of the Past. *I'd spend hours looking at it. I also spent time with his photo album and became fascinated by his travels to remote parts of the world. Spitzbergen was one of them, an icy place foreign to the Sydney world which was my home. I feel my grandfather with me still as I make my way through explorations in life.*

Long conversations occur between generations, extending beyond death. When we maintain a living relationship with the past, we continue a personally creative conversation. If traditions become intransigent and dogmatic, they lose the sense of being in conversation with the present.

Whether at the level of parents, clinical practice or government, there is a need to shape experience to foster the health and well-being of those in receipt of care. There are dilemmas over care or control. People in government feel a political imperative to exercise some control over human behaviour. This is soundly based in the sense that there need to be limits in place to maintain safety. There is no freedom without responsibility (Frankl, 1992). However, too often such control is exercised in ways that are repressive or manipulative, rather than promoting individual well-being. The biggest single preventative advance that could occur in relation to health and well-being relates to changes in lifestyle that are a product of self-actualization, that is to say, in people taking care of themselves in cohesive harmony with their community.

When psychoanalysis became prominent in the 20th century, it has been argued that classical analytic understanding of drive theory was used by politicians, propagandists and advertisers to influence people so that at least some desires might be satisfied, thereby keeping them "politically quiet" (Curtis, 2002). A consumer society is one where people are encouraged to consume rather than think or cooperate. This sells people short in terms of communicative exchange.

It seems likely that language evolved in response to new biological capacities for shared attention, communicative expression of inner life and collaborative engagement with others towards shared purpose. Cooperative social engagement is how we have evolved to live. Rather than drive satisfaction, the older notion of eudaimonia, reflecting integrity in relational life and following a path morally motivated towards the common good, would reflect a more lasting and achievable kind of contentment for individuals, that would also benefit society as a whole.

External realities aren't always sufficient to sustain relational life. Empathic apprehension is important but often needs an investment of imagination for life to become liveable. Sometimes, the maintenance of an *illusion* of safety when external conditions may not, in fact, be safe may be achieved through imagination.

An evocative representation of this is found in the film *Life Is Beautiful*, for which Roberto Benigni won an Oscar. It is inspired by the stories of Rubino Salmoni and Luigi Benigni (Roberto's father). The story is of a child's survival of in a Nazi concentration camp, achieved through his father's sustained effort at creating an illusion that what was occurring in the concentration camp was a game, even though the actual reality was brutal (Benigni & Cerami, 1997). The drama culminates in the murder of the father, while his son later reflects that the imaginative world of his father's creation was "*his gift to me*", as he looks back on the events from an adult perspective (ibid.).

The gift was protection of the child-self from trauma, in circumstances of extreme adversity. The gift is also a story, created prospectively and spontaneously, in response to a situation from the realm of horror. We need not only to recognize patterns of trauma but also to work towards the creation of illusions that foster growth. This is the demand, one might say, of intersubjective reality. The sharing of dreams may foster such creations. The task is essentially symbolic, in that it involves the creative use of language, rather than simply literal replication of facts and events.

Individuals find themselves in the space between the affordances of the environment and the actions, signs and feeling that are bodily contributions to the stream of consciousness and development of self. When there is a strong prevailing worldview espoused by the society into which one is born, this will be a substantial, although essentially symbolic, affordance with which the individual will have to reconcile. The complexity of this task is simpler in the case of a single community worldview.

At the time of his birth in the 4th century, St Augustine was already born into a time of competing worldviews. By the time St Augustine wrote the *Confessions*, his writing takes the form of a dialogue with God, representing his effort to reconcile himself with the received wisdom of the Bible (St Augustine, 2006). When St Augustine says, "we learn kindness from our very weakness" (ibid.), he refers to a universal truth emphasizing the vulnerable state in which all human life starts and to which we always remain subject. He is not, as many do, using *weakness* in a pejorative sense. Rather he sees it as having a central value, fostering kindness and care in human societies.

While the *Confessions* is a dialogue generated within a social environment less heterogeneous than modern developed societies, the dialogue includes recognition of other worldviews and the need for the individual to select from competing messages. A more homogeneous worldview is found in Indigenous Australia in the *Dreaming*. With the arrival of outside influence, the dreaming worldview still existed but could no longer exist as "total" worldview. Now many worldviews, religious and secular are confronted as external actualities by individuals, even though they are intersubjective realities rather than objective facts. In the face of this confusion we are susceptible to loss of balance and the sense of feeling lost.

Finding one's self requires creative, prospective effort in the development of a match between feeling and verbal expression. Change requires *exchange* with the peopled environment, providing contributions from other selves who become part of the process of transformation. Without these exchanges the individual is left in a solipsism dominated by repetitive thought and behaviour. Traditionally, this interpersonal process was facilitated by rituals, supporting relevant life stage transitions (i.e. "rites of passage"). It has become increasingly left to individuals to explore ways of developing an effective personal order that sustains balance in the relationship between self and world. Scientific views, extremely influential in modern societies, can have the effect of reducing experience to "objective reality". Nonetheless, to be useful, science still needs to be interpreted by individuals. The need for patients to digest what is actual and factual in their lives and to personalize it at the level of affective-conceptual integration, can be understood as a transformation of the lifelessness of pure objectivity, towards the ownership of personal value, ascending to what is personally concrete, in the sense of being felt and recognized as *me*. This is a process of symbolic transformation.

The challenge of translating individual process to communal and intercultural processes is debatable and daunting. If we allow for the possibility of a long conversation between peoples, perhaps we admit of the possibility of an exchange associated with growth. The timescale is likely to be long. Recognizing that *The Dreaming* might speak to our condition in the modern world could be an example of a long conversation worth having. An advance, in terms of civilization, on processes of domination and subjugation.

In language we find the syntax that allows higher consciousness and the storied self. *The Dreaming* understands the importance of stories of *belonging* not only to the *mob* but also to the *land*. Traditional song-lines reflect paths individuals follow in living, creative relationship with the land. Cultural stability and the sense of the world that *somehow holds us all*, contrasts with modern cultures, bent on competition and "progress" where objectivity trumps subjectivity in society's processes of evaluation, missing the affective heart of significance, what really matters to people. A culture which supports self would be a culture that supports personal dreaming, allowing creative engagement with the world around us.

Surely this is the great human dream. Dreams of dominance are in the end empty when it comes to the real challenge of living together cooperatively. The great dream is of unity in our humanity and diversity, with freedom in our particularity. *Dreaming* as *worldview* restores balance by recognizing the uniquely human contribution to a world and cosmos that seem to belittle us in their enormity.

In the spirit of this book, I draw things to a close with recounting of an experience that led to an encounter with wisdom from another time and place that spoke to me in the present, summing up what constitutes a balance between *self* and *other*.

> *I met with a Jewish friend who told me of some events that were being held in Sydney's Jewish Museum. I mentioned that I'd never been although I had thought of visiting. While I consider myself agnostic, I have both Jewish and Christian heritage. In any case, my wife and I made a visit. The foyer provides a vista onto many of the displays on various levels of the museum. Its walls had quotes, written in relief, from many sources, some modern, some*

ancient. One of these stood out to me and I found myself "hearing" it in my mind after I left the place, and subsequently. It read,

> *"If I am not for myself, who will be for me?*
> *If I am only for myself, what am I?*
> *If not now, when?"*
>
> Hillel HaGadol

This was written in the century before the common era.

There are long conversations going on all the time. If we listen, perhaps we will find the resources that bring our lives into balance. Finally, when the dreaming comes to an end in death, the personal conversation of the *little life* ends in silence. Perhaps a silence leavened by the knowledge that the human conversation continues.

There is only one human being and we find it in the dream.

References

Alighieri, D. (c.1310), *Inferno (The Divine Comedy: 1)*, trans. and ed. Kirkpatrick, R. London, Penguin, 2006.
Anderson, T. & Shotter, J., *Don't Think, Look!* (on a "Wittgensteinian" approach to therapy) Paper presented at the EAP Congress, Cambridge, 14th August, 2006.
Appelhans, B.M. & Luecken, L.J., Heart Rate Variability as an Index of Regulated Emotional Responding. *Review of General Psychology*, 2006; 10(3):229–240.
Aristotle, *Metaphysics*, Book H 1045a 8–10 (quote taken from Wikipedia). http://en.wikipedia.org/wiki/Emergence
Aristotle, *Poetics*, trans. Health, M. London, Penguin, 1996.
Atkinson, J., *Trauma Trails*. Melbourne, Spinifex Press, 2002.
Atzil, S., Gao, W., Fradkin, I. & Barrett, L.F., Growing a Social Brain. *Nature Human Behaviour*, 2018. https://doi.org/10.1038/s41562-018-0384-6
Audi, R. (ed.), *The Cambridge Dictionary of Philosophy*. Cambridge, Cambridge University Press, 1995.
Austin, M.A., Riniolo, T.C. & Porges, S.W., Borderline Personality Disorder and Emotion Regulation: Insights from the Polyvagal Theory. *Brain and Cognition*, 2007; 65:69–76.
Bains, P., *The Primacy of Semiosis: An Ontology of Relations*. Toronto, University of Toronto Press, 2006.
Baldwin, J.M., *Thoughts and Things*, Vol. 1. London & New York, Macmillan, 1906.
Bannan, N. & Woodward, S., Spontaneity in the Musicality and Music Learning of Children. In, Malloch, S. & Trevarthen, C. (eds.), *Communicative Musicality: Exploring the Basis of Human Companionship*, Vol. 21 (pp. 465–494). Oxford, Oxford University Press, 2009.
Bargh, J.A. & Chartrand, T.L., The Unbearable Automaticity of Being. *American Psychologist*, 1999; 54(7):462–479.
Barral, C. & Meares, R., The Holistic Project of Pierre Janet, Part Two: Oscillations and Becomings: From Disintegration to Integration. Chapter 9 In, Craparo, G., Ortu, F. & van der Hart, O. (eds.), *Rediscovering Pierre Janet: Trauma, Dissociation, and a New Context for Psychoanalysis*. London, Routledge, 2019.
Barthes, R., *S/Z*. New York, Farrar, Straus & Giroux, 1974.
Bateson, G., (1954), A Theory of Play and Fantasy. In, Innis, R.E. (ed.), *Semiotics, an Introductory Anthology*. Bloomington, IN, Indiana University Press, 1985.
Baum, A.L., Carroll's *Alices*: The Semiotics of Paradox. *American Imago*, 1977; 34:86–108.

Beckett, S., et al., *Our Exagmination Round His Factification for Incamination of Work in Progress*. With Letters of Protest by G.V.L. Slingsby and V. Dixon. Paris, Shakespeare and Company, 1929; London, Faber & Faber, 1929.

Benigni, R. & Cerami, V., *Life Is Beautiful* (Screenplay). Film, Cecchi Gori Pictures, Prod. Brashchi, G., Dir. Benigni, R., 1997.

Benjamin, J., *Shadow of the Other: Intersubjectivity and Gender in Psychoanalysis*. New York, Routledge, 1998.

Benjamin, J., Beyond Doer and Done to: An Intersubjective View of Thirdness. *The Psychoanalytic Quarterly*, 2004; 78:5–46.

Benjamin, R., Unconscious Relational Traumatic Memory and Its Relevance to "Everyday" Clinical Psychiatry. *Australasian Psychiatry*, 2013; 21:321–325.

Bennett, M., Criminal Law as It Pertains to "Mentally Incompetent Defendants": A McNaughton Rule in the Light of Cognitive Neuroscience. *Australia and New Zealand Journal of Psychiatry*, 2009; 43:289–299.

Bennett, M. & Hacker, P.M.S., Philosophical Foundations of Neuroscience: The Introduction. In, Bennett, M., Dennett, D., Hacker, P. & Searle, J. (eds.), *Neuroscience and Philosophy*. New York, Columbia University Press, 2007.

Berthold, D., Talking Cures: A Lacanian Reading of Hegel and Kierkegaard on Language on Madness. *Philosophy, Psychiatry, & Psychology*, 2009; 16:299–311.

Billman, G.E., Heart Rate Variability: A Historical Perspective. *Frontiers in Physiology*, 2011; 2:86–97.

Blair, D. (ed.), *The Pocket Macquarie Dictionary*. Sydney, The Jacaranda Press, 1982.

Bollas, C., Why Oedipus? Chapter 7 In, *The Christopher Bollas Reader*. London & New York, Routledge, 2011.

Bowden, A.R., *A Psychotherapist Sings in Aotearoa*. Plimmerton (Wellington), Caroy Publications, 2001.

Bowlby, J., *Attachment, Separation, and Loss*, Vols 1, 2 & 3. London, The Hogarth Press & The Institute of Psycho-Analysis, 1969, 1973 & 1980.

Bowlby, J., *Attachment*. Pelican, Harmondsworth, Middlesex, 1984.

Bowlby, J., *A Secure Base: Parent-Child Attachment and Health Development*. London, Routledge, 1988.

Brandchaft, B., The Negativism of the Negative Therapeutic Reaction and the Psychology of the Self. In, Goldberg, A. (ed.), *The Future of Psychanalysis* (pp. 327–359). New York, International Universities Press, 1983.

Brandchaft, B., Doctors, S. & Sorter, D., *Towards and Emancipatory Psychoanalysis*. New York, Taylor & Francis, 2012.

Brazelton, T.B., Evidence of Communication during Neonatal Behavioural Assessment. In, Bullowa, M. (ed.), *Before Speech: The Beginning of Interpersonal Communication*. Cambridge, Cambridge University Press, 1979.

Broca, P., Anatomie compare des circonvolutions cerebrales: Le grand lobe limbique et la scissure limbique dans la serie des mammiferes. *Rev Anthropol*, 1878; 1:385–498.

Browning, M.M., Feeling One's Way in the World: Making a Life. *International Journal of Psychoanalysis*, 2017; 98(4):1075–1095.

Buber, M., *I and Thou*. Edinburgh, T & T Clark, 1937.

Buber, M., *Between Man and Man*, trans. Gregor-Smith, R. London, Routledge, 1947.

Buckley, T., Stannard, A., Bartrop, R., McKinley, S., Ward, C., Mihailidou, S., Morel-Kopp, M., Spinaze, M. & Tofler, G., Effect of Early Bereavement on Heart Rate and Heart Rate Variability. *American Journal of Cardiology*, 2012; 110:1378–1383.

Budgen, F., (1934), *James Joyce and the Making of Ulysses*. London, Oxford University Press, 1972.
Bullowa, M., Prelinguistic Communication: A Field for Scientific Research. In, Bullowa, M. (ed.), *Before Speech: The Beginning of Interpersonal Communication*. Cambridge, Cambridge University Press, 1979.
Burgess, A., *Shakespeare*. London, Jonathan Cape, 1970.
Butt, D.G., Some Basic Tools in a Linguistic Approach to Personality. In, Christie, F. (ed.), *Literacy in Social Processes*. Melbourne, Centre for Studies of Language Education, 1990.
Butt, D.G., Method and Imagination in Halliday's Science of Linguistics. In, Hasan, R., Matthiessen, C.M.I.M. & Webster, J.J. (eds.), *Continuing Discourse on Language: A Functional Perspective*, Vol. 1. London, Equinox, 2005.
Butt, D.G., *"Mysterious Butterflies of the Soul": One Linguistic Perspective on the Efficacy of Meaning in the "Mind-Brain" System*. Keynote address, "Voices Around the World", 35th International Systemic Functional Linguistics Congress, Macquarie University, Sydney, 21st July, 2008.
Butt, D.G., Fahey, R., Feez, S., Spinks, S. & Yallop, C., *Using Functional Grammar: An Explorer's Guide*, 2nd Edition. Sydney, National Centre for English Language Teaching and Research, Macquarie University, 2000.
Butt, D.G., Henderson-Brooks, C., Moore, A., Meares, R., Haliburn, J., Korner, A. & Eyal, R., Motivated Selection in Verbal Art, "Verbal Science", and Psychotherapy: When Many Methods Are at One. In, Yan, F. & Webster, J.J. (eds.), *Deploying Systemic Functional Linguistics*. London, Continuum, 2012.
Butt, D.G. & Lukin, A., Stylistic Analysis: Construing Aesthetic Organization. In, Halliday, M.J.K. & Webster (eds.), *Systemic Functional Linguistics, Companion Volume*. London, Continuum, 2009.
Butt, D.G., Moore, A.R., Henderson-Brooks, C., Meares, R. & Haliburn, J., Dissociation, Relatedness, and "Cohesive Harmony": A Linguistic Measure of "Fragmentation". *Linguistics and the Human Sciences*, 2007/10; 3(3):263–293.
Calvin, W.H., *How Brains Think: Evolving Intelligence, Then and Now*. New York, Phoenix, 1996. **Note:** Page references taken from the Kindle Edition of this book, where the notation is in terms of "Location" rather than page (hence, "Loc").
Cammell, P., *Reinterpreting the Borderline: Heidegger and the Psychoanalytic Understanding of Borderline Personality Disorder*. London, Rowman & Littlefield, 2016.
Cardinal, M., *The Words to Say It*, trans. Goodheart, P. London, Picador, 1984.
Cardoso, S.H. & Sabbatini, R.M.E., The Animal That Weeps. *Accessed on Dana Foundation Website*, 2002. www.dana.org/news/cerebrum/detail.aspx?id=1740
Caspi, A. & Moffitt, T. E., All for One and One for All. Mental Disorders in One Dimension. *American Journal of Psychiatry*, 2018, 175; 9:831–844. https://doi.org/10.1176/appi.ajp.2018.17121383
Charon, R., *Narrative Medicine: Honoring the Stories of Illness*. Oxford & New York, Oxford University Press, 2006.
Chomsky, N., *The Logical Structure of Linguistic Theory*. New York & London, Plenum Press, 1975.
Church of England (1662), *The Book of Common Prayer*. London: Everyman's Library (published 1999), ISBN 1-85715-241-7.
Cole, R.B., *Essentials of Respiratory Disease*. London, Pitman Medical, 1975.

Cross, I., Communicative Development: Neonate Crying Reflects Patterns of Native Language Speech. *Current Biology*, 2009; 19:R1078–R1079.
Damasio, A., *The Feeling of What Happens*. London, Vintage, 2000.
Damasio, A., *Self Comes to Mind: Constructing the Conscious Brain*. London, Vintage, 2012.
Darwin, C., (1872), *The Expression of the Emotions in Man and Animals*. London, HarperCollins, 1998.
Deacon, G., The Science of Human Relationships. *Nature*, 1945; 155:649–652.
Delbridge, A., (ed.), *The Macquarie Dictionary*, Sydney, Macquarie Library Pty Ltd, 1981.
Detre, T., The Future of Psychiatry. *American Journal of Psychiatry*, 1987; 144:621–625.
Deutscher, G., *The Unfolding of Language*. New York, Holt, 2005.
Diagnostic and Statistical Manual of Mental Disorders: DSM 1, 1st Edition, Washington, American Psychiatric Association, 1952.
Diagnostic and Statistical Manual of Mental Disorders: DSM IV^{TM}, 4th Edition, Washington DC, American Psychiatric Association, 1994.
Diagnostic and Statistical Manual of Mental Disorders: DSM-5, 5th Edition, Arlington, VA, American Psychiatric Association, 2013.
Dobzhansky, T.G., Mankind Evolving: The Evolution of the Human Species. *The Eugenics Review*, 1962; 54(3):168–169.
Doidge, N., *The Brain That Changes Itself*. New York, Viking Penguin, 2007.
Dolen, G., Darvishzadeh, A., Huang, K.W. & Malenka, R.C., Social Reward Requires Coordinated Activity of Nucleus Accumbens Oxytocins and Serotonin. *Nature*, 2013; 501:179–184.
Dunbar, R., *Grooming, Gossip, and the Evolution of Language*. Cambridge, MA, Faber & Faber, 1996.
Edelman, G.M., Personal Communication. Cambridge, July, 2006.
Edelman, G.M., *Second Nature: Brain Science and Human Knowledge*. New Haven & London, Yale University Press, 2006.
Edelman, G.M. & Tononi, G., *Consciousness: How Matter Becomes Imagination*. London, Penguin, 2000.
Ellenberger, H.F., *The Discovery of the Unconscious: The History and Evolution of Dynamic Psychiatry*. New York, Ingram, 1981.
Emde, R.N., The Pre-Representational Self and Its Affective Core. *Psychoanalytic Study of the Child*, 1983; 38:165–192.
Emde, R.N., Kubicek, L. & Oppenheim, D., Imaginative Reality Observed during Early Language Development. *International Journal of Psychoanalysis*, 1997; 78:115–133.
Fair, D.A., Cohen, A.L., Dosenbach, N.U.F., Church, J.A., Miezin, F.M., Barch, D.M., Raichle, M.E., Petersen, S.E. & Schlaggar, B.L., The Maturing Architecture of the Brain's Default Network. *Proceedings of the National Academy of Sciences U.S.A.*, 2008; 105(10):4028–4032.
Fairbairn, R., *Psychoanalytic Studies of the Personality*. London, Tavistock, 1952.
Fernald, A., Human Maternal Vocalizations to Infants as Biologically Relevant Signals: An Evolutionary Perspective. In, Barkow, J.W., Cosmides, L. & Tooby, J. (eds.), *The Adapted Mind: Evolutionary Psychology and the Generation of Culture* (pp. 391–428). Oxford, Oxford University Press, 1992.
Fernandez-Armesto, F., *Truth*. London, Black Swan, 1997.
Fernandez-Armesto, F., *Out of Our Minds: What We Think and How We Came to Think It*. London, One World, 2019.

Fonagy, P., Gergely, G., Jurist, E.L. & Target, M., *Affect Regulation, Mentalization, and the Development of Self.* New York, Other Press, 2002.

Frances, A., Saving Normal: An Insider's Revolt against Out-of-Control Psychiatric Diagnosis, DSM-5, Big Pharma and the Medicalization of Ordinary Life. *Psychotherapy in Australia*, 2013; 19:14–18.

Frankl, V., *Man's Search for Meaning.* Boston, Beacon Press, 1992.

Frayn, M., *The Human Touch: Our Part in the Creation of a Universe.* London, Faber and Faber, 2006.

Frenkel, O., Phenomenology of the "Placebo Effect": Taking Meaning from the Mind to the Body. *Journal of Medicine and Philosophy*, 2008; 33:58–79.

Freud, S., (1895), Project for a Scientific Psychology. In, *The Standard Edition of the Complete Psychological Works of Sigmund Freud*, Vol. 1 (pp. 281–397). London, Hogarth, 1950.

Freud, S., (1900), The Interpretation of Dreams. In, *The Standard Edition of the Complete Psychological Works of Sigmund Freud*, Vols. 4 & 5. London, Hogarth, 1953.

Freud, S., (1905), Three Essays on the Theory of Sexuality. In, *The Standard Edition of the Complete Psychological Works of Sigmund Freud*, Vol. 7 (pp. 135–221). London, Hogarth, 1953.

Freud, S., (1911), Formulations on the Two Principles of Mental Functioning. In, *The Standard Edition of the Complete Psychological Works of Sigmund Freud*, Vol. 18 (pp. 1–64). London, Hogarth, 1955–64.

Freud, S., (1915), Instincts and Their Vicissitudes. In, *The Standard Edition of the Complete Psychological Works of Sigmund Freud*, Vol. 14 (pp. 109–140). London, Hogarth, 1957.

Freud, S., (1920), Beyond the Pleasure Principle. In, *The Standard Edition of the Complete Psychological Works of Sigmund Freud*, Vol. 18 (pp. 1–64). London, Hogarth, 1955–64. Page refs from, Freud, S., *On Metapsychology.* London, Penguin, 1984.

Freud, S., (1921), Group Psychology and the Analysis of the Ego. In, *The Standard Edition of the Complete Psychological Works of Sigmund Freud*, Vol. 18 (pp. 65–144). London, Hogarth, 1955.

Freud, S., (1923), The Ego and the Id. In, *The Standard Edition of the Complete Psychological Works of Sigmund Freud*, Vol. 19 (pp. 1–66). London, Hogarth, 1949.

Freud, S., (1933), New Introductory Lectures on Psychoanalysis. In, *The Standard Edition of the Complete Psychological Works of Sigmund Freud*, Vol. 22, lecture 31, The Dissection of the Psychical Personality, London, Hogarth, 1964. Page references given are to the copy of "New Introductory Lectures". www.scribd.com/doc/31127291/Freud-New-Introductory-Lectures-on-Psycho-Analysis-1933a

Fukuyama, F., *The Origins of Political Order.* New York, Farrar, Straus & Giroux, 2011.

Gallese, V., Fadiga, L., Fogassi, L. & Rizzolatti, G. Action Recognition in the Premotor Cortex. *Brain*, 1996; 119:593–609.

Gelven, M., *A Commentary on Heidegger's Being and Time.* De Kalb, IL, Northern Illinois University Press, 1989.

Gevirtz, R., The Promise of HRV Biofeedback: Some Preliminary Results and Speculations. Biofeedback, Fall, 2003.

Goehler, L.E., Vagal Complexity: Substrate for Body-Mind Connections? *Bratislasvske Lekarske Listy* [*Bratislava Medical Journal*], 2006; 107:275–278.

Goldberg, E., *The Wisdom Paradox.* New York, NY, Gotham Books, 2005.

Goleman, D., *Emotional Intelligence.* New York, Bantam Books, 1995.

Goodman, R.B., *Wittgenstein and William James.* Cambridge, Cambridge University Press, 2002.

Gratier, M. & Apter-Danon, G., The Improvised Musicality of Belonging: Repetition and Variation in Mother-Infant Vocal Interaction. In, Malloch, S. & Trevarthen, C. (eds.), *Communicative Musicality: Exploring the Basis of Human Companionship*, Vol. 14 (pp. 301–330). Oxford, Oxford University Press, 2009.

Greenspan, S.I. & Shankar, S.G., *The First Idea: How Symbols, Language and Intelligence Evolved from Our Primate Ancestors to Modern Humans*. Cambridge, MA, Da Capo Press, 2004.

Gregory, R.L., *The Oxford Companion to the Mind*. Oxford, Oxford University Press, 1987.

Grenyer, B.F.S., The Clinician's Dilemma: Core Conflictual Relationship Themes in Personality Disorders. *Acparian*, 2012; 4:24–26.

Hales, S., *Statistical Essays II, Haemastaticks*. London, W. Innys & R. Manby, 1773.

Halliday, M.A.K., *Learning How to Mean: Explorations in the Development of Language*. London, Edward Arnold, 1975.

Halliday, M.A.K., How Do You Mean? In, Davies, M. & Ravelli, L. (eds.), *Advances in Systemic Linguistics: Recent Theory and Practice*. London, Pinter, 1992.

Halliday, M.A.K., On Language in Relation to the Evolution of Human Consciousness. In, Allen, S. (ed.), *Of Thoughts and Words: Proceedings of Nobel Symposium 92: The Relation between Language and Mind*. River Edge, NJ, Imperial College Press, 1995.

Halliday, M.A.K., *Text and Discourse*. London, Continuum, 2002.

Halliday, M.A.K. & Matthiessen, C.M.I.M., *An Introduction to Functional Grammar*, 3rd Edition. London, Hodder Arnold, 2004.

Harari, Y.N., *Sapiens: A Brief History of Humankind*. London, Vintage, 2011.

Harris, R., *Language, Saussure and Wittgenstein*. London, Routledge, 1988.

Hasan, R., *Language, Society and Consciousness*. London, Equinox, 2005.

Hasan, R., (2011), Linguistic Sign and the Science of Linguistics: The Foundations of Applicability. In, Fang, Y. & Webster, J. (eds.), *Developing Systemic Functional Linguistics*. London, Equinox, 2013.

Hassabis, D., Kumaran, D. & Maguire, E.A., Using Imagination to Understand the Neural Basis of Episodic Memory. *The Journal of Neuroscience*, 2007; 27:14365–14373.

Hegel, G.W.F. (1807), *Phenomenology of Spirit*, trans. Miller, A.V. Oxford, Oxford University Press, 1977.

Heidegger, M., (1927), *Being and Time*, 7th Edition, trans. Macquarrie, J. San Francisco, Harper and Row, 1962.

Heidegger, M., *Basic Writings: From Being and Time (1927) to the Task of Thinking (1964)*, ed. Krell, D. New York, Harper and Row, 1977.

Heisenberg, W., Ueber die Grundprincipien der "Quantenmechanik". *Forschungen und Fortschritte*, 1927; 3(11) S 83 Z: 602–603.

Henderson-Brooks, C.K., *What Type of Person Am I, Tess? The Complex Tale of Self in Psychotherapy*. Ph.D. thesis, Macquarie University, 2006.

Hirsch, J.A. & Bishop, B., Respiratory Sinus Arrhythmia in Humans: How Breathing Pattern Modulates Heart Rate. *American Journal of Physiology*, 1981; 241:H620–H629.

Hobson, R., *Forms of Feeling*. London, Tavistock, 1985.

Holmes, J., *John Bowlby and Attachment Theory*. London, Routledge, 1993.

Hon, E.H. & Lee, S.T., Electronic Evaluations of Fetal Heart Rate Patterns Preceding Fetal Death, Further Observations. *American Journal of Obstetrics and Gynecology*, 1965; 87:814–826.

Innis, R.E., Introduction. In, Innis, R.E. (ed.), *Semiotics, an Introductory Anthology*. Bloomington, IN, Indiana University Press, 1985.

Jackson, J.H., *Selected Writings of John Hughlings Jackson*, Vols. 1 & 2, ed. Taylor, J. London, Hodder, 1931–2.
James, W., (1890), *The Principles of Psychology*, Vol. 1. New York, Dover, 1950.
James, W., (1892), Psychology: Briefer Course: The Stream of Consciousness. In, James, W., *Pragmatism and Other Writings*. (ed. Gunn, G.). New York, Penguin, 2000.
James, W., (1899), On a Certain Blindness in Human Beings. In, James, W., *Pragmatism and Other Writings*. Penguin, Harmondsworth, Middlesex, 2000 (page refs from this volume).
James, W., (1902), *The Varieties of Religious Experience*, Centenary Edition. London & New York, Routledge, 2002.
James, W., (1904), Does Consciousness Exist? In, Wilshire, B.W. (ed.), *William James, The Essential Writings*. Albany, State University of New York Press, 1984.
Jaspers, K., *General Psychopathology*. (1963 translation). Baltimore, Johns Hopkins University Press, 1997.
Joyce, J., Letter to Stanislaus, Feb. 11, 1907. In, Gilbert, S. (ed.), *Letters of James Joyce*, Vol. 1 (p. 213). New York, Viking Press, 1966.
Jung, C.G., (1923), Psychological Types. In, Staub de Laszlo, V. (ed.), *The Basic Writings of C.G. Jung*. New York, The Modern Library, 1959.
Jung, C.G., (1934), Archetypes of the Collective Unconscious. In, Staub de Laszlo, V. (ed.), *The Basic Writings of C.G. Jung*. New York, The Modern Library, 1959.
Kaehler, S.D., Fuzzy Logic: An Introduction: Part 1. *Encoder, The Newsletter of the Seattle Robotics Society*, March, 1998.
Kagan, J., *What Is Emotion?* New Haven and London, Yale University Press, 2007.
Kemp, A.H., Quintana, D.S., Gray, M.A., Felmingham, K.L., Brown, K. & Gatt, J., Impact of Depression and Antidepressant Treatment on Heart Rate Variability: A Review and Meta-Analysis. *Biological Psychiatry*, 2010; 67:1067–1074.
Kendler, K., Hettema, J.M., Butera, F., Gardner, C.O. & Prescott, C.A., Life Event Dimensions of Loss, Humiliation, Entrapment, and Danger in the Prediction of Onsets of Major Depression and Generalized Anxiety. *Archives of General Psychiatry*, 2003; 60:789–796.
Kenwright, D.A., Bahraminasab, A., Stefanovska, A. & McClintock, P.V.E., The Effect of Low-Frequency Oscillations on Cardio-Respiratory Synchronisation. *European Physical Journal B: Condensed Matter and Complex Systems*, 2008; 65:425–433.
Khan, M.M.R., Introduction. In, Winnicott, D.W. (ed.), *Through Paediatrics to Psycho-Analysis*. New York, Basic Books, 1975.
Kierkegaard, S., *Kierkegaard's journals and papers*, 6 vols, trans. Hong, H. & Hong, E. Bloomington, Indiana University Press, 1967.
King James Version (KJV), *The Holy Bible*, Revised Edition. London, The British and Foreign Bible Society, 1956.
Kirkpatrick, R., (trans. & ed.), *Inferno (The Divine Comedy: 1, Dante Alighieri)*. London, Penguin, 2006.
Kohut, H., *The Analysis of Self*. New York, International Universities Press, 1971.
Kolasz, J. & Porges, S., Chronic Diffuse Pain and Gastrointestinal Disorders after Traumatic Stress: Pathophysiology from a Polyvagal Perspective. *Frontiers in Medicine: Hypothesis and Theory*, 2018; Open Access, doi: 10.3389/fmed.2018.00145
Korner, A., Liveliness. *Australian and New Zealand Journal of Psychiatry*, 2000; 34:731–740.
Korner, A. The Phenomenology of Feeling. In, Meares, R. & Nolan, P. (eds.), *The Self in Conversation*, Vol. 1. Sydney, ANZAP Books, 2002.

Korner, A., Language as Metaphorical Environment. In, Meares, R. & Nolan, P. (eds.), *The Self in Conversation*, Vol. 2. Sydney, ANZAP Books, 2003.

Korner, A., Living the World Knot: Towards a Reconciliation of the Brain, Mind and the Living Environment. *International Journal of Psychotherapy*, 2008; 12:26–38.

Korner, A., Language and the Personality Conundrum: Developing a Science of Personality. In, Meares, R. & Nolan, P. (eds.), *The Self in Conversation*, Vol. 7. Sydney, ANZAP, 2008.

Korner, A., Dreaming as Worldview. *ANZAP Bulletin, (Special Supplement), "Conversations in Dreaming"*, 2011; 20(3):22–26.

Korner, A., *Analogical Fit: Dynamic Relatedness in the Psychotherapeutic Setting (with Reference to Language, Autonomic Response, and Change in Self-State)*. Thesis submitted in accordance with the requirements of Doctor of Philosophy, Sydney, Macquarie University, 2015.

Korner, A., Heart to Heart: The Associative Pathway to Therapeutic Growth. *International Journal of Psychotherapy, Counselling & Psychiatry: Theory, Research and Clinical Practice*, 2018; 3, April. http://ijpcp.com/

Korner, A.J., Bendit, N., Ptok, U., Tuckwell, K. & Butt, D., Formulation, Conversation and Therapeutic Engagement. *Australasian Psychiatry*, 2010; 18:214–220.

Korner, A.J., Gerull, F., Meares, R. & Stevenson, J., The Nothing That Is Something: Core Dysphoria as the Central Feature of Borderline Personality Disorder: Implications for Treatment. *American Journal of Psychotherapy*, 2008; 62:377–394.

Korner, T., Making Conscious Identifications: A Means of Promoting Empathic Contact. *ANZ Journal of Psychiatry*, 1993; 27:115–126.

Kotani, K., Tachibana, M. & Takamasu, K., Investigation of the Influence of Swallowing Coughing and Vocalization on Heart Rate Variability with Respiratory-Phase Domain Analysis. *Methods of Information in Medicine*, 2007; 46:179–185.

Kreibig, S.D., Autonomic Nervous System Activity in Emotion: A Review. *Biological Psychiatry*, 2010; 84:394–421.

Kripke, S.A., *Wittgenstein: On Rules and Private Language*. Oxford, Blackwell, 1982.

Kriss, S., Book of Lamentations. *Psychotherapy in Australia*, 2013; 20:52–54.

Lacan, J., *The Seminars of Jacques Lacan, Book XI: The Four Fundamental Concepts of Psycho-Analysis*, trans. Grigg, R. New York, Norton, 1964.

Lacan, J., *Ecrits*, trans. Fink, B. New York, Norton, 1966.

Lacan, J., *The Language of the Self*, trans. Wilden, A. Baltimore, The Johns Hopkins University Press, 1968.

LaGasse, L.L., Neal, A.R. & Lester, B.M., Assessment of Infant Cry: Acoustic Cry Analysis and Parental Perception. *Mental Retardation and Developmental Disabilities Research Reviews*, 2005; 11:83–93.

Lamb, S., *Pathways of the Brain*. Philadelphia, Benjamins, 1999.

Lambert, M. (ed.), *Bergin and Garfield's Handbook of Psychotherapy and Behavioural Change*, 6th Edition. Hoboken, NJ, John Wiley & Sons, 2013.

Lambert, M., Introduction and Historical Overview. Chapter 1 In, Lambert, M. (ed.), *Bergin and Garfield's Handbook of Psychotherapy and Behavioural Change*, 6th Edition. Hoboken, NJ, John Wiley & Sons, 2013.

Larsen, W.J., *Human Embryology*, 3rd Edition. New York, Elsevier, 2001.

Le, N., *The Boat*. Camberwell, VIC, Penguin, 2008.

Le Doux, J.E., Emotion Circuits in the Brain. *Annual Review of Neuroscience*, 2000; 23:155–184.

Lemke, J., Material Sign Processes and Emergent Ecosocial Organization. In, Andersen, P.B., Emmeche, C., Finnemann, N.O. & Christiansen, P.V. (eds.), *Downward Causation: Minds, Bodies and Matter*. Aarhus, Aarhus University Press, 2000.

Levenson, E.A., *The Purloined Self: Interpersonal Perspectives in Psychoanalysis*. London & New York, Routledge, 2017.

Lewis, D. (Daniel), Marshall turns his kicking around, but was happier to meet Lleyton, p. 28, *The Sydney Morning Herald*. 16 August 2010.

Lewkowicz, D.J. & Ghazanfar, A.A., (2006), The Decline of Cross-Species Intersensory Perception in Human Infants. National Academy of Sciences of the USA, 2010. http://pnas.org/content/103/17/6771.full.

Lewontin, R., *The Triple Helix*. Cambridge, MA, Harvard University Press, 2000.

Lichtenberg, J.D., *Psychoanalysis and Motivation*. Hillsdale, NJ, The Analytic Press, 1989.

Lingiardi, V., *Challenging Oedipus in Changing Families*. Paper presented at RANZCP Faculty of Psychotherapy Conference, Barcelona, 13th July, 2019.

Luborsky, L., Measuring a Pervasive Psychic Structure in the Psychotherapy: The Core Conflictual Relationship Theme. In, Freedman, N. & Grand, S. (eds.), *Communicative Structures and Psychic Structures*. New York, Plenum Press, 1977.

Luepnitz, D.A., Thinking in the Space between Winnicott and Lacan. *International Journal of Psychoanalysis*, 2009; 90:957–981.

Lyons-Ruth, K., Implicit Relational Knowing: Its Role in Development and Psychoanalytic Treatment. *Infant Mental Health Journal*, 1998; 19:282–289.

Lyons-Ruth, K., Dutra, L., Schuder, M.R. & Bianchi, I. From Infant Attachment Disorganization to Adult Dissociation: Relational Adaptations or Traumatic Experiences? *Psychiatric Clinics of North America*, 2006; 29:63–86.

MacLean, P.D., Brain Evolution Relating to Family, Play and the Separation Call. *Archives of General Psychiatry*, 1985; 42:405–417.

MacLean, P.D., Evolution of Audiovocal Communication as Reflected by the Therapsid-Mammalian Transition and the Limbic Thalamocingulate Division. In, Newman, J.D. (ed.), *The Physiological Control of Mammalian Vocalization* (pp. 185–201). New York, Plenum, 1988.

MacMurray, J., *Persons in Relation*. London, Faber & Faber, 1961.

Mahler, M., Pine, F. & Bergman, A., *The Psychological Birth of the Infant*. London, Hutchinson, 1975.

Main, M., Kaplan, N. & Cassidy, J., Security of Infancy, Childhood, and Adulthood: A Move to the Level of Representation. In, Bretherton, I. & Waters, E. (eds.), *Growing Points of Attachment Theory and Research*. Chicago, University of Chicago Press, 1985.

Malloch, S., *Communicative Musicality: Theory and Practice in Psychotherapy*. Seminar, Australian and New Zealand Association of Psychotherapy, 18th February, 2012.

Malloch, S. & Trevarthen, C. (eds.), *Communicative Musicality: Exploring the Basis of Human Companionship*. Oxford, Oxford University Press, 2009.

Malloch, S. & Trevarthen, C., Musicality: Communicating the Vitality and Interests of Life. In, Malloch, S. & Trevarthen, C. (eds.), *Communicative Musicality: Exploring the Basis of Human Companionship*. Oxford, Oxford University Press, 2009.

Malloch, S. & Trevarthen, C., The Human Nature of Music. *Front. Psychol.*, October, 2018. www.frontiersin.org/people.u/58154

Mampe, B., Friederici, A.D., Christophe, A. & Wermke, K., Newborns' Cry Melody Is Shaped by Their Native Language. *Current Biology*, 2009; 19:1994–1997.

Marci, C.D., Ham, J., Moran, E. & Orr, S.P. Physiologic Correlates of Perceived Therapist Empathy and Social-Emotional Process during Psychotherapy. *Journal of Nervous and Mental Disease*, 2007; 195:103–111.

Marek, M., Task Force of the European Society of Cardiology and the North American Society of Pacing and Electrophysiology: Heart Rate Variability: Standards of Measurement, Physiological Interpretation, and Clinical Use. *Circulation*, 1996; 93:1043–1065.

Mariani, R., Maskit, B., Bucci, W. & De Coro, A., Linguistic Measures of the Referential Process in Psychodynamic Treatment: The English and Italian Versions. *Psychotherapy Research*, 2013; 23:430–447.

Martel, F., *In the Closet of the Vatican*. London, Bloomsbury Continuum, 2019.

Mason, C., *Ulysses: A Map of the Human Body from the Ear to the Rear*. Bloomsday, 16th June, Kerry Packer Auditorium, Prince Alfred Hospital, Sydney, 2008. www.bloomsdaysydney.com/publications/styled-2/a_map_of_the_human_body2008.html, 2014.

Maturana, H.R., Biology of Language: The Epistemology of Reality. In, Miller, G.A. & Lenneberg, E. (eds.), *Psychology and Biology of Language and Thought: Essays in Honor of Eric Lenneberg* (pp. 27–63). New York: Academic Press, 1978.

Maturana, H.R. & Verdan-Zoeller, G., *The Origin of the Humanness in the Biology of Love*. Exeter, Imprint Academic, 2009.

McGilchrist, I., *The Master and his Emissary*. New Haven, Yale University Press, 2009.

McGilchrist, I., *The Divided Brain and the Search for Meaning: Why Are We So Unhappy? (ebook)*. New Haven, Yale University Press, 2012.

McGinn, M., *Routledge Philosophy Guidebook to Wittgenstein's and the Philosophical Investigations*. London, Routledge, 1997.

McLean, L. & Korner, A., Dreaming the (Lost) Self in Psychotherapy: Beings in Body spacetime in Collision, Confusion and Connection. In, *(e-book), Inter-Disciplinary.net*. Oxfordshire, Freeland, 2013. www.inter-disciplinary.net

McLeod, J., Qualitative Research: Methods and Contributions. Chapter 3 In, Lambert, M. (ed.), *Bergin and Garfield's Handbook of Psychotherapy and Behavioural Change*, 6th Edition. Hoboken, NJ, John Wiley & Sons, 2013.

McWilliams, N., *Paper presented for the Section of Psychotherapy, RANZCP*, University of Sydney, Sydney, August, 2010.

Meares, R., The Fragile Spielraum: An Approach to Transmuting Internalisation. In, Golberg, A. (ed.), *The Realities of Transference: Progress in Self-Psychology*, Vol. 6 & 7 (pp. 69–89). Hillsdale, NJ, Analytic Press, 1990.

Meares, R., Episodic Memory, Trauma and the Narrative of Self. *Contemporary Psychoanalysis*, 1995; 31:541–555.

Meares, R., The Self in Conversation: On Narratives, Chronicles and Scripts. *Psychoanalytic Dialogues*, 1998; 8:875–891.

Meares, R., The "Adualistic" Representation of Trauma: On Malignant Internalization. *American Journal of Psychotherapy*, 1999a; 53:392–402.

Meares, R., Hughlings Jackson's Contribution to an Understanding of Dissociation. *American Journal of Psychiatry*, 1999b; 156:1850–1855.

Meares, R., *Intimacy and Alienation*. London, Routledge, 2000.

Meares, R. *The Metaphor of Play*, 3rd Edition. Hove, Routledge, 2005.

Meares, R., Attacks on Value: A New Approach to Depression. *Psychotherapy in Australia*, 2006; 12:62–68.

Meares, R., *A Dissociation Model of Borderline Personality Disorder*. New York, W.W. Norton, 2012.

Meares, R., *The Poet's Voice in the Making of Mind*. London, Routledge, 2016.
Meares, R., The Interpersonal Construction of the Human Brain-Mind System. In, Benjamin, R., Haliburn, J. & King, S. (eds.), *Humanising Health Care in Australia*. London & New York, Routledge, 2019.
Meares, R., Bendit, N., Haliburn, J., Korner, A., Mears, D. & Butt, D., *Borderline Personality Disorder and the Conversational Model: A Clinician's Manual*. New York, Norton, 2012.
Meares, R., Butt, D., Henderson-Brooks, C. & Samir, H., (2005b) A Poetics of Change. *Psychoanalytic Dialogues*, 2005; 15:661–680.
Meares, R. & Jones, S., Analogical Relatedness in Personal Integration or Coherence. *Contemporary Psychoanalysis*, 2009; 45(4):504–519.
Meares, R. & Lichtenberg, J., The Form of Play in the Shape and Unity of Self. *Contemporary Psychoanalysis*, 1995; 31:47–64.
Meares, R. & Orlay, W. On Self Boundary: A Study of the Development of the Concept of Secrecy. *British Journal of Medical Psychology*, 1988; 55:305–316.
Meares, R., Schore, A. & Melkonian, D., Is Borderline Personality Disorder a Particularly Right Hemispheric Disorder? A Study of P3a Using Single Trial Analysis. *Australian and New Zealand Journal of Psychiatry*, 2011; 45:131–139.
Melkonian, D., Similar Basis Function Algorithm for Numerical Estimation of Fourier Integrals. *Numerical Algorithms*, 2009, 10.1007/s11075-009-9324-x
Melkonian, D., Korner, A., Meares, R. & Bahramali, H., Increasing Sensitivity in the Measurement of Heart Rate Variability: The Method of Non-Stationary RR Time-Frequency Analysis. *Computer Methods and Programs in Biomedicine*, 2012; 108:53–67.
Menninger, K., *The Vital Balance*. New York, Viking Press, 1963.
Merleau-Ponty, M., (1945), *Phenomenology of Perception*, trans. Smith, C. London, Routledge & Kegan Paul, 1962.
Miller, G.A., The Magical Number Seven, Plus or Minus Two: Some Limits on our Capacity for Processing Information. *Psychological Review*, 1956; 63:81–97.
Morrison, S.E. & Salzman, C.D., Re-Valuing the Amygdala. *Current Opinion in Neurobiology*, 2010; 20(2):221–230.
Murray, L., *Taller When Prone*. Melbourne, Black Inc., 2010.
Napaljarri, P.R. & Cataldi, L. (trans.), *Warlpiri Dreamings and Histories. Yimikirli*. Walnut Creek, CA, Altamira Press, 2003.
Newman, J.D., Vocal Communication and the Triune Brain. *Physiology & Behavior*, 2003; 79:495–502.
Newman, J.D., Neural Circuits Underlying Crying and Cry Responding in Mammals. *Behavioural Brain Research*, 2007; 182:155–165.
Newman, J.D. & Bachevalier, J., Neonatal Ablations of the Amygdala and Inferior Temporal Cortex Alter the Vocal Response to Social Separation in Rhesus Macaques. *Brain Research*, 1997; 758:180–186.
Niedtfeld, I. & Schmahl, C. Emotion Regulation and Pain in Borderline Personality Disorder. *Current Psychiatry Reviews*, 2009; 5:48–54.
Norcross, J.C., *Psychotherapy Relationships That Work*, 2nd Edition. New York, Oxford University Press, 2011.
Norcross, J.C. & Lambert, M., Compendium of Evidence-Based Relationships. *Psychotherapy in Australia*, 2013; 19:22–26.
Ogden, T.H., Analysing Forms of Aliveness and Deadness of the Transference-Countertransference. *International Journal of Psycho-Analysis*, 1995; 76:695–709.
Ogden, T.H., *This Art of Psychoanalysis*. London, Routledge, 2005.

Orange, D.M., *Thinking for Clinicians: Philosophical Resources for Contemporary Psychoanalysis and the Humanistic Psychotherapies*. New York, Routledge, 2010.

Orloff, J., *Emotional Freedom*. New York, Three Rivers Press, 2010.

Osborne, N., Towards a Chronobiology of Musical Rhythm. In, Malloch, S. & Trevarthen, C. (eds.), *Communicative Musicality. Exploring the Basis of Human Companionship* (pp. 301–330). Oxford, Oxford University Press, 2009.

Otti, A., Guendel, H., Laer, L., Wohlschlaeger, A.M., Lane, R.D., et al., I Know the Pain You Feel: How the Human Brain's Default Mode Predicts Our Resonance to Another's Suffering. *Neuroscience*, 2010; 169:143–148.

Panksepp, J., The Power of the Word May Reside in the Power of Affect. *Integrative Psychological and Behavioural Science*, 2008; 42:47–55.

Panksepp, J. & Biven, L., *The Archaelogy of Mind: Neuroevolutionary Origins of Human Emotions*. New York, W.W. Norton, 2012.

Panksepp, J. & Burgdorf, J., "Laughing" Rats and the Evolutionary Antecedents of Human Joy? *Physiology and Behaviour*, 2003; 79:533–547.

PDM Task Force, *Psychodynamic Diagnostic Manual*. Silver Spring, MD, Alliance of Psychoanalytic Organizations, 2006.

Peirce, C.S., (1897), Logic as Semiotic: The Theory of Signs. In, Innis, R.E. (ed.), *Semiotics, an Introductory Anthology*. Bloomington, IN, Indiana University Press, 1985.

Pennebaker, J.W., *The Secret Life of Pronouns*. New York, Bloomsbury Press, 2011.

Phillips, A., *On Balance*. London, Hamish Hamilton, 2010.

Piaget, J., *The Construction of Reality in the Child*. London, Routledge & Kegan Paul, 1954.

Pinyerd, B.J., Infant Cries: Physiology and Assessment. *Neonatal Network*, 1994; 13(4):15–20.

Poirier, S., "This Is Good Country: We Are Good Dreamers": Dreams and Dreaming in the Australian Western Desert. In, Lohmann, R.I. (ed.), *Dream Travellers*. New York, Palgrave MacMillan, 2003.

Porges, S.W., *Method and Apparatus for Evaluating Rhythmic Oscillations in Aperiodic Physiological Response Systems*. United States Patent: Patent No. 4,510,944; Apr. 16, 1985.

Porges, S.W., The Polyvagal Theory: Phylogenetic Substrates of a Social Nervous System. *International Journal of Psychophysiology*, 2001; 42:123–146.

Porges, S.W., *The Polyvagal Theory*. New York, W.W. Norton, 2011.

Porges, S.W., *The Pocket Guide to the Polyvagal Theory*. New York, W.W. Norton, 2017.

Porges, S.W. & Dana, D., *Clinical Applications of the Polyvagal Theory: The Emergence of Polyvagal-Informed Therapies*. New York, W.W. Norton, 2018.

Porges, S.W., Personal Communications, 2019.

Porges, S.W., Doussard-Roosevelt, J.A. & Maiti, A.J., Vagal Tone and the Physiological Regulation of Emotion. In, Fox, N.A. (ed.), *Towards a Developmental Science of Politics*, Vol. 59, No. 2–3: 167–186, 1994 (the Monographs of the Society for Research in Child Development Series).

Porges, S.W. & Lewis, G.F., The Polyvagal Hypothesis: Common Mechanisms Mediating Autonomic Regulation, Vocalizations and Listening. In, Brudzynski, S.M. (ed.), *Handbook of Mammalian Vocalization*. London, Elsevier, 2010. DOI: 10.1016/B978-0-12-374593-4.00025-5

Project Gutenberg ebook edition, 2010. http://www.gutenberg.org/files/1826/1826-h/1826-h.htm

Raichle, M.E., MacLeod, A.M., Snyder, A.Z., Powers, W.J., Gusnard, D.A. & Shulman, G.L., A Default Mode of Brain Function. *Proceedings of the National Academy of Sciences U.S.A.*, 2001; 98:676–682.

Raichle, M.E. & Snyder, A.Z., A Default Mode of Brain Function: A Brief History of an Evolving Idea. *NeuroImage*, 2007; 37:1083–1090.

Redding, P., *The Logic of Affect*. Ithaca, Cornell University Press, 1999.

Reed, E., *Encountering the World: Toward an Ecological Psychology*. New York, Oxford University Press, 1996.

Reilly, K.J. & Moore, C.A., Respiratory Movement Patterns during Vocalizations at 7 and 11 Months of Age. *Journal of Speech, Language and Hearing Research*, 2009;52:223–229.

Ricks, D., Making Sense of Experience to Make Sensible Sounds. In, Bullowa, M. (ed.), *Before Speech: The Beginning of Interpersonal Conversation*. Cambridge, Cambridge University Press, 1979.

Ricoeur, P., *Freud & Philosophy: An Essay on Interpretation*. New Haven & London, Yale University Press, 1970.

Ricoeur, P., *The Rule of Metaphor. The Creation of Meaning in Language*, trans. Czerny, R. London, Routledge, 1977.

Rizzoli, G.S., The Critique of Regression: The Person, the Field, the Lifespan. *Journal of the American Psychoanalytic Association*, 2016. http://journals.sagepub.com/doi/full/1 0.1177/0003065116679111?utm_source=Adestr...

Rogers, R. & Hammerstein, O., (1945), You'll Never Walk Alone. In, *Reader's Digest, Treasury of Best Loved Songs*, New York, Reader's Digest Association, 1972.

Rubia, K., The Neurobiology of Meditation and Its Clinical Effectiveness in Psychiatric Disorders. *Biological Psychiatry*, 2009; 82:1–11.

Sackett, D., Rosenburg, W., Muir-Gray, J., Haynes, R. & Richardson, W., Evidence Based Medicine: What It Is and What It Isn't. *British Medical Journal*, 1996; 312:71–72.

Samuels, A., *A New Therapy for Politics?* London, Karnac, 2015.

Sapir, E., The Unconscious Patterning of Behavior in Society. In, Mandelbaum, D.G. (ed.), *Selected Writings of Edward Sapir in Language, Culture and Personality*. Berkeley & Los Angeles, University of California Press, 1951.

Sartre, J., *No Exit*. New York, Samuel French, 1958.

Sartre, J., *Nausea*. New York, New Directions Publishing Corp., 1964.

Saussure, F. de, *Course in General Linguistics*, trans. Baskin, W. New York, Columbia University Press, 1959.

Schore, A.N., *Affect Regulation and the Origin of the Self*. Hillsdale, NJ, Lawrence Erlbaum Associates, 1994.

Schore, A.N., *The Science of the Art of Psychotherapy*. New York, W.W. Norton, 2012.

Schumann, J.H., A Linguistics for the Evolution and Neurobiology of Language. *Journal of English Linguistics*, 2007; 35:278–287.

Schwerdtfeger, A. & Friedrich-Mai, P., Social Interaction Moderates the Relationship between Depressive Mood and Heart Rate Variability: Evidence from an Ambulatory Monitoring Study. *Health Psychology*, 2009; 28(4):501–509.

Shanahan, D., *Language, Feeling and the Brain: The Evocative Vector*. New Brunswick, NJ, Transaction Publishers, 2007.

Shankly, B. (Bill), Quote (c. 1961) from Website. www.shankly.com/article/2517

Shapiro, J.A., *Evolution: A View from the 21st Century*. Upper Saddle River, NJ, FT Press Science, 2011.

Shelley, M., (1818), *Frankenstein, or, the Modern Prometheus*. London, Penguin, 1992.

Siegel, D.J., *The Developing Mind*, 2nd Edition. London & New York, The Guilford Press, 2015.
Sims, A., *Symptoms in the Mind*. Leeds, University of Leeds Press, 1988.
Smith, O.B., The Social Self of Whitehead's Organic Philosophy. *European Journal of Pragmatism and American Philosophy*, 2010; 2(1):1–15.
Soanes, C. & Stevenson, A., *Oxford Dictionary of English (Kindle Default Dictionary)*. Oxford, Oxford University Press, 2011.
Solms, M., *The Feeling Brain: Selected Papers on Neuropsychoanalysis*. London, Karnac, 2015.
Solms, M., The Hard Problem of Consciousness and the Free Energy Principle. *Frontiers in Psychology: Psychoanalysis and Neuropsychoanalysis*, 2019. https://doi.org/10.3389/fpsyg.2018.02714. www.frontiersin.org/articles/10.3389/fpsyg.2018.02714/full
Spitz, R., Anaclitic Depression. In, *The Psychoanalytic Study of Child*, Vol. 2, p. 313. I. New York, International Universities Press, 1946.
St Augustine, G., *Confessions*, trans. Wills, G. London, Penguin, 2006.
Stern, D. (Daniel), *The Interpersonal World of the Infant*. New York, Basic, 1985.
Stern, D. (Daniel), *The Present Moment*. New York, W.W. Norton, 2004.
Stern, D.B. (Donnel), Dissociated and Unformulated Experience: A Psychoanalytic Model of Mind. In, *The Self in Conversation*, Vol. 5. Sydney, ANZAP, 2006.
Stevenson, R.L., (1886), The Strange Case of Dr Jekyll and Mr Hyde. In, Harman, C. (intro.), *The Strange Case of Dr Jekyll and Mr Hyde and Other Stories*. London, Everyman (J.M. Dent), 1992.
Stevenson, R.L., The Lantern-Bearers: Essay in *Across the Plains*. Quoted in James, W. (1899), On a Certain Blindness in Human Beings. In, James, W., *Pragmatism and Other Writings*. Harmondsworth, Middlesex, Penguin, 2000.
Stocker, M. (with Elizabeth Hegeman), *Valuing Emotions*. Cambridge, Cambridge University Press, 1996.
Stolorow, R.D. & Atwood, G., Three Realms of the Unconscious. In, *Contexts of Being: The Intersubjective Foundations of Psychological Life*. New York, The Analytic Press, 1992.
Strachey, J., Sigmund Freud: A Sketch of His Life and Ideas. In, *Two Short Accounts of Psycho-Analysis*. London, Pelican, 1962.
Taylor, C., *The Language Animal: The Full Shape of the Human Linguistic Capacity*. Cambridge, MA, Belknap Press of Harvard University Press, 2016.
Thibault, P.J., *Brain, Mind, and the Signifying Body*. London, Continuum, 2004.
Thomas, P., Bracken, P. & Timimi, S., The Limits of Evidence-Based Medicine in Psychiatry. *Philosophy, Psychiatry and Psychology*, 2013; 19:295–308.
Tolpin, M., Doing Psychoanalysis of Normal Development: Forward Edge Transferences. Chapter 11 in, *Progress in Self Psychology*, 2002; 18:167–190.
Tomasello, M., *Origins of Human Communication*. Cambridge, MA, The MIT Press, 2010.
Tomkins, S., *Shame and Its Sisters: A Silvan Tomkins Reader*, eds. Sedgwick, E.K. & Frank, A. Durham & London, Duke University Press, 1995.
Trevarthen, C., Conversations with a Two-Month Old. *New Scientist*, 1974; 62:230–235.
Trevarthen, C., Early Attempts at Speech. In, *Child Alive: New Insights into the Development of Young Children*. London, Temple Smith, 1975.
Trevarthen, C., Communication and Cooperation in Early Infancy: A Description of Primary Intersubjectivity. In, Bullowa, M. (ed.), *Before Speech: The Beginning of Human Communication* (pp. 321–347). London, Cambridge University Press, 1979.
Trevarthen, C., Making Sense of Infants Making Sense. *Intellectica*, 2002; 34:161–188.

Trevarthen, C., Shared Minds and the Science of Fiction: Foreword to. In, Zlatev, J., Racine, T.P., Sinha, C. & Itkonen, E. (eds.), *The Shared Mind: Perspectives on Intersubjectivity*. Amsterdam & Philadelphia, John Benjamins Publishing Company, 2008.

Trevarthen, C., Awareness of Infants: What Do They, and We, Seek? *Psychoanalytic Inquiry*, 2015; 35:395–416.

Trevarthen, C., Preface: The Psychobiology of the Human Spirit. In, Apter, G., Devouche, E. & Gratier, M. (eds.), *Early Interaction and Developmental Psychopathology, Volume 1: Infancy*. Switzerland, Springer Nature AG, 2019.

Tronick, E.Z., Dyadically Expanded States of Consciousness and the Process of Therapeutic Change. *Infant Mental Health Journal*, 1998; 19:290–299.

Tronick, E.Z., Als, H., Wise, S. & Brazelton, T.B., The Infant's Response to Entrapment between Contradictory Messages in Face-to-Face Interaction. *Journal of American Academy of Child Psychiatry*, 1978; 17:1–13.

Vygotsky, L., (1934), *Thought and Language*. Cambridge, MA, MIT Press, 1986.

Wachtel, P.L., *Relational Theory and the Practice of Psychotherapy*. New York, The Guilford Press, 2008.

Whelan, M., The Work of Ronald Fairbairn: Fairbairn's Critique of Freud and Abraham. *Psychoanalysis Downunder*, 2003. www.psychoanalysisdownunder.com.au/downunder/backissues/issue4/359.fairb

Whitehead, A.N., *Process and Reality: Corrected Edition*, eds. Griffin D.R. & Sherburne, D. New York, Free Press, 1978.

Wikipedia, *Protagoras*, 2012. http://en.wikipedia.org/wiki/Protagoras

Wikipedia, *Oedipal Complex*, 2012. http://en.wikipedia.org/wiki/Oedipus_complex

Wikipedia, *Arthur Stace*, 2019. https://en.wikipedia.org/wiki/Arthur_Stace

Wiktionary, 2013. http://en.wiktionary.org/wiki/infant

Willems, R.M. & Hagoort, P., Neural Evidence for the Interplay between Language, Gesture, and Action: A Review. *Brain and Language*, 2007; 101:278–289.

Williams, L.M. & Gordon, E., Dynamic Organization of the Emotional Brain: Responsivity, Stability, and Instability. *Neuroscientist*, 2007; 13:349–370.

Williams, P., Isolation. *Psychoanalytic Dialogues*, 2019; 29:1–12. https://doi.org/10.1080/10481885.2018.1560873

Wilshire, B.W., *William James the Essential Writings: Introduction*, ed. James, W. the essential writings (ed. Wilshire B.W.). Albany, State University of New York Press, 1984.

Winnicott, D.W., (1950–55), Aggression in Relation to Emotional Development. In, *Through Paediatrics to Psycho-Analysis: Collected Papers*. New York, Basic Books, 1975.

Winnicott, D.W., (1956), Primary Maternal Preoccupation. In, Winnicott, D.W. (ed.), *Through Paediatrics to Psycho-Analysis*. New York, Basic Books, 1975.

Winnicott, D.W., (1960), The Theory of the Parent-Infant Relationship. In, *The Maturational Processes and the Facilitating Environment*. London, Hogarth, 1965.

Winnicott, D.W., (1963), Communicating and Not Communicating Leading to a Certain Study of Opposites. In, *The Maturational Processes and the Facilitating Environment*. London, Hogarth, 1965.

Winnicott, D.W., (1971), *Playing and Reality*. London, Routledge, 1991.

Wittgenstein, L., *Philosophical Investigations*, 2nd Edition. Oxford, Basil Blackwell and Mott, 1958.

Wittgenstein, L., (1921), *Tractatus Logico-Philosophicus*. London, Routledge, 2001.

Wood Jones, F., (1931), Of Words and Little Emotions. In, F. Wood Jones (ed.), *Unscientific Essays* (pp. 14–24). London, Arnold.
Wright, A., *Carpentaria*. Sydney, Giramondo, 2006.
Zadeh, L.A., Fuzzy Sets. *Information and Control*, 1965; 8:338–353.
Zanarini, M.C. & Frankenburg, F.R., Emotional Hypochondriasis, Hyberbole and the Borderline Patient. *The Journal of Psychotherapy Practice and Research*, 1994; 3:25–36.

Index

Note: Page numbers in *italic* indicate figures and page numbers in **bold** indicate tables.

accommodation 4, 103
Adult Attachment Interview (AAI) 48
affect 15, 21, 28, 30, 68–69; *see also* feeling
affective (emotional) investment 2, 24, 26, 48, 57, 104, 143, 147–148, 154, 169
affective core 67, 81
affective expression/experience 15, 68–69
affectively toned complexes 170
affective neuroscience 13
affective pattern recognition 21
affect regulation 20, 146, 170, 173
affect reorganization 115
afferent networks 18
Alice in Wonderland and language underground 60
alienation 29, 160, 178–182
Alighieri, Dante 172
allostasis/allostatic process 17, 82
alone togetherness 28, 133
analogical fit 19, 33–37, 40, 139
analogical relatedness 173
analogical relationship 71
analogue 35–36, 65, 69
analogue scale 36, 65, 136–137
analogy 30, 33–36, 40, 42, 65–66, 72–74, 77, 85, 113, 143, 173
analytic thinking 173
apperception 14–15, 18, 66–68, 70, 77, 79, 84, 106, 109
approximate responses 77
archetypes 161
Aristotle 104, 138
"ascending to the concrete" 109, 148–151, 157
assimilation 103
association 2, 46, 54, 82, 140–141

associative power 140
asymbolic code 105
asymbolic consciousness 95
asymmetry 4, 8–9, 23, 28, 155
Atkinson, J. 148–149
Atwood, G. 52
Augustine, St. 187
autobiographical memory 2–3, 54, 70, 96–97, 109
autonomic nervous system (ANS) 50, 58, 70–71, 73, 77–81, 94, 137
autonomic response to communication 50–51, 66, 82–83, 105–106, 121
autopoiesis 17
Axis of Simultaneities 86–87
Axis of Successions 86–87

Barthes, R. 105
Bateson, G. 93
being-in-relatedness 3
Being and Time (Heidegger) 40
Benjamin, J. 145–146
Benjamin, R. 179, 181
Bennett, M. 94
best fit concept 74
birth practices 5–6
bodily syntax 170
body-mind 83
bonds/bonding 5–7, 17, 52, 79–80, 92, 125
brain: Broca's area 12; cry and 12–14; emotional processing and 75; function 12, 20, 44, 74; lateralization 12; left hemispheric influence 14, 84, 142–143, 170–171; limbic system 13–14, 66, 146; mind connection and 74; neuronal selection and 74; perception and 45;

plasticity of 59; relationship with mind and environment 44, 74; right hemispheric influence 12, 14, 67, 84, 142, 170; social engagements and 67, 142
brain-mind connection 12, 74
brain-mind-environment relationships 44, 74
brain-mind as facilitator 12
Brandchaft, B. 146
breathing: cardio-respiratory apparatus and 70–72, 126; concept of, traditional 64; consciousness and 65–66, 83–84; feeling and 66–68; heart rate and 72–73; Respiratory Sinus Arrhythmia and 72, 120, 123–124, *124*; rhythm of 62, 103; transition 71, *124*, 125; unconsciousness and 65
breathless stases 64
Buber, M. 35, 147–148

calling, human 4
cardio-respiratory apparatus (CRA) 70–73, 126
Carpentaria (Wright) 177–178
cathecting 143; *see also* affective (emotional) investment
Change in Self Experience Rating Scale (CSERS) 118–123, *120*, 127–128, 130, 134–138
chronicles 70, 110, 112–113, 160
"chunking" of consciousness 67
civilization 163, 183, 188
collective unconscious 161
communicants 1, 49, 93
communication: asymmetry in 8–9; audio-vocal in forerunners of mammals 22; autonomic response to 50–51, 66, 82–83, 105–106, 121; birth practices and 6; "core self" in 14; cry and response pattern and 7; embodiment of 76, 104–106; facial expressions and 8, 18, 29, 80, 92–93, 104, 170; gestures 5, 7–8, 16, 18, 49, 53, 56, 61, 89, 92, 100, 104–105, 170; of infant 7–8; language and 34; of non-human primates 22; reciprocal 13, 35; as resonating social exchange 70; right hemisphere influence in 141–142; sense modalities in 70; social engagement and, facilitating 8; symbolic in 90; *see also* communicative exchange; conversation; cry
communicative embodiment 76, 104–106

communicative exchange: asymmetry in 8–9; complexity of, modelling 29–30; in consumer society 186; cry and 1, 5–9, 14, 56; definition of concept 1–2; evolution of 12–17; feeling and 1–2, 170; iconic 11, 53, 55–58, 88–89, 92, 98; indexical 6, 11, 52, 53, 55–58, 89, 97–98, 115, 170; information unit in 101; life-long 163; linguistics of 98–101; proto-conversation in 100; psychotherapy and 31; resonance and 2–3; resonant self and 2–3; response and 5–9; rhythm in 62; self and, growth of 17–19, 39–40; self-state and 57–58; shaping by 2; significance and, social 49; social engagement and 72; symbolic 55–58; transactions in 100–101, **100**; transformation and 163–164; unconsciousness and 117; *see also* communication; conversation
communicative musicality 52
complexity (of feeling) 95–97
Confessions (Augustine) 187
consciousness: affect and 21; asymbolic 95; breathing and 65–66, 83–84; "chunking" of 67; feeling and 1, 48, 143; higher 12, 39, 43–44, 55, 57, 59, 75, 103, 188; intersubjective 102; meaning making and 109–110; neuroscientific model of 43–44; object 109, 135–136; present moment and 67; primary 55, 57, 74–75; self and 107, 136; as stream 39; subject 109, 135–136; traumatic 95, 107, 112; unhappy 38, 166
conscious states 58, 116, 123; *see also* consciousness
consensuality 17
conservation of relationship 183
conversation: in Conversational Model 181–182; given and new structure of 30, 85, 115, 151–159; intercultural 177–178, 188; inter-generational knowledge and 163; intersubjective research and, shift to 33–34; language and 100–101; as natural form of language 90; in psychotherapy 2, 85, 91; self and 136; singularity and 30; time frames and 102; units 91; *see also* communicative exchange; long conversation
conversational analysis (CA) 100, 118, 119

Conversational Model (CM) 34, 85, 88, 90, 107, 110, 145, 181–182
Core Conflictual Relationship Theme approach 118
core self 14, 19
core vulnerability 136
Course in General Linguistics (Saussure) 86
creation stories 64, 163, 165–166
creative third concept 8
cry: brain and 12–14; call and 5, 16–17; communicative exchange and 1, 5–9, 14, 56; as emotional expression, complex 9–12; evolution of 14–17; as first language 6, 11–14; healthy 13; human existence and 3–4; human interactions and 3–4; as mood sign 6, 93; neuroscience of 12–14; overview 1; of patient 136; pattern of response and 6–7, 174; power of human 6; prolonged 10; psychotherapy and 9, 136; reception of 12–14; of self 136; as sign 11, 56; significance of 4; social engagement and 10; unconsciousness of 5–6, 10, 56, 71–72, 93, 100; vulnerability expressed by 3–4

Dadirri ("deep listening") 149
Damasio, A. 19–20
Darwin, C. 15
dasein ("being-there") 39–40
death-feigning behaviour 80–82
default network (DN) 20–21, 29–30
Deutscher, G. 104
diachrony 86–90, 114
"*Dis*" 160
dis-integration 4, 166, 168–170
dis-social 170–173
dissociation 14, 61, 81, 108, 131, 133, 148, 158, 163, 166–171
Divine Comedy, The (Dante) 172
Dobzhansky, T.G. 83
dominance, dreaming of 188
Dorsal Motor Nucleus of the Vagus (DMNV) 79
double life 168–171
dreaming/dreams 148–151, 182–184, *185*, 186–189
Dreaming, The (Australian Indigenous tradition) 87–88, 160–161, 166, 177–178, 184, 187–188
"drive-defence" model 106–107
drive theory/drives 26–27, 186
DSM-5 46, 181

DSM IV™ 181
DSM series 181
dyadic relatedness 167

ectoderm 12
Edelman, G.M. 59, 67, 103
ego 34, 93, 142–144, 146–170
Ego and the Id, The (Freud) 143
embodied interaction 63
embodied mind 37–44
embodiment: of communication 76, 104–106; of stories 85; of the symbolic 106–108
emergent self 5, 17–19, 22–23, 35, 42, 51, 115, 135–136, 140–141
emotion *see* feeling
emotional (affective) investment 2, 24, 26, 48, 57, 104, 143, 147–148, 154, 169
emotional expression in living language 14–17
emotional fractal 49
emotional processing 75; *see also* feeling
empathy 50, 115, 148, 155, 171
empiricism 148
environment-mind-brain relationship 44, 74
eternity 176–177
eudaimonia 186
Evidence-Based Medicine (EBM) 180–181
evoked response potential (ERP) 123
evolution: of communicative exchange 12–17; of cry 14–17; Darwinian theory of 165; of humans 21–24, 62, 106; of role transformations 1; of significance 21–24; social engagement and 62, 106
evolutionary duplicity 97
existence, human 3–4, 65

face-brain-heart 29, 108
facial expressions 8, 18, 29, 80, 92–93, 104, 170
failure to thrive 18, 110
Fairbairn, R. 27
feeling: breathing and 66–68; communicative exchange and 1–2, 170; complexity of 95–97; consciousness and 1, 48, 143; developmental course; as evaluative system 79; forms of 2, 16, 29, 63, 96; fuzzy logic and 84; heart and, working with 62–63; as integration of information 66; James and 41; language and 1, 137; limbic system and 14; "little emotions" 96–97;

meaning making and 95–97; Meares's stages of 96–97; measuring 36, 82; narrative and, regulation through 68–70; neural organization of 14, 20–21, 95; overview 62; of participation 20; perception and 58, 108, 143; personal knowing of 183; philosophical considerations 37–44; physiological correlates of 82–84; psychotherapy and 2, 16, 62, 82–84; rhythms and, bodily 62–63; self-states and 66–68; social engagement and 84, 147, 168; value system and 52, 66, 68, 107; visceral 22; voice of, true 19; *see also* affect
feeling-toned complexes 161
first-person perspective/experiences 33, 40, 55
flexibility 58–61
flights and perchings 39, 151
formal thinking 173
forms of feeling 2, 16, 29, 63, 96
formulation 47, 52, 90–91, 165
forward edge transference 135
Frankenstein (Shelley) 64, 171
Frederick II 32, 110
free association 33–34, 141
freeze behaviour 80–82
Freud, S. 25–26, 45, 75, 115, 142–146, 173
fuzzy logic 76–77, 84, 110, 112, 119
fuzzy scripts 84

General Images of Affect 68–69, 170
gestures 5, 7–8, 16, 18, 49, 53, 56, 61, 89, 92, 100, 104–105, 160, 170
good enough fit concept 76–77

Halliday, M.A.K. 59, 97–98, 101
heart: affective 147; cardio-respiratory apparatus and 70–73, 126; expressions using 63; feeling and working with 62–63; Heart Rate Variability and 72–73, 82, 116–117, 120–121; "measuring" 73–75; rate 72–73; rhythm of 72
Heart Rate Variability (HRV) 72–73, 82, 116, 120–121
Hegel, G.W.F. 31, 38, 42–43, 109, 140, 144–145, 167
Heidegger, M. 31, 38–40, 42
Heisenberg, W. 90
higher consciousness 12, 39, 43–44, 55, 57, 59, 75, 103, 188
Hillel HaGadol 188–189
Hobson, R. 34–35

homeostasis/homeostatic process 17–19, 29, 67, 76, 80–82, 103, 122–123, 141
human existence 3–4

iconic communicative exchange 11, 53, 55–58, 92, 98
iconic relationship between sign and object 89–90
id 46, 143–144, 147
idealism 43
I-it configuration 35
imagination 2–3, 60, 92, 95, 115, 157, 165, 171, 173, 186
I-me duality 34
immobilization/immobilization without fear 80
impinging narrative 69–70, 112
implicit memory 18, 39, 48, 70, 74, 170, 182
indexical communicative exchange 6, 11, 52–53, 55–58, 97–98, 115, 170
indexical relationship between sign and object 89
infant-carer relationship 3–4, 8, 18, 24–25, 27, 49, 56, 62, 170, 174; *see also* cry; proto-conversation
Inferno (Dante) 160, 172
information units 101–103, 151
inhibition 68, 143, 167, 170
instantiation 22, 33, 59, 87, 113–114, 139, 151–154, 159
integration: affective-conceptual 182, 188; of experience 17–19, 30; feeling as 66; of forms of feeling 141; of language 55, 68–69; in psychotherapy, successful 182; reciprocal engagement and 4; secrets and loss of 169; of self 17–19, 21, 141; sexuality and 168; significance and, measuring 126; social 55, 166; trauma and neural 21; of value system 145; whole person 11, 20
intercultural conversation 177–178, 188
inter-generational knowledge 163
internalization of language 54
internal working model 48, 69, 86
interoception 80–81
interpenetrated relationships 71
interpersonal metafunctions 99–100, 114–115, 137; *see also* language and interpersonal metafunction
interpersonal neurobiology 74
Interpretation of Dreams, The (Freud) 142
intersubjective consciousness 102

intersubjective research on self-states: background to 62; Change in Self-Experience Rating Scale and 118–123, *122*, 127–133, *134*, 136–138; concept of 30; conversation and, shift to 33–34; emergence of self 135–136; Heart Rate Variability and 116–117, 120–121, 123–125, *124*; overview 116–118; paradigm 116–117; psychotherapy and 116; speaking/listening on autonomic function 125–126, *126*; vulnerable self, transformation of 116, 133–135; *see also* self-states
intersubjectivity 18, 97, 102, 117, 174–175
isolation call 6, 10, 71, 111
I-thou configuration 35, 150

James, W. 31, 34, 38–39, 41–42, 46–47, 59, 65–66, 67, 113–114, 165
Jaspers, K. 164
Jekyll and Hyde 163, 171–172
Joyce, J. 50–51
Jung, C.G. 90

Kagan, J. 15–16
Kierkegaard, S. 144–145

Lacan, J. 87, 144–145
language: acquisition of 22, 28, 54, 92; analogical fit and 34–37; changes in self-states and 137; as common property 4; communication and 34; complexity of 16; as concrete entity 113–115; conversation and 100–101; defining, challenge of 15–16; development of 28, 52–53, 107; diachronic dimension of 89, 142; emotional expression in living, complex 14–17; as essential to humans 32; evolutionary 87–88; experiential metafunctions 99; feeling and 1, 137; flexibility and 58–61; games 41–43, 107–108; Heidegger's view of 40; indexical 6; integration of 55, 68–69; internalization of 54; interpersonal metafunctions 99–100, 114–115, 137; linguistics and 59, 117; lived experience of significance and 140–141; living 14–17, 31–34, 55; logical metafunctions 99; meaning making and 15–16; metaphor's role in 90; mood signs and 15; musicality of 2; narrative style of 173; as network of differences in value 113; objective/adaptive 88; personal realization and 175–176; person and 51–52, 59; phonology and 16; play and 141; poetic 88; pronoun use 136, 143, 147; proto-conversation and potential of 32; psychotherapy and 33, 45; public domain and 139; redundancy and 59–61; relationship with 60; representations 114; resonance and 90; resonant self and 51–52; rhythm 57, 62, 94, 103; in role transformation 24; safety and, sense of 28, 73; self and 16, 33, 35, 51–52, 60; signs and 56, 87, 89; social aspect of 35; social engagement and 107; spatiality of 54; static 87; subject and, concept of 98–99; symbolic 5, 22, 52, 71, 104, 137; symbolic world and 22, 52–53; synchronic dimension of 89, 142; syntactic 140; syntax and 52, 54, 188; as system of pure values 87; taboos and 28; transformation and 58–61; unconscious relationship of individual to 44, 88; unit of, basic 100; urbanization and 88; vagal tone and 83, 123–124; as value system 87; verbal equations and 135–136; Wittgenstein's view of 41–43; written 101, 107
"language underground" 15–16, 60
"languaging" 2
Levenson, E.A. 164
Levinas, E. 7
lexicogrammar 16
life 44, 55, 64, 75, 168–171
Life Is Beautiful (film) 186–187
linguistic analysis/structure 14, 59, 77, 98–101, **100**, 117, 147
linguistics *see* language; Systemic Functional Linguistics (SFL)
linguistic metafunctions 99–100, 114–115
listening 125–126, *126*, 149
liveliness 44–46, 56, 74, 84, 118
living language 14–17, 31–34, 55
living symbols 1, 8, 11, 90, 92, 145
living text 17
logos 24
long conversation: about alienation 178–182; creation stories and 165–166; with deceased 184, 186; defining 163–164; development and 173–177; dis-integration and 168–170; dis-social and 170–173; double life and 168–170; dreaming of better worlds and 182–184, *185*, 186–189; horror of trauma and 170–173; intercultural conversation and

177–178; overview 163; about suffering 178–182; trauma zone and 166–168; worldview and 163–165

Madonna and Child with Book (Raphael painting) 184, *185*
Mahler, M. 52
marked responses 94
marking 93–95, 100–101
master-slave dialectic 38
materialism 43
maturational process 93
mature self 57, 75, 104, 115, 148
McGilchrist, I. 183
meaning making: consciousness and 109–110; concrete entities and 113–115; consciousness and 109–110; diachrony and 86–90; feeling and 95–97; flexibility in 59; indexical communicative exchange and 97–98; language and 15–16; linguistics of communicative exchange and 98–101, **100**; mood signs and 93–94, 100–101, 106; narrative and, building 101–103; overview 85; personal 33; play and 91–95; proto-language and 97–98; proto-self and 104–106; self and 85–86; self-states and 33, 103; signs and 89–91; story types and 110–113; of suffering 165; symbolic 53, 92, 106–108; in symbolic world 85–86; symbols and 89–91; synchrony and 84–90; *see also* significance
meaning units 72
Meares, R. 29–30, 69–70, 88, 96, 167
medical model 178
"me" experience 39, 169–170
memory 2–3, 18, 39, 54, 56, 60, 70, 96–97, 109, 140
mental models 21, 39
mental space 28–29, 40
mental triad relationships 74
mereological fallacy 39
Merleau-Ponty 18
meronymy 38–39
metaphor: of analogical fit 34, 40; analogical relatedness and 173; in creation stories 165; "dead" 137; experience and, actual 24; fitting experience and 90; Freudian "I" 143, 146; Jamesian's stream of consciousness 39; of limbo 133; in measuring feeling 82; moving 90, 134; Oedipal complex and 26; metaphorical "tree" 114; in

politics 24; in psychotherapy 33–34, 63, 90, 133–135, 157, 159, 179; role of in language 90; in science 24; of self in adversity 133–134; spatial 113; in symbolic world 85–86; syntactic language and 140
mind 28, 37–44, 73–75, 83, 147, 179
mind-body 83
mind-brain connection 74
mind-brain-environment relationship 44, 74
mind-brain relationships 74
mobility/mobilization 4, 32, 73, 79, 81, 84, 106–108, 128, 131, 134
moments of meeting 45
monadic relatedness 167
mood signs 6, 15, 56, 93–94, 100–101, 106, 128, 136
moral third concept 8, 145–146
motivated selection 60–61, 151
motivation for speech 13
motivational system 13, 17, 52
motivation for speech 13
moving metaphor 90, 134
musicality 2, 52, 59, 62, 94, 102
mutual relatedness 5
mythos 24

narcissism, resistance of 173
narrative: building 101–103; clause selection in 152–159; feeling regulation through 68–70; impinging 69–70, 112; knowledge 19; story type 110, 113; structure 102; traumatic 70; units 85, 103, 105, 116, 152–159; vocalization and form of 71–72; *see also* stories
negative therapeutic reaction 146
neoteny 10
neural network 1; *see also* brain; *specific system*
neuroception 79, 106, 108–109
neuronal selection 74
nonverbal communication *see* facial expressions; gestures
"not me" experience 39, 169–170
nuclear script 70
Nucleus Ambiguus (NA) 79

object consciousness 109, 135–136
Oedipus complex 25–28
"On a Certain Blindness in Human Beings" (James) 59
orienting response 78–79
other 17–19, 22, 79, 108, 118, 175, 188–189

Paedomorphism 10
parasympathetic nervous system (PNS) 50, 71–72, 76, 106, 108, 121, 134
parasympathetic response 50, 134
participant observer role of therapist 179
Peirce, C. S. 5, 11, 56
perception: of animals 95; autonomic nervous system and 58; brain and 45; of causal connection 40; feeling and 58, 107, 143; Freud's view of 143; internal working models and 48; of meaning 40; of physicality of humans 183; Redon painting and 174–175; right hemisphere of brain and 142; of safety 18, 79, 83–84, 93, 186; symbols and action separated from 104; of time by child 96; value to, imbuing 66; whole person phenomenon and 11, 14–15
person: dynamic progression of 53–55; intersubjectivity and 117; language and 51–52, 59; mature 54–55; as self-organizing system 30, 50, 54, 68, 163; term of 3; *see also* self
personality 45–48, 51, 53–55, 58
personal realization: dreaming and 148–151; instantiation and 139, 151–154, 159; interpersonal experience and 4; language and 175–176; metaphorical "tree" and 114; non-linear path of 4; overview 139; presence of others and 175; prospective self and 160–162; realizations and 139, 155; recognition and 16, 139, 153–154, 156–159; self-growth and 16, 141–148, 156–159; self as second nature 139–141; spiral growth in meaning and 151–159
personal self 46–51
phenomenal awareness 55
phenomenological research 117
Phenomenology of Spirit (Hegel) 38
Phillips, A. 28
phonemes 72
phonology 16
Piaget, J. 103
plasticity of brain 59
play: capacity for development of 44; combat 94; emergence of 6–7; field of 94–95; language and 141; meaning making and 91–95; mutual 174; following proto-conversation 57; in psychotherapy 95–96; purpose of 29; reality versus 94–95; rough and tumble 57, 94, 184; safety and 93–95, 104; symbolic 54, 57, 94
playspace 29
Pleasure Principle 45, 75, 118, 143
poetic language 88
Poetics (Aristotle) 104, 110, 138
Poet's Voice in the Making of Mind, The (Meares) 96
Polyvagal Theory (PVT) 62–63, 78–80, 84, 106, 116, 125–126, 135
Porges, S.W. 62, 80, 83, 107, 123
power/empowerment 68–69
presentification 47
present moment 47, 67, 78, 116, 121, 137
primary consciousness 55, 57, 74–75
primary maternal preoccupation 24–25
primary process 46, 142–143, 145
primates, non-human 22
probability theory 76
pronoun use 136, 143, 147
prospective self 139, 160–162
proto-conversation: balance and 160; in communicative exchange 100; in Conversational Model 182; defining 16–17, 91; dyadic relatedness and 167; indexical communicative exchange and 97–98; language and, potential of 32; other and 18; play following from 57, 91–95; proto-language and 91, 97; self and 18; self development and 115; significance and 170
proto-language 19, 53, 91, 97–98
proto-self 19, 53, 104, 114, 167
proto-symbolic capacity/exchange 53, 56
psyche (soul) 11–12, 35, 64, 110–111, 182
psychoanalysis 26, 51–52, 86–87, 135, 144, 146, 186; negative therapeutic reaction and 146
psychotherapy: analogue in 36; analogy in 33–37; asymmetric relationships and 8; change and 61; communicative exchange and 31; conversation in 2, 85, 91; cry and 9, 136; CSERS application in 127–136, *134*; as embodied interaction 63; embodied mind and 37–44; embodied text and 46–48; emotional complexity and, capturing 16; empathy and 115; feeling and 2, 16, 62, 82–84; forms of feeling and 29; growth from 141–148; intersubjective research on self-states and 116; journey/process of 110, 114; language

and 33, 45; measurement in 76–78; metaphor in 33–34, 63, 90, 133–135, 157, 159, 179; misunderstandings and, correcting 42; moments of meeting and 45; narrative form and 91; necessity of 43; outcome 29, 73, 83, 116, 180; personal knowledge and, gaining 38–39; personal self and 46–49; philosophical assumptions and 37–44; play in 95–96; problems in 37; reciprocal communication and 13, 35; relational orientation and, shift to 44–45; research 116; safety and, personal 77, 106, 141, 186; self in 139; signs in 89–91; successfully 95, 182; symbols in 89–91; transformation and 115–116; unconscious motivation in 24, 84

qualitative research 117

radical empiricism 148
Reality Principle 45, 118, 143
realizational model of meaning 59
realizations 139, 155; *see also* personal realization
realization of value *see* meaning making
real play room 29
re-association 108, 171
recognition 5, 16, 139, 153–154, 156–159
redemption 176
Redon painting 174–175, *175*
redundancy (linguistic) 59–61
re-entry loop 67
referential reorganization 173
reflective function 98, 104, 137
relational trauma 168
relationships: all or nothing 76; analogical 71; asymmetry in 4, 8, 155; brain-mind 74; brain-mind-environment 44, 74; conservation of 183; family 25–28; infant-carer 3–4, 8, 18, 24–25, 27, 56, 62, 170, 174; internal 76; interpenetrated 71; with language 60; mind-brain 74; moral third concept and 8; Oedipus complex and 25–28; seeking 37; significance in 1, 21–24, 125
religion 38, 165, 184
reorganization 115, 170
resemblances *see* metaphors
resonance 2–3, 79, 90, 126
resonant self: analogical fit and 34–37; autonomic response and, whole-body 50–51; communicative exchange and 2–3; embodied mind and 37–44; embodied text and 46–48; flexibility and 58–61; language and 51–52; liveliness of being and 44–46; living language and 31–34; overview 31; personality and 46–48; personal selves and 48–51; philosophical considerations and 37–44; progression of personality and 53–55; self-states and, emergence of 55–58; significance and, early investment in 48–49; in symbolic world 52–53; whole-body autonomic response and 50–51; zone of proximal development and 59–61
resonating system 14, 103
respiration *see* breathing
Respiratory Sinus Arrhythmia (RSA) 72, 120, 123–124, *124*
response: approximate 77; autonomic, to communication 50–51, 66, 82–83, 105–106, 121; communicative exchange and 5–9; as first language 6; orienting 78–79; of other 30, 118; overview 1; parasympathetic 50, 134; pattern of cry and 6–7, 174; of self 118, 147–148; significance of 4; startle 79; of therapist 136; true rejoinder and 150
revocability 114
Ricoeur, P. 90, 172–173
right hemispheric influence in communication 141–142
role transformation/transition 1, 22–24, 174
Roosevelt, F.D. 183
Russell, B. 41

safe other 79
Safe and Sound protocol 83
safety: apperception and 106; autonomic nervous system and 71, 76; evolutionary value and 83; Heart Rate Variability and sense of 72; infant's illusion of 18, 93; language and sense of 28, 73; marking and 93; mental space and, creating 104; neuroception of 106, 108; perception of 18, 79, 83–84, 93, 186; play and 93–95, 104; Polyvagal Theory and 79, 81; psychotherapy and personal 77, 106, 141, 186; reward-related stimuli and 75; social engagement and 106–108; transformation and 112
Sapir, E. 77
Sarrasine (Balzac) 105
Sartre, J-P. 160

Saussure, F. de 52, 86–87, 89–90, 113–115, 137
Schenker analysis 110
script: change in 85–86; fuzzy 84; nuclear 70; story type 110, 112; traumatic 69–70, 112, 162
secondary process 46, 139, 142–143
second nature 139–141, 182
seduction theory 25–27
seeking system 38, 45, 140
self: accommodation of 103; assimilation of 103; autonomous 61; call of 30; care 23; communicative exchange and growth of 17–19, 40–41; complexity of, neural ontology of 19–21; consciousness and 107, 136; conversation and 136; core 14, 19; cry of 136; *dasein* and 39–40; default network and 20–21; development of 17, 19–21, 40–41, 54–55, 75, 106, 115, 135, 137, 139; dynamic progression of 53–55; as embodied text 1, 46–48, 64, 161–162; emergent 5, 17–19, 22–23, 35, 42, 51, 115, 135–136, 140–141; finding 187–188; first-person experience and 40; growth of 17–19, 38–40, 86, 141–148, 156–159, 173; Heidegger's view of 42; I-me duality and 34; integration of 17–19, 21, 141; intersubjectivity and 117; James's view of 42, 46–47; language and 16, 33, 35, 51–52, 60; mature 57, 75, 104, 115, 148; meaning making and 85–86; with mental space 28–29, 40; mutual relatedness and 5; other and 17–19, 188–189; personal 46–51; personality and 51; physiological correlates of 82–84; private experience of 139; as process 17, 38; prospective 139, 160–162; proto 19, 53, 104, 114, 167; proto-conversation and 18; in psychotherapy 139; resonant 2–3; response of 118, 147–148; as second nature 139–141, 182; as self-organizing system 30, 50, 54, 68, 163; singularity of 1; spiral growth of 17, 82; stories and 160; term of 3; trajectory of 55–58; verbal 19; vulnerable 116, 132–133, 136, 182; well-being of 1; Wittgenstein's view of 42–43; *see also* person; resonant self
self-organizing system, self as 30, 50, 54, 68, 163

self-realization 58, 61; *see also* personal realization
self-states: changes in 117–118, 121–122, **122**, 127, 129, 133, 137; communicative exchange and 57–58; complexity of 138; conscious state versus 58, 116, 123; feeling and 66–68; higher order, creating 55; meaning making and 33, 103; measuring 103, 118–123, *120*, 127–128, 130, 134–138; resonant self and emergence of 55–58; self and, development of 137; *see also* intersubjective research on self-states
self-talk 54
self-world relatedness 168
semantic memory 109
semantics 16, 21
semiosis 5, 56–57
semiotic act 32–33
sensorimotor sequences 140
separation call 6, 10, 71, 111
sexual abuse 62, 168
sexual drive 25–27
sexuality 168
Shakespeare, W. 86, 89
shame 170
Shankly, B. 161–162
Shelley, M. 64, 171
Siegel, D.J. 74
significance: calling and 4; communicative exchange and social 49; of cry 4; evolutionary perspective of 21–24; evolution of 21–24; "felt" 56, 59; infant's with carer 168; integration and measuring 126; interpersonal metafunction and 100; investment in, early 48–49; language and lived experience of 140–141; proto-conversation and 170; in relationships 1, 21–24, 125; of response 4; sequence of relational 23; symbolic perspective of 24–29; *see also* meaning making
signs: cry as 11, 56; iconic relationship between object and 89–90; indexical relationship between object and 89; language and 56, 87, 89; meaning making and 89–91; mood 6, 15, 56, 93–94, 100–101, 106, 128, 136; in psychotherapy 89–91
Similar Basis Function (SBF) 123
singularity 1, 7, 30, 117, 141, 147
smart vagus 79, 80, 82, 121
smile 93

social engagement: brain and 67, 142; communication and facilitating 8; communicative exchange and 72; cooperative 186; cry and 10; evolution of humans and 62, 106; face-brain-heart and 29; feeling and 84, 147, 168; Freud's view of 144; growth of 66; inter-relation of mind and body and 83; language and 107; motivation for 66; parasympathetic nervous system and 50; Polyvagal Theory and 62, 78–80, 106–107, 125–126, 135; as primary motivator 147; receptive processes and 18; safety and 106–108; self and, development of 106
soul (*psyche*) 11–12, 35, 64, 110–111, 182
sound units 72
speech 13, 30, 72, 87, 125–126, *126*; *see also* language
spiral growth in meaning 151–159
spiral growth of self 17, 82
spirit 64, 97, 149, 160, 178
spirituality 163
splitting 39, 167
Stace, A. 176–177
startle response 79
static language 87
Stern, D. 18–19, 67, 101
still-face experiment 6, 170
stimulus-organism-response (SOR) paradigm 71
stimulus-response (SR) paradigms 71
stories: animation of symbols and 11; chronicle story type 110, 112–113, 160; creation 64, 163, 165–166; development of 85; embodiment of 85; narrative story type 110, 113; no story type 110–111, 160; realization of 161–162; script story type 110, 112; self and 160; *see also* narrative
subject, concept of 98–99
subject consciousness 109, 135–136
suffering 165, 178–182
superego 142, 144, 146
survival of the fittest 165
symbolic attitude 36, 59, 90, 92
symbolic communicative exchange 55–58
symbolic development 91–95
symbolic embodiment 106–108
symbolic language 5, 22, 52, 71, 104, 137
symbolic meanings 53, 92, 106–108
symbolic medium 32
symbolic milieu 85–86, 139

symbolic play 54, 57, 94
symbolic transformation 24, 28–29, 188
symbolic world 22, 52–53, 85–86
symbols: animation of 11; formation of 104; living 1, 8, 11, 90, 92, 145; meaning making and 89–91; perception separated from action and 104; in psychotherapy 89–91
sympathetic nervous system (SNS) 50, 71, 78–79, 81, 106–108, 131
synchrony 82, 84–90
Systemic Functional Linguistics (SFL): clause in 67, 99, 114–115; information unit in 101–103; interpersonal metafunction in 100, 114–115; linguistic metafunction in 99–100, 114–115; present moment and 67; subject in 99

taboos 28
textual metafunction 99, 114–115
therapsids 22
threat 76, 79–82, 108
timelessness 24, 53, 87, 177
Tomkins, S. 15, 26, 68
transformation: communicative exchange and 163–164; in human development 22–23; language and 58–61; psychotherapy and 115–116; role 1, 22–24, 174; safety and 112; of suffering 166; symbolic 24, 28–29, 92, 188; of vulnerable self 133–135
transition: to adulthood 23, 167, 174; breathing 71, 124, *124*; patient's 155, 158; from pre-symbolic to symbolic 52; between self-orientation and other-centeredness 23; to verbal self 19
trauma: alienation due to 29; blame and 168; characteristics of environment of 92; disruption of existence and 2; horror of 111, 170–173; impact of 28–29, 160, 163; neural integration and 21; personal growth and 32–33; protection from 186–187; recognizing 29; relational 168; sexual abuse 168; shame and 170; unconsciousness and 28, 166; zone of 166–168
traumatic consciousness 95, 107, 112
traumatic events 92, 170; *see also* trauma
traumatic script 69–70, 112, 162
triadic relatedness 167, 171
true rejoinder 150
turn construction unit 100
turn-taking 67

uncertainty 37, 90
Uncertainty Principle 90
unconsciousness: autonomic nervous system and 77–78, 83; breathing and 65; collective 161; communicative exchange and 117; of cry 5–6, 10, 56, 71–72, 93, 100; growth of self and 86, 148; internal relatedness and 48; language underground and 60; location of, unknown 143–144; motivated selection and 151; motivation in psychotherapy 24, 84; neuroception and 106; Oedipal complex and 25–26; recall 60; relationship of individual to language and 44, 88; trauma and 28, 166
unhappy consciousness 38, 166
unpleasure 75

vagal brake 81, 106
vagal tone 83, 123–124
vagus nerve 18, 22, 50, 73, 78–80
value system: affect system and 52, 66; autonomic nervous system and 58, 94; core vulnerability and 136; external 58; feeling and 52, 66, 68, 107; integration of 145; internal 58, 107, 117, 137, 145, 147; language as 87; memory and 140; perception and 58; *see also* meaning making
variants 26, 69
verbal equation 135–136
verbal self 19
vitality affects 45, 48, 101
vocal expression 56, 71, 94
vocalization 13, 71–73, 108
vocal production/reception 12–13
vulnerability 3–4, 7–8, 136
vulnerable self 116, 132–133, 136, 182

Weltanschaung ("world outlook") 164
Whitehead, A.N. 47
Winnicott, D.W. 44, 77, 93
Wittgenstein, L. 31, 38, 41–44, 77
world knot 109
worldview 48, 61, 88, 93, 140, 148, 163–165, 177–178, 183, 187–188
Wright, A. 177–178
written language 101, 107

zone of proximal development 59–61, 91